The Kin
Who Count

FAMILY AND SOCIETY
IN OTTOMAN ALEPPO,
1770–1840

Margaret L. Meriwether

UNIVERSITY OF TEXAS PRESS
AUSTIN

Requests for permission to reproduce material from this work
should be sent to Permissions, University of Texas Press,
Box 7819, Austin, TX 78713-7819.

∞ The paper used in this publication meets the minimum
requirements of American National Standard for Information
Sciences—Permanence of Paper for Printed Library Materials, ANSI Z39.48-1984.

Library of Congress Cataloging-in-Publication Data
Meriwether, Margaret Lee.
    The kin who count : family and society in Ottoman
Aleppo, 1770–1840 / Margaret L. Meriwether. — 1st ed.
        p.   cm.
    Includes bibliographical references (p.   ) and index.
    ISBN 0-292-75223-7 (alk. paper). — ISBN 0-292-75224-5
(pbk. : alk. paper)
    1. Family—Syria—Aleppo—History. 2. Marriage—
Syria—Aleppo—History. 3. Family—Middle East—
History—18th century.   4. Family—Middle East—
History—19th century.   5. Marriage—Middle East—
History—18th century. 6. Marriage—Middle East—
History—19th century.   I. Title.
HQ663.7.Z9A776   1999
306.85′095691′3—dc21   98-41120

Contents

Preface

This book has been in preparation for a long time. My interest in the notables of Aleppo and in family history dates back almost twenty years, to when I was in graduate school. At that time there was little interest in family history among historians of the Middle East. As a result, the doctoral dissertation that I completed was more about notables than about the family. Since that time I think I have developed a better sense of how we can use the sources available to us to do family history. In part this is because serious study of Middle Eastern family history has begun in recent years, and my thinking about the historical and methodological issues involved in studying the family has been greatly influenced by this work. So this book is about families who happen to be notables. My hope is that it will be a contribution to the emerging literature on the family in the Ottoman period. I have tried to write a book that will be useful to Middle Eastern scholars interested in families, in gender, and in Ottoman cities, and at the same time accessible to nonspecialists and to students.

Over the years I have benefited from the support and guidance of many people. Tom Naff, Basim Musallam, Abdul-Karim Rafeq, and the late Albert Hourani were particularly important in the early stages of this project in helping me define my interests, preparing me to do archival research, and sharing their vast knowledge of Ottoman and Syrian history with me. Elizabeth Fernea, Judith Tucker, Bahram Tavakolian, Jim Reilly, André Raymond, and Muriel Joffe have at various times encouraged me to continue with this project. Special thanks to the staffs of the Department of Antiquities and Dar al-Watha'iq al-Ta'rikhiyya in Damascus. As anyone who has done historical research in Syria knows, our work has benefited enormously from their help and hospitality and the ease of accessibility to the archives, not to mention the numerous cups of coffee to see us through a long morning of poring over the court registers.

Finally, this book would never have been done without the support of my family. My parents gave all their children the best possible education and the sense of independence to pursue whatever we wanted to do. My husband and son have had to live with this project hanging over our heads for many years. As a token of my love for and gratitude to them, I dedicate this book to my mother, to Mike and Patrick, and to the memory of my father.

Note on Transliteration

The Arabic terms and names in this book have been transliterated according to a modified version of the system used by the *International Journal of Middle East Studies*. Diacritical marks have been omitted except for medial hamza (᾿). The Arabic letter ῾ayn has been indicated as ῾. Words of Arabic or Turkish origin that have come into general use in English, like "ulema" or "mufti," are treated as English words, and are spelled according to common English spelling, like "Koran." Other Arabic or Turkish terms are italicized and briefly defined the first time they are used.

INTRODUCTION

> *The thing which has become clear is that family history*
> *is inextricably involved in the great issue of the change*
> *from traditional to modern society. No other question*
> *is more important to historians of the West than the*
> *causes, nature, timing, and consequences of this transi-*
> *tion. . . . There is hardly a single one of these transfor-*
> *mations in which the family has not played a key role*
> *as agent, subject, catalyst, or transmitter of changing*
> *values and experience.*[1]

In this statement, Lawrence Stone sums up the historiographical impact
of twenty years of intensive research on the European family in the past.
Historical studies of the European family have a long pedigree, but it is
only with the enormous production of family historians in recent decades
that family history has come into its own. Its contribution is best reflected
in the extent to which it has been "mainstreamed." Most historians now
recognize the connection between family history and the major structural transformations of European society. Yet despite the impact that
family history has had in reshaping historical studies, Stone concludes his
assessment by arguing that we still have few indisputable answers about
the family in the past. What we have learned, however, is what questions
to ask.[2]

Stone's comments on the state of European family history underscore
the challenges that confront historians who wish to study the family, especially in regions for which serious study of family history is just begin-

ning. Until a few years ago, there was no family history of the Middle East. There were some histories of families, but these did not deal with the family as an institution, its evolution over time, nor the relationship between the family and society. This gap in the historical studies of the Middle East is now starting to be filled as historians are being attracted to the study of the family from a variety of backgrounds. For example, scholars interested in women's history find that they need to better understand the functioning of the family as a whole in order to understand the position of women within it. Demographic historians find that basic questions about population change are intimately tied to the behavior of families.[3]

Uncovering the history of the Middle Eastern family is not an easy task. Complex problems of interpretation and methodology, often daunting to European family historians with a rich diversity of sources appropriate to the task and with an established historiographical framework in which to work, pose even greater obstacles to students of the Middle Eastern family. *How* to study the family—the methodological issues involved—is complicated by the limited nature of the source material, especially before the end of the nineteenth century. *Why* study the family and how to interpret what we find are hindered by certain underlying assumptions that have not been easy to discard: that the "Islamic" family was a monolithic and unchanging institution, at least until the forces of modernization affected the Muslim world in the twentieth century, and that family life is "private" and therefore not a suitable subject for historical research. Few people would any longer admit to believing these statements, yet such assumptions still linger in subtle and not-so-subtle forms.

The growing theoretical and methodological sophistication of Middle Eastern historical studies, however, can help us overcome both the methodological and conceptual obstacles. Like the history of gender or the reconstruction of culture, both of which seemed impossible to study in any meaningful way for the premodern and early modern periods just a short time ago, family history *is* possible, as recent research is revealing. A major task for Middle Eastern family historians now is compiling basic information about the family, a process that is just beginning. We still have very little data on marriage and divorce, household structure, inheritance, economic ties, affective relations, and kinship roles for most regions of the Middle East and from different time periods. Another major task is to identify the questions we want to ask. As Stone indicates, this is a critical step in moving forward in our understanding of the family. Identifying the right questions and documenting the family go hand in hand. We have to ask the right questions to be able to collect the evidence; at the same time, the more we learn about the family, the more we can refine our questions and ask more meaningful ones.

The research done to date has begun the process of identifying key questions and amassing evidence. Thanks to the pioneering work of Alan Duben, the best-developed line of inquiry so far concerns household structure and formation. Following the work done by historians of other regions on comparative household structures, Duben's basic question has focused on the type of household system found in the Turkish areas of the Ottoman Empire and during the early republican years, a question intertwined with issues of family size and the nature of the domestic cycle—that is, age of marriage, place of residence after marriage, and the timing of household fission. Duben indicates that both simple and multiple-family households existed.[4] Although it is too early to tell if one type was more prevalent, Haim Gerber hypothesizes that "the nuclear family was much more widespread in the past than commonly realized."[5] We may never be able to answer the question of which type predominated before the modern period, given the nature of our sources before the late nineteenth century. Our task, however, is to identify what patterns existed, where they existed, and the reasons for these patterns. To what extent did household type vary by class, region, ethnicity, distance from the center, location (urban vs. rural), and the conditions of the local economy?[6]

A second line of inquiry focuses on marriage. Much of what was written about marriage in the past dealt with the legal strictures surrounding this institution, with particular attention to polygamy and concubinage, divorce, and the control of the marriages of females, that is, those aspects of the law that placed women in a clearly subordinate position. Recent research has refocused the discussion in two directions. First, it has looked at marriage law not just as legal text but as it was interpreted and executed by judges and muftis.[7] Second, it has paid more attention to marriage practices, which were affected by a variety of other variables besides the provisions of Islamic law. Judith Tucker has identified some of the important questions to ask: How significant was the exchange of *mahr* (dower)? How common was polygamy? How permanent were marriages, with particular attention to the issue of divorce? What was the age of marriage? How common was cousin marriage? Underlying all these questions is the connection between these features of the institution of marriage and the position of women within the family: that is, to what extent was marriage another way of controlling and limiting the autonomy of women or, alternatively, a means by which women were provided with some economic security and some control over their own lives? There was no single answer to this, according to Tucker. The impact of marriage practice on women was a mixed bag and depended largely on class position.[8] Moreover, marriage was only one of a number of family relationships in which women were involved. Their relationship to their children and to their parents and other relatives played a role in how they interacted with their husbands.[9] While Tucker's work focuses on marriage in the early modern period, Beth Baron and Duben and Behar explore the nature of marriage ties in Cairo and Istanbul respectively, as marriage practices began to change under the impact of the social transformations in the late nineteenth and early twentieth centuries. They discuss the transition to more companionate marriages in which bride and groom have greater freedom to choose a spouse.[10] Other information on marriage practices emerges from general overviews on women. We are only beginning to answer these questions about marriage, few of which have simple answers.

A third line of inquiry focuses on the role of the family in structuring gender relations. It was through the family that socialization about gender roles took place and male-female, male-male, and female-female relationships were defined and internalized. The debate about gender and patriarchy is therefore inseparable from discussion of the family. Much of this debate centers around whether something called "Islamic patriarchy" as a form of "classical patriarchy" existed. If so, what were its characteristics and how important was this gender ideology, as opposed to material factors, in determining the position of females?[11] According to the model of Islamic patriarchy, the family was patrilineal, endogamous, patrilocal, and extended, and it held property jointly—all features that were grounded in the family and personal status laws of the *shariʿa*.[12] These characteristics of the Islamic patriarchal family are seen as necessarily connected, even by historians such as Gerber who question whether such a family type was the norm in the past.[13] Understanding basic features of family life—principles of descent, marriage, household, and inheritance—and the distribution of power within families is intricately linked to determining the nature of the patriarchal system. How were power and authority distributed and resources allocated among males and females within the family and among generations? Through the control of marriage and maintenance of extended family households, were the rights of individuals, especially women, being entirely subordinated to the interests of the family? In other words, was the family the perpetuator of patriarchy, an oppressive institution for females as well as for younger and weaker males, as the model of Islamic patriarchy implies?[14]

This research on household, marriage, and the connection between family structure and the gender system is only the beginning of the inquiry into these issues. It represents the tip of the iceberg in terms of the range of questions that can and should be asked about the historical Middle Eastern family, and it raises as many questions as it answers. At the same time, three critical points are underscored by the research done so far. The first is that we should not take anything for granted. All our assumptions and generalizations about the Middle Eastern family in the past need to be reexamined in light of solid historical evidence. Seemingly true generalizations—that households in the past were large, that age of marriage was young, that kinship ties were more important than other social ties—are being challenged as archival research sheds doubts on their universal application. Many of these assumptions may prove to be true for some groups in some places at some times; it does not necessarily follow that they were always true. Rather, they remain hypotheses to be tested.

The second point, related to the first, is the diversity of family arrangements. The myth of a monolithic "Islamic" or even "Middle Eastern" family is made very clear in this research. Household patterns varied from one region to the next; within one small city marriage practices varied significantly by class. It is probably best to stop using terms such as "Islamic" and "Middle Eastern" and to find different labels that more accurately reflect this diversity by firmly anchoring discussions of the family in a particular region and time. What ties much of the recent research together is the focus on the family in the Ottoman Empire between 1600 and 1914, or what we might call the early modern period and the first decades of the modern era. This is in fact a historiography of the Ottoman family. This is not to suggest that there was such a thing as a monolithic "Ottoman" family, any more than there was or is an "Islamic" or "Middle Eastern" one. The Ottoman Empire was characterized by a diversity of social patterns, religious and ethnic groups, ecological and economic zones, and political arrangements between center and provinces that reflected the flexibility that was one of the Empire's great strengths. Given this, there is unlikely to be a single "Ottoman" family. However, Ottoman rule provided an overarching political structure, a unified system of law, and widely shared social norms and cultural values to the peoples of the Empire and a well-known political and economic context in which to explore the diverse forms of the Ottoman family. Once the similarities and differences among families in this specific historical context have been adequately identified and explained, researchers will be in a better position to compare family patterns in the Ottoman Empire to those of other Middle Eastern and Islamic countries and to analyze the extent to which the cultural values and ideology embedded in a shared religious system, and the structural features imposed by similar environmental constraints, affected these patterns.

The third point underscored by recent research is the danger of assuming changelessness in the family. Scholars of the Middle East acknowledge that profound changes have taken place in the family as the region has undergone social transformation in the last two hundred years, sometimes at the risk of ignoring continuities with the past. Many also appear to believe that little change took place in the family before that time, in part because such change is hard to uncover. Labels like "Islamic" or "classical" patriarchy aggravate the problem by emphasizing similarities across time and space and reinforcing a sense of changelessness. Differences are subsumed to what are seen as more profound similarities.

Some historians of gender are beginning to challenge the view that premodern gender relations were changeless. Implicit in this rejection of an unchanging gender system is a recognition that the family also changed over time. Mervat Hatem has been particularly critical of the failure of scholars who are concerned with questions of patriarchy to anchor their discussions of these issues in a specific historical context and to explore how patriarchal systems differed and how change occurred within them.[15] She and others link changes in the family to changes in the state by exploring the connections between the decentralization of the Ottoman Empire and changes in the gender system. In the case of Egypt, Hatem argues that the weakening of the Ottoman state led to larger kinship structures giving way to a family type in which the power of the patriarch over his extended household was greatly expanded. In return for continued allegiance to the Ottoman state, the state agreed to give the patriarchs a free hand.[16] Linda Schilcher sees a similar connection in Syria between weakening Ottoman control and changes in the family. She argues that the patriarchal extended family emerged there in the late seventeenth century. The rise of the notables, a consequence of the redistribution of power between center and provinces, led to the emergence of this particular family pattern.[17]

Two other historians of Egypt take a different view. They agree that the loosening of Ottoman authority was a catalyst for changes in gender relations and in the family. They, however, do not believe that it led to a more patriarchal family. Instead, these changes gave women more room to negotiate with husbands and fathers, greater autonomy within the family, and increased opportunities to amass wealth that in turn provided them more leverage with significant males. These advantages were lost with state centralization and modernization in the nineteenth century.[18]

We know too little about the family and the patriarchal system in the premodern and early modern periods to begin to resolve such a debate. Nevertheless, the theoretical issue raised—about the relationship between changes in the state and changes in the family—is critical, and these studies offer exciting ideas. They are important for stimulating further research and for their attention to change and to connections between state structures, economic conditions, and family patterns.

The ultimate goal of an emerging history of the Middle Eastern family should be to arrive at an understanding of the evolution of the family and kinship in the various regions of the Middle East and to uncover the relationships between change in the family and other kinds of change. If the study of the family fulfills its potential, historical studies in the future will seem incomplete without thorough attention to the family. Achieving this goal, however, can only be done through a step-by-step process. We need to establish some basic "facts" about the family—size, structure, marriage patterns, economic arrangements, affective relationships—through careful, detailed case studies of the family at different times and in different places, and to place these family facts in historical context. Then we can begin to generalize in a meaningful way, to make comparisons, to see change over time, to determine which variables were critical in family formation and change, and to understand the intricate link between the evolution of the family and the transformation of Middle Eastern society since 1500. This study of upper-class families in late Ottoman Aleppo attempts to be one of the building blocks from which we can construct a family history of the Middle East.

FRAMEWORK OF THE STUDY

The family is a complex institution. This most basic point must be kept in mind and forms the underlying assumption of this study. Even when looking at families among one class in a limited period of time, the diversity of family types and the flexibility of family arrangements can seem to defy generalization. The sources of this complexity grow out of the processes of family life and the role of the family as the primary social institution. In the past, as today, families changed over time. As society changed, so did family structure and relationships. As a pivotal institution, the family was both responsive to and an agent of change. Change in the family occurred not only in the framework of historical time but also on a constant basis in the framework of "domestic" time: families were in a constant state of evolution over the course of the domestic cycle as children were born and grew up, married, started families of their own, and as parents aged and died. This complexity and the accompanying difficulties of studying the family in the past are compounded by the ambiguities surrounding our sense of what constituted the family. The term itself is an imprecise one in English, referring to everything from the "isolated" nuclear family to everyone related by blood and marriage. Although more precise in naming relatives, Arabic terms for family are also ambiguous.[19]

The problem for the historian is how to do justice to this complexity and at the same time establish some basic facts and draw meaningful conclusions about families. In this study, I propose to focus on three aspects of family life: household, marriage, and inheritance. The household, as the fundamental framework for family life, will be the subject of Chapter 2. Which family members shared a residence and for how long are critical questions for understanding the family. This chapter will focus on the formation and breakup of households and compare these patterns to those in other parts of the Ottoman Empire and to cultural ideals.

Chapter 3 will focus on marriage patterns and practices among these families, with particular attention to the much-discussed issues of polygyny, divorce, and the mahr and the effect of these practices on the nature and strength of the marriage bond. Because marriage created a political, social, and economic alliance between families, at least at the level of the upper class, it was a pivotal institution in defining significant social and family relationships and establishing social boundaries.

Chapters 4 and 5 will examine the transmission of wealth from one generation to the next. The two principal means of doing this in Aleppo were the Islamic inheritance system and the religious endowment, although premortem transfers through gifts to brides, property sales, and cash exchanges occurred with some regularity. Chapter 4 will look at devolution through the inheritance system, focusing on the relationship between law and practice and the impact of inheritance strategies on family structure. Chapter 5 will look at the use of family religious endowments as another inheritance strategy and examine whether this form of devolution had fundamentally different consequences for the family. To provide the context for discussions of household, marriage, and inheritance, Chapter 1 will discuss Aleppo's notables as a social group and as patrilineages.

Forming households, arranging marriages, and passing wealth from one generation to the next were the most important decisions facing any family. The choices made reveal family strategies for achieving certain goals within the opportunities available to and limits placed on them by many variables, including how much wealth and what type of resources they controlled, the state of the economy, political conditions, gender and age structure within the family, and rates of fertility and mortality. Some of these factors were within the family's control; others clearly were not. These decisions were rarely simple, and they had consequences for family structure and relationships at the time and in future generations. They involved delicate negotiations, the balancing of competing and sometimes conflicting interests and priorities, and efforts to minimize the tensions that surrounded such processes. On occasion, the sources allow us to see these processes directly; more often they reveal the results in indirect ways. From these results, patterns emerge that allow us to make some generalizations about the nature of the household and the practice of marriage and inheritance in eighteenth- and nineteenth-century Aleppo.

Knowing who lived together, who married whom and for how long, and who got a piece of the patrimonial pie lays the foundation for constructing a better understanding of the Aleppo family in the past. Focusing on household, marriage, and inheritance also reveals much about the interaction among kin, the nature of their relationships, and the dynamics of family life that allow us to go beyond mere description of these institutions. Through this interaction insights emerge about three major historical issues that form the themes of this book. The first theme is fam-

ily and law. The impact of Islamic law on women, the gender system, and
the family has been the subject of some very interesting studies in recent
years. Much of this work challenges the view of Islamic law as highly
mysogynist and as a key institution in perpetuating female subordination.[20] My own thinking about issues of law and family has been greatly
influenced by this work. This study, however, does not foreground law as
these other works do. Rather, in looking at marriage and inheritance
practices as revealed through the *mahkama shar'iyya* (Islamic court) records, I treat law as one factor among others that influenced these practices and patterns.

The second theme is the relationship between the nature of the family and the gender system. The debate about family and patriarchy was
discussed in the previous section. What does a case study of upper-class
families in Aleppo contribute to this debate? Did the way in which
households were structured, marriages arranged, and inheritance controlled reveal a patriarchal and patrilineal family living under a single roof
and dominated by a powerful head who monopolized control of economic resources and placed severe restrictions on the economic and social autonomy of family members, especially women? Or did the realities
of everyday life place limits on the ability to form such families and result
in a less lopsided balance between genders? The evidence from upper-
class families is very important to this debate. Although the elite formed
only a small part of the population, and their wealth, power, and status allowed them to lead lives very different from the rest of the population,
their lifestyle and values, in theory at least, embodied ideals to which
other classes aspired, and therefore their family arrangements had "practical and ideological effects beyond class boundaries."[21]

The third and most important theme is what constituted the family. Family historians would most like to know what the family meant
to people at the time. Unfortunately, we cannot ask these eighteenth-
century Aleppo notables, nor have they left records that allow us some
window into what they considered the family, as did some individuals in
Renaissance Italy, for example.[22] However, as they bought and sold property, formed new households, married, settled inheritances, feuded with
each other, received appointments to offices, assumed the guardianship of
minors, and went about the business of everyday life as it appears in the
court records, we see these families "in action." What emerges from these
activities are patterns that suggest an idea of what the "family" was. On
one level it did not have clearly defined boundaries. Each individual in-

habited several family "circles." Two of these circles, representing the largest and the smallest kinship structures, had more or less clearly defined boundaries: the lineage and the conjugal family (i.e., husband, wife or wives, and children). The lineage included all who shared the family name, including distant relatives, and it could be quite large. The use of the same last name identified a biological relationship and implied recognition of kinship. At the other end of the scale, the conjugal family was bound by the rights and obligations and perhaps ties of intimacy and affection between husbands and wives and parents and children. The conjugal families were the building blocks of the domestic unit. But these two "family circles" were not the only ones. There was the family as defined by law, which may only have become relevant when inheritances were distributed or the guardianship of children was decided. There was the residential family or household, which may have incorporated non-kin in a familial relationship. There was the affinal family created through marriage. But it is not clear that any of these circles alone would have been considered the "family" to which one belonged, in the eyes of Aleppo's elite. Everyone was involved in multiple ties of kinship that changed over his or her lifetime. These family circles overlapped, but they were not necessarily identical. Who formed part of these different family circles? How important were they, and under what circumstances did different types of kinship ties become critical?

By looking at interactions among family members as they formed households, arranged marriages, and passed wealth from one generation to the next, we can begin to see which family connections appeared to be strongest. Which family members were most likely to reside in the same household? Which were chosen as marriage partners in endogamous marriages? Which family members were actually tied together as heirs or beneficiaries of religious endowments? As these relationships emerge, some of the most important family ties are revealed and the boundaries of the family delineated. This is not to say that these boundaries were rigid or impermeable, or that other meaningful kinship ties were precluded. But it means that certain types of kinship interaction were more frequent and centered around the most critical aspects of family life and in effect defined the family in a way that would have made sense to individuals at the time. The main purpose of this study, then, is to attempt to identify the boundaries of the family among the notables of Aleppo and to define family structure in those terms. In other words, who were the "kin who counted"?

SOURCES AND METHODOLOGY

The growing interest in Middle Eastern family history is clear evidence of the importance of the issues of concern to family historians. However, historians interested in studying the Middle Eastern family, especially for any time period before the twentieth century, face significant methodological challenges, including the daunting prospect of limited sources, even the best of which are problematic; determining how to use the available sources with few models to guide them; and formulating questions that can be answered and say something meaningful about the family. Because of these methodological problems, it is important to discuss the sources on which this study is based and how they will be used.

For European historians who study the family, there is almost an embarrassment of riches in source materials. Even for the premodern period, manorial roles and household accounts, parish and notary records, and diaries and letters are available in large numbers, and a key question for the historian is how to select from this richness. Middle Eastern historians are not so lucky. Despite the abundance of literary and archival sources for premodern history, relatively few can yield much information on the family. One major exception to this rather discouraging picture are two kinds of legal sources: the *fatwa* documents (legal opinions by muftis) and the records of the mahkama shar'iyya. This study is based on the latter.

The value of the Islamic court archives for family history lies in the nature of Islamic law and the institutionalization of the legal and judicial system under the Ottomans. The keystone of the Islamic legal system, family law is minutely detailed and explicit on the rights and obligations of family members with regard to marriage and divorce, inheritance, custody of children, parentage, and relationships between spouses. Consequently, the whole range of family matters was subject to the courts and to judges who were administering this law. In this capacity, judges served not only as arbitrators in civil litigation as it concerned family law, but also as the equivalent of notary publics in the West, registering marriages, divorces, inheritance settlements, and guardians. Moreover, cases that were not specifically tied to family law, but that affected and revealed relationships within the family, such as property and commercial transactions, came before the judge for registration or resolution. In all cases, kinship relationships were carefully recorded because of the concern about family matters.

Although the Ottomans did much to regularize the judicial system and although *qadi*s (judges) had jurisdiction over a range of legal matters, what was actually recorded, the form in which it was recorded, the amount of information that was included about participants and issues, and of course, what has survived varied from one Ottoman city to another. For example, although marriages were registered with the qadi in eighteenth-century Aleppo, marriage contracts are not found in the existing records. Marriage contracts have survived for many other places, however, including Cairo and many towns in Palestine.[23] The content and form of these records were influenced by such factors as the effectiveness of Ottoman control in different periods, the real power and authority of the qadi, the importance of the city, and the competence of the clerks.

In assessing the usefulness and reliability of these sources, the historian is confronted with two problems common to all scholars who use legal sources. The first is the question of how extensively the courts were used. Many matters were undoubtedly settled within the family or through informal networks of arbitration at the neighborhood level.[24] Moreover, it is possible that there is a class bias in the recorded cases. As in our own legal system, those who could afford the fees, who were literate and familiar with the law and often had connections with the judicial hierarchy, and who had the most to gain from a duly registered and legally binding contract or settlement of litigation would have been most likely to use the courts. Nevertheless, scholars who have examined these sources have generally come to the conclusion that people registered contracts and brought disputes to be resolved on a routine basis, especially in the larger Ottoman cities. The most persuasive support for this conclusion comes from Haim Gerber's analysis of who used the courts in Bursa. He classified a sample of cases according to the social background of the participants and found that most of them were not from the elite. Moreover, in cases that did involve the elite, most were brought to court by the "social underdog." Gerber concludes that "the court is seen mainly as a tool of the common people to defend a modicum of legal rights."[25] While a similar breakdown of the background of the litigants is not available for other courts, the sheer number of cases in any one year in a city like Aleppo or Cairo suggests that they were widely used by individuals from a range of ethnic, religious, and socioeconomic groups. People seemed to have faith in the courts as vehicles for achieving their goals.[26]

The second problem is the extent to which what was recorded in the sources reflected reality. Were the decisions rendered in any case actually implemented? A brief consideration of our own legal system is enough to suggest how frequently the actual implementation of a decision fails to follow the ruling of the judge. However, to some extent this is less problematic than it might appear at first. Much of the value of these sources lies less in the final decisions rendered by the qadis and more in the issues raised and detailed information provided.[27] Moreover, whether a decision was implemented can be confirmed in some cases by subsequent entries in the registers dealing with the same piece of property. A more complicated issue is that of legal fiction. It is possible that fictitious contracts or property sales were registered to serve the particular purposes of the parties involved. For example, a wealthy merchant might register the sale of property to a religious leader to avoid the threat of confiscation, without the property ever changing hands in reality. This type of methodological problem has been raised in the case of historians using notary records in Renaissance Italian cities.[28] We have no way of knowing whether such legal fictions took place nor any means of weeding them out if they did. It is important to note the problem, but we must simply live with the doubt.

Despite the problems posed by the sources and the limitations inherent in the evidence, the religious court archives remain an enormously rich source for the study of the Ottoman family in the early modern period. The very weaknesses of these records as evidence can also be their strengths, since the need to confront their limits forces one to be as creative as possible in devising ways of using them. The great volume of cases and the sheer amount of detail contained in most of them pose real dilemmas of sampling and selecting. At the same time, it is this volume and detail that make the sources so useful, opening, as they do, a window into the social and cultural world of Ottoman urban society unavailable in other sources.

There are a number of different ways to use these sources to study the family. For purposes of this study, I have chosen to concentrate on those families with family names. In the Ottoman Empire of this period, that means elite families.[29] Evidence about family life in other classes will be included at times to provide comparison, but the main focus of the study will be confined to one group. The most important reason for choosing this focus is that it allows us to identify individuals. Consistent social identification, apart from religious affiliation, is missing from these records. A study of the elite, with its family names, allows us to overcome the problem posed by the general anonymity of the sources. This in turn allows us to use two methodologies that minimize some of the problems posed by the sources and maximize their potential: family reconstitution and historical ethnography.

Family reconstitution, a technique devised by European demographic historians utilizing parish registers of births, deaths, and marriages to establish some basic facts about family size and structure, is essentially a technique of genealogical reconstruction, piecing together information about the family from a variety of sources.[30] Reconstructing families in this way makes it possible to resolve questions that we would otherwise be unable to answer, including the approximate size of the lineages and individual families that made up these lineages when we have no reliable statistical data available. It also shows the structure and delineates the boundaries of the lineage, the largest kin group. In addition, being able to answer many basic questions about households, marriage, and inheritance depends on knowing the precise relationship among kin. Determining the frequency and significance of cousin marriage, tracing the changes in residence that indicate the formation of new households, and knowing who among the potential heirs actually inherited require a knowledge of genealogical relationships that only become clear through reconstructing the family.

Historical ethnography, as described by Diane Owen Hughes, is the "study of the cumulative experiences of individuals to construct societal models."[31] Hughes proposed such a methodology for utilizing the notary records of medieval and Renaissance Italy, documents with many similarities to the religious court archives. It involves tracking the behavior of individuals over time in their everyday lives as recorded by the notaries. By studying those Aleppo individuals with family names, it is possible to trace the activities of members of each family through the sources. Single entries, which by themselves are relatively meaningless, become significant when put in the context of all other cases in which that individual was involved. Similarly, the recorded activities of an individual may have little significance alone, but take on new importance when placed side by side with the activities of other family members. In this way, the fragmented, but detailed, nature of the information in the sources can be placed in a meaningful context. We see these families "in action." Patterns emerge that shed light on basic institutions of family life. These documents are also what Andrejs Plakans calls "interaction" documents, windows through which we can see family members interacting with each other.[32] They make it possible to see which family members interacted most frequently, what kinds of issues brought them together, and what kinship roles they seem to be playing. As we see which kin have the closest and most frequent contact, we can begin to define the boundaries of the effective family. Tracing families through the sources and being able to study families across generations helps avoid a static approach that obscures the dynamics of family formation and interaction.

Since the main purpose of this study is to attempt to understand important family ties and identify the boundaries of the effective family, one other methodological issue needs to be addressed: the question of terminology. The problem of using an imprecise term like *family* to describe and analyze such a complex institution has already been alluded to, although I have continued to use the term rather indiscriminately in this study to refer to all who share a common family name as well as other kinds of kin groups. For stylistic purposes, it will continue to be used in this way occasionally, and the context should make that clear. Nevertheless, for analytical purposes, it is necessary to have a more precise vocabulary to talk about the different family circles in which these notables operated. It is important to be able to use a vocabulary that is appropriate to the way in which Middle Easterners of the time would have understood the family and at the same time use terminology that allows us to put the Aleppo family of the Ottoman period in comparative context.

Arabic is more helpful than English, both in naming kin and describing kinship groups, since it is more precise about the relationship between individuals and groups of relatives. For example, it uses different terms for paternal and maternal aunts/uncles. However, it still falls short of providing a clear terminology in which to discuss family structure and relationships. Ambiguity arises because there is considerable regional and even class variation in the use of these terms today, and there may well be important differences between how terms are used today and how they were used in the past. Moreover, like English, some of the most basic Arabic terms to designate kin groups can have multiple meanings.

For understanding historical usage of kinship terms in Syria, the best source is perhaps Kazem Daghestani, who surveyed the Syrian Muslim family in the 1920s and made careful note of the way kinship terms were used. Usage at that point was probably similar to what it had been a hun dred years earlier. Two Arabic terms were commonly used to denote significant family groupings among the great "bourgeois" families of the urban centers—that is, the kind of families who are being studied here. The term ʿaʾila (or ʿāla) was used to designate the group consisting of all males and females from the same *souche* (origin) who shared the same family name and were tied together by consanguine relationships through the males—in other words what we would call a lineage in English. Subdivisions of the lineage were called *bayt* in Arabic. According to Daghestani, division of the ʿaʾila occurred when the family grew too large. Each bayt, headed by one or more males and including his or their wives and children, became an independent economic unit and usually, though not always, lived in a separate household.[33] While the meaning of bayt in this sense and the relationship between ʿaʾila and bayt seems clear at first glance, a closer look reveals some ambiguity. Some lineages were subdivided into separate branches, with each branch consisting of several families or households, but others were not. Did bayt refer to branches of the lineage or to the households or conjugal families that made up each branch? There is also the confusion between bayt used in the figurative sense of family and bayt used to designate a physical structure, the house itself, and/or those people who lived in it, the household, who may or may not have been part of the family. Another term, *dar,* was also used to refer to the house as a physical structure and in a more figurative sense, as in the "house" of Osman. Moreover, both ʿaʾila and ʿāla could mean the conjugal family as well as the lineage. So although Arabic does make some more precise distinctions among levels of kinship organization, the ambiguity in the vocabulary of family and kinship is not eliminated and so does not fully resolve the problem of how to talk about "family" with greater clarity.

Nevertheless, in general the language used by the religious courts seems to make the distinction between ʿaʾila and *bayt* on the one hand and *bayt* and *dar* on the other, using ʿaʾila to indicate a larger kin group, *bayt* a smaller one, and *dar* to designate the actual physical house. In doing so, it presumably reflected some of the distinctions that society as a whole made about the kinds of kinship groups. With that in mind, I have chosen to use the term *lineage* as a translation of ʿaʾila and to refer to the largest kinship group among these families: all individuals who shared the same family name. This is not a completely satisfactory term since *lineage* is often used in the Middle Eastern context to refer to corporate groups and may suggest connotations about kinship organization that are not appropriate here. Still, it is clear from the use of family names and other evidence that these patrilineal descent groups were recognized and those connections considered important. What to call the subdivisions of the lineage is more problematic. As indicated above, the term *bayt* can refer to anything from a basic family group of parents and children to a large extended grouping consisting of several generations and several degrees of kinship. Despite this imprecision, *bayt* will be translated as "branch" when referring to a distinct subdivision of the patrilineage. The term *family* will refer to individual units of the lineage or branch. The phrases *elementary family* or *conjugal family* will be used to refer to husband, wife or wives, and children.[34] The term *extended family* will refer to parents and children plus father's parents, siblings, and siblings' children. These terms will be used when talking about families as economic associations or social networks as well as residential units. When talking about households, however, the terminology preferred by scholars interested in comparative household structures will be used: *simple households* to refer to those with only one resident elementary or conjugal family, and *multiple households* to describe those with more than one conjugal family, consisting of either father and married sons and their families or brothers and their families.

THE HISTORICAL CONTEXT

The century from 1750 to 1850 was a time of upheaval and transition in the Ottoman Empire. Two key processes reshaped the Empire: (1) the integration of the empire into the world economy with European expansion, and (2) political decentralization, followed by a more or less effective recentralization with the reforms of the Tanzimat. A major urban center like Aleppo did not remain isolated from the turmoil produced by these changes. How fundamentally Aleppo was affected by the structural changes in the empire, however, is a subject of some debate. The impact of these changes on provincial society throughout the empire depended on a number of factors: the perceived importance of the region to Istanbul, its value to the Europeans as a source of raw materials and markets, the structure of the local economy, and the response of local society. After 1750 political events moved rapidly. Nevertheless, this did not necessarily mean that social structure or cultural values and attitudes kept pace or that basic institutions like the family were transformed. In fact it is almost impossible to find evidence that change occurred in these areas. In his study of Aleppo in the middle of the eighteenth century on the "eve of modernity," Abraham Marcus demonstrates a remarkable stability in the basic social order and continuity in attitudes, values, and worldview.[35] Social and cultural changes that grew out of the processes of economic and political change would not become obvious until later in the nineteenth century. But the beginnings of a major social transformation were already underway beneath this surface continuity. Political events and economic changes were affecting different social groups, including the elite, in a variety of ways and having an impact on their decisions and behavior, including the strategies they used in setting up households, making marriages, managing family resources, and handling family relationships. It is important, then, to summarize briefly the wider political and economic developments as they affected Aleppo and its elite.

The political decentralization of the empire had its roots in changes that occurred in the sixteenth century, such as the influx of New World silver and the resulting inflation, the effective end to acquisition of new land and resources through conquest, and a revolution in military technology. The financial crisis and changes in the military that followed profoundly affected land administration and the collection of revenues. These became the purview of tax farmers, drawn more and more from local notables. In contrast to the "classical" empire of the sixteenth century and to the smaller but recentralized state of the post-Tanzimat period, the Ottoman state of the seventeenth and eighteenth centuries experienced a shift of power from the center to the periphery. The notables, through their increasing control of local surpluses and acquisition of offices formerly reserved for imperial officials, were able to wield considerable power. Although they rarely rebelled openly against Ottoman authority, the notables, rather than Istanbul, often called the shots.

The impact of the shift of power to the periphery was not uniform throughout the empire, nor was it a unilinear process. Karl Barbir has argued convincingly that the Ottoman government was able to regain control of Damascus in the first half of the eighteenth century after being forced to make concessions to local notables in the latter part of the seventeenth. It was only after 1760 that the Ottomans effectively "lost" control of the province to local forces.[36] In Aleppo, the Ottoman government never lost control to the extent that it did in Damascus and other places after the middle of the eighteenth century. No local dynasty like the

'Azm governors in Damascus was able to dominate the city and act autonomously. As André Raymond has pointed out, "The province of Aleppo was undoubtedly the only one governed, more or less constantly, by pashas sent by the Porte."[37] Aleppo was closer to both Istanbul and the frontiers of the empire than Damascus and so had greater strategic importance. Moreover, it had always been a more "Ottoman" city, with an elite oriented to Istanbul and a heterogeneous and cosmopolitan population. It was also more directly linked by commercial ties to the Anatolian heartland of the empire.

Central control in Aleppo did weaken somewhat after 1760. The political instability that plagued the city between 1760 and 1820 reflected the inability of the imperial government to rule as effectively as before.[38] Three groups competed for power: the Janissaries (members of the Ottoman infantry corps), the *ashraf* (literally, descendants of the Prophet; in Aleppo they formed the basis of a political faction during this period), and Ottoman officials. The Janissaries and ashraf represented local groups in competition with each other while trying to take advantage of the problems of the Ottoman state. Except for a brief period between 1808 and 1812, however, when the Janissaries virtually ruled the city, Ottoman authority, although sometimes shaky, was nevertheless real. Imperial officials were able to govern the city and beat back every challenge to Ottoman authority by using effective strategies of exile, extortion, and cooption, as well as playing the other two factions off against one another. This latter strategy was particularly effective, since the competition between the two groups was so intense.

Ottoman attempts to destroy the Janissaries and ashraf, to regain full control of Aleppo, and to forge a new relationship with it began as early as 1813. These initial efforts were met with resistance from groups whose interests were threatened by them, culminating in an open revolt in 1819. With some difficulty, the Ottomans put down this uprising. Through punishment and conciliatory gestures, they continued their efforts to establish authority more tightly. The coming of the Egyptian occupation in 1831 interrupted this process but also represented a period of direct governmental control and left a legacy on which the Ottomans could build once their power was reestablished in 1839. Two policies introduced by the Egyptians—direct taxation and conscription—were continued by the Ottoman government. The creation of a modern army and a new fiscal system were key components of Ottoman reform and critical to the reestablishment of strong central authority in the provinces and were thus strongly opposed by many groups in Aleppo. Fueled by worsening economic conditions, local resentment against these policies culminated in the riots of 1850 that took the form of antigovernment and anti-Christian violence.[39] The Ottomans restored order relatively quickly, and within months the city had returned to "normal." Ottoman taxation and conscription policies continued as before. With the successful suppression of this revolt, Ottoman recentralization in Aleppo was effected.

This process of decentralization and recentralization in the Ottoman Empire occurred at the same time that it was undergoing profound economic change, and the two processes were closely connected. The distinctive feature of this transitional period in Ottoman economic history was the growing involvement of the empire in a world market increasingly dominated by Europe. The impact of this involvement on local economies varied. In the case of Aleppo, the accepted wisdom has been that it went into economic decline as trade routes shifted and a new relationship with Europe evolved. In the course of the seventeenth century, according to Niels Steensgaard, an Asian trade revolution occurred as the Muslim-dominated caravan trade was overtaken by European-dominated sea trade. Aleppo's decline began early in the seventeenth century as this commercial revolution got under way. It continued steadily through the eighteenth century and reached its culmination in the nineteenth when coastal cities replaced inland cities as the dominant commercial centers in the Middle East.[40] But this interpretation has been challenged by a number of recent studies. Without denying the extent to which the city's economic history was affected by changes in the world economy, the newer studies see the decline thesis as too simplistic to adequately explain the complex process of economic change that Aleppo underwent. They question the timing of these changes, the relative importance of internal and external factors in effecting them, and the tendency to tie Aleppo's economic fate to fluctuations in international commerce at the expense of ignoring commercial activities more important for the economic vitality of the city. Bruce Masters, who has done the definitive study of the economic history of Aleppo between 1600 and 1750, generally accepts Steensgaard's thesis, but sees the decline of the caravan trade, at least as it affected Aleppo, as not occurring until the mid–eighteenth century.[41] Antoine Abdel-Nour argued that the health of a city's economy depended much more on what it produced and on its regional commercial networks, and that Aleppo was able to withstand the consequences of a reduced role in international trade because it remained the center of an important and varied zone of production and commerce.[42]

The complexities of the situation and the difficulty of making easy generalizations are apparent in looking at the critical period between 1700 and 1850. In 1700, at least on the surface, the caravan trade was still going strong, and Aleppo was an equal, if not dominant, partner with the Europeans in this trade. By 1850, the city was well integrated into the European-dominated world economy. I suggest, tentatively—because, except for the first half of the eighteenth century, this period has not been subjected to in-depth study—that one can identify four different economic stages during this 150-year period. Looking at this transition in terms of different stages can reveal a great deal about the timing, relative importance of internal and external factors, and impact of these changes on the population of Aleppo.

The first half of the eighteenth century was a time of solid economic prosperity in the city. The population continued to grow as it had in the seventeenth century, though not as rapidly. Although much uncertainty surrounds the various estimates of the city's population, Abdel-Nour argued for these: approximately 60,000 in the late sixteenth century; 78,000 in the late seventeenth century; and 100,000 in 1750.[43] The growth in population throughout this period was the result of constant migration to the city from other areas. Migrants came from distant parts of the Islamic world, such as India and North Africa, as well as from regions closer to the city. The importance of Aleppo as a commercial center, and the opportunities it provided for achieving fame and fortune, brought this steady stream of migrants. Christians from eastern Anatolia and Iran fueled this migration in the seventeenth century, and as a result, the Christian population of Aleppo almost doubled between 1600 and 1683. In the first part of the eighteenth century, Christian migration had slowed but not stopped; the Christian population had grown by fifty percent by 1750. Tribesmen and peasants from the mountains and villages linked to Aleppo by commercial and political ties were also among the early-eighteenth-century newcomers.[44] So were Muslim merchants from more distant areas of the Islamic world. Several of the wealthiest and most influential families of the late eighteenth century had been established by merchants who had arrived from Basra, the Hijaz, and North Africa in the first decades of the eighteenth century.[45]

Population growth by itself is not sufficient evidence of economic growth, but other indications of wealth and prosperity suggest that it continued to be "pull" factors rather than "push" factors that were bring-ing large numbers to the city. One important indication of this was the urban development and expansion that took place in the early eighteenth century. For the first time since the sixteenth century major urban de-velopment or redevelopment took place in the central quarters of the city. Three local leaders—a locally born Ottoman governor, ʿUthman Pasha; a distinguished ʿalim (religious scholar; singular of ulema), Ahmad Taha; and a wealthy merchant, Hajj Musa Amiri—each built a new monu-ment. The endowments used to support these monuments included the construction or reconstruction of markets and commercial buildings in the quarters of Dakhil Bab al-Nasr, Jallum, and Suwayqa Hatim. Vacant land within the city walls was built over, and the largely Christian quar-ters to the north of the walls, and the eastern quarters in which most of the residents involved in the caravan and grain trade lived, continued to expand, indicating both the need for new residential and commercial buildings and the wealth to finance this construction.

The relatively high rate of social mobility also suggests new wealth coming into the city during this period and is not consistent with a city in economic decline. New fortunes were being made. As will be dis-cussed in greater detail in Chapter 1, many of the upper-class families of the late eighteenth and early nineteenth centuries acquired their fortunes and began the process of acquiring high social status in the early eigh-teenth century. Nor was economic prosperity confined to the rich. Aleppo had a substantial class of "men of modest substance," small prop-erty owners who also participated in the general prosperity.[46] The active buying and selling of real estate, much of it by groups other than the wealthy, reveals the wide distribution of property ownership across soci-ety and therefore of some means to make such purchases. So does the proliferation of religious endowments (waqfs) during this period. Less than a hundred new endowments were created in the seventeenth cen-tury, but five hundred were established in the eighteenth century, most of them modest endowments established by small property owners either for their own families or to serve some charitable purpose. Population growth, urban development, considerable social mobility, and the wide-spread distribution of prosperity were all dependent on the availability of economic opportunities and of wealth and do not suggest a city in eco-nomic decline.

Wealth came into the city from two principal sources. Commerce continued to generate wealth as it had since the sixteenth century, although the relative importance of the different commercial networks of which Aleppo was part was shifting. The first half of the eighteenth century saw Aleppo's decline as the entrepôt for the export of Iranian silk to Europe, a decline reflected in the shrinking number of British merchant houses in the city (from eight to two). The loss of the silk trade resulted primarily from the decline in demand, as new sources of better-quality silk emerged. The disruption of the silk trade resulting from the Ottoman-Iranian wars of the 1740s dealt a blow to the already declining trade from which it never recovered. However, the loss of this silk trade was not the economic blow that historians have usually suggested.[47] Our dependence on European sources for Aleppo's economic history has tended to exaggerate its importance in the economy. It was probably much less important than the city's links to Anatolia, Iraq, and eastern and southern Asia. The lack of statistics on this trade makes it impossible to establish definitely the relative importance of these two commercial sectors, although Abdel-Nour points out that Aleppo's exports to Europe after the second half of the seventeenth century were dominated by the products of its agricultural hinterland rather than by goods in transit from the East.[48]

At the same time, new wealth was being generated by sources other than commerce. With the decentralization of the empire described above, revenues that had once been destined for Istanbul now found their way into the pockets of the local elite and into the urban economy. Masters has pointed out that Muslim merchants were much more likely to put their wealth into these lucrative new investments than to reinvest it in commerce, partly to diversify their economic base and partly to take advantage of the potentially high rate of return on these investments.[49] The end of the silk trade did not have much impact on merchants' ability to find profitable investments and to increase their fortunes.

Underlying this general prosperity, however, were structural changes described by Masters and going beyond the end of the silk trade with Iran. One was that international trade was increasingly in the hands of the Europeans and their Christian agents. Syrian Christians took over trade between Aleppo and Egypt, for example. Goods from India more often arrived in Aleppo through Iskenderun, to which port they had been brought on European ships. This meant widening horizons and greater prosperity to the Christian communities of the city. It also meant the loss of commercial opportunities for Muslims, a loss that affected not so much the wealthy, who found other outlets for their capital, as the ambitious poor, who had been able to use commerce as a means of acquiring some wealth and social mobility.[50] However, the impact of these structural changes was not yet apparent in the general prosperity of the early eighteenth century.

The decade of the 1760s marked the beginning of a new phase in Aleppo's economic history. It was at this point that the changes underway before 1750 began to have a visible impact on the city, although calling this period after 1760 a time of economic "decline" fails to capture the contradictory forces at work. All evidence suggests that the volume of trade into and out of the city remained high and may have grown in the second half of the century. The French stepped in to replace the British as Aleppo's major European trading partner, and French trade with Aleppo expanded rapidly until the end of the eighteenth century. Trade with its own hinterland, other regions of the empire, and points east—always the mainstay of the city's commerce—also continued to thrive, although the lack of statistics frustrates efforts to confirm the impressions of contemporary observers to this effect. Observers in the late eighteenth and early nineteenth centuries commented on the flourishing state of trade in the city, reflected in the wealth of merchants and the abundance of goods in the market. Arabian coffee; tobacco and pipes from Iran; and spices, shawls, carpets, and Indian textiles from further east were found in great quantity in the markets of Aleppo, and trade with Anatolia and Egypt was brisk. The importance of the trade in these items was reflected in the revenues they produced for local customs officials. For the most part these goods were brought in for local consumption, a sign of a prosperous upper class that was interested in and could afford to purchase such items. As Masters indicates, many of these items, especially from further east, were being carried on European ships, but there is also evidence that the caravan trade, which had revived after 1745, continued to grow and expand into the nineteenth century.[51] Contemporary observers noted the number of caravans that continued to carry goods to Aleppo's traditional trading areas.[52] Hanna Batatu argues that trade through Iraq remained vigorous because of the "richness of the inter-Muslim" trade, despite the impoverishment of the countryside, pillaging tribesmen, and rapacious sheikhs and officials. Aleppo remained a key link in this commercial network.[53] Bedouin incursions and the unsettled state of the frontier periodically disrupted this trade and affected the city negatively, but it could also work to the advantage of Aleppo's commercial community at other times. In the early years of the nineteenth cen-

tury, when the cross-desert trade to Damascus was interrupted by
Bedouin and Wahhabi attacks, this trade was rerouted through Aleppo
and further increased the volume of trade in the city.[54]

The continued briskness of trade coexisted with more troubling signs
that boded ill for the future, however. To begin with, the trade with Europe now had a clearly "colonial" character. Aleppo's role, instead of being that of middleman in international trade, shifted to being an exporter
of raw materials. In particular, the expansion of the French cotton indus-
try created a large demand for raw cotton that was exported from Aleppo
at an increasing rate through the rest of the century.[55] Other developments were also indicative of troubled times. The population continued
to grow, but most of the migrants were peasants and tribal people from
the surrounding countryside, who were fleeing rural misery and insecurity rather than coming to seek the opportunities to be had in the city.
The worsening conditions in its hinterland, reflected in this migration,
began to negatively affect the city's overall economy. This migration also
resulted in a serious shortage of housing and terrible overcrowding in the
poorer areas of the city.[56] The intensified factional fighting in the city between the Janissaries and ashraf during this period also reflected a general
sense of economic insecurity and greater competition for resources in the
wake of worsening conditions in the countryside.

As these problems came to a head in the second decade of the nineteenth century, Aleppo experienced a real economic downturn. A third
stage in the city's economic history began at this time, when its economic
prosperity came to an end. Between 1813 and 1825 political factors and
a series of natural disasters negatively affected the economic strength of
the city. The factional fighting that Aleppo had been experiencing since
the 1760s (as discussed above) had occasionally led to disruption in trade
and temporary halts to production in the city, but overall it had had a
relatively minor impact until the second decade of the nineteenth century. John Barker, the British consul in Aleppo in the early years of the
nineteenth century, commented on how little the factional rivalry in the
city had affected its social and economic life up to that point.[57] After
1813, however, this changed as the struggle between the Janissaries and
the Ottoman government became more bitter and its effects more widely
felt. According to one chronicler, conditions in 1813 were so bad that if
women wanted to go to the baths, they had to go in groups of ten or
more for their safety.[58] The 1819 revolt that resulted from this intense
struggle was very destructive, with parts of the city virtually destroyed by

Ottoman artillery. It was only settled after four months and left serious economic repercussions. Before Aleppo had time to recover from this upheaval, a major earthquake hit in 1822, destroying large parts of the city and causing many casualties. It was followed by a series of aftershocks that continued to bring down buildings already weakened by the original quake. Two years later Aleppo experienced its first cholera epidemic, in which hundreds of people were killed. The combined effect of these events led to significant depopulation in the city and a major disruption of commercial and productive life. The long-term economic consequences were apparent in the fact that even ten years after the earthquake, large parts of Aleppo were still in ruins. There was not enough money to engage in major rebuilding projects.[59]

Given time, Aleppo might well have recovered from this series of disasters. However, these problems coincided with the major reorientation of the economy of the eastern Mediterranean. The weaknesses in Aleppo's economy made it particularly vulnerable to new economic forces in the region. The 1830s and 1840s marked the transition to a colonial economy in many parts of the Middle East, including Aleppo; by 1850 Aleppo showed many of the signs characteristic of this type of economy.[60]

The decisive event that marked the transition to this new economic stage was the Egyptian invasion in 1831, which affected Aleppo's economy in several different ways. The presence of the Egyptians revived the economy, as Muhammad ʿAli's government stimulated production in Syria—even though the primary impetus was to supply Egypt with necessary raw materials rather than to benefit Syria. Second, and more important in the long run, the Egyptian occupation affected Aleppo's economy by the revival of trade with Europe. After a decline in trade between Europe and Aleppo in the last years of the eighteenth and early years of the nineteenth centuries, European, and especially British, interest in commercial contacts with Aleppo reemerged in the 1820s. Direct trade between England and Aleppo reappeared in 1828, and by 1832 there were three British merchant houses in the city; in 1835 a British consul was reappointed to the city.[61] The policies of the Egyptian government facilitated greater European involvement in the economy. Muhammad ʿAli was anxious to win the support of the British for his position in Syria, and he hoped to do this by allowing the British access to Syrian markets. The rapid expansion of British trade and the consequences of this for Aleppo's economy were a direct result of the stance of the Egyptian government.

By the time Egyptian forces left Aleppo in 1839, its integration into the European-centered world economy was irreversible.

The impact of this integration became clearly apparent when Aleppo erupted into riots in 1850, the most startling aspect of which was the killing and plundering directed at the city's Christian population. These events are well known and viewed as a harbinger of the more extensive outbreak of communal violence in other parts of Syria ten years later. However, Bruce Masters has recently offered a new interpretation of this outbreak. While previous interpretations have emphasized the role of outsiders, resentment by local notables of changes coming from Istanbul, or long-standing Muslim hostility toward Christians, Masters argues that "the Events represented a partial collapse of the old order, conditioned by the empire's incorporation into the world system."[62] By paying careful attention to the identity of the attackers and the victims, Masters is able to pinpoint the causes of the outbreak. It was only the Muslims of the eastern quarters of the city who attacked, and it was only the Christians of the northern suburb of Judayda who were attacked. These were the groups whose position in the city had been most radically affected by economic change resulting from integration into the world market. The Muslims of the eastern quarters, whose livelihoods depended on the caravan trade and the provincial grain trade, had suffered from the decline of the caravan trade and a series of disastrous harvests. The burden of direct taxation and the abolition of the Janissary corps that had provided protection for, and corporate identity to, many inhabitants of these quarters intensified the economic hardships they experienced. On the other side, it was the Christians of the northern suburbs who benefited most from changing conditions. Their economic and political status was improving significantly with their increased commercial contacts with Europe and the protection of European powers operating in the empire, and culturally they were moving further away from their fellow Aleppines and closer to their European contacts. The root causes of the 1850 violence, therefore, were the economic dislocations caused by Aleppo's integration into the world capitalist system and the social and cultural tensions produced by the changing social order.[63]

Throughout this period, political and economic change in Aleppo interacted with and reinforced each other. In the eighteenth century, political change gave local residents access to resources that were formerly dominated by the state and brought new wealth into the region. At the same time, economic change created some uncertainty and sent people scurrying for safer ways of protecting their wealth. This resulted in increased competition for land and its products and was an underlying cause of the factional struggle in the city. Even so, political and economic changes moved at different paces. Despite the political instability of the period, economic prosperity continued and guaranteed social stability as well. This was reflected in the lack of structural change in society, although opportunities for social mobility and the assimilation of new families into the elite became more common. Traditional attitudes and values similarly remained intact. The shifting trade routes and early stages of Aleppo's integration into the world economy had as yet had little impact on the city.

Economic change and political instability began to have a major impact on traditional social structure in the first decades of the nineteenth century. These developments could no longer be absorbed and deflected by a basically stable social order, and the impact was reflected in changes in the elite. Although the elite was still composed of many of the same families, the change was apparent in the smaller size of the group, the number of downwardly mobile families, the slowed rate of recruitment into the group, and the redistribution of wealth and power among these families. The changing nature of the economy left those who controlled its resources in a potentially vulnerable position, while at the same time it opened up new opportunities. The task facing those who already controlled wealth was how best to preserve it in these circumstances and how, if possible, to take advantage of the changing economy. The strategies they used to accomplish this task were intricately linked to family organization and structure and affected, and were affected by, family relationships. In the following chapter, we will look more closely at Aleppo's notables and begin the examination of the elite family.

One   # FAMILY AND LINEAGE
Aleppo's Notables

O n the surface, traditional urban social structure was still intact in late-eighteenth- and early-nineteenth-century Aleppo, but the apparent stability of the social order and continuity in attitudes, values, and worldview masked profound changes already under way that would undermine these in the course of the nineteenth century. While on one level factional fighting might have been business as usual in the eighteenth century, it was a symptom of more profound socioeconomic changes on another. The effects of structural changes in the economy and readjustment of relationships between the provinces and the central government were already felt in the political and economic environment of Aleppo by the early nineteenth century.

One major transformation of the nineteenth century would be the emergence of a new class system out of the old social order, redefining social categories and changing relations among different social groups. At the top would be an upper class whose outlines were only beginning to become clear in the late eighteenth and early nineteenth centuries, the period under study here. It is this social group whose family patterns will be explored in later chapters. The idea of family and the ordering of early modern Ottoman provincial society were closely linked. The upper stratum of this society consisted of a group of families—in effect, patrilineages. These patrilineages were the largest kinship structures, and they provided a sense of identity to their members and conferred social status on them. This chapter will discuss who belonged to this group, the social bases of elite status, and the concept and meaning of the lineage as a

family group, within the context of the relationship between changes
within the class of notables and changes in the social order of Aleppo.

THE NOTABLES
IN OTTOMAN HISTORY

The social order of premodern and early mod-
ern Islamic society was anchored by an urban elite that occupied the top
stratum of local society and acted as mediators between the population
and the government. This elite, usually called the notables (in Arabic,
aʿyan), existed as an identifiable group as early as the ninth century, and
its formation was closely linked to the evolution and functioning of the
city in Islamic society and the distinctive political structures in which it
was embedded.[1] The role and composition of this elite varied over time
and from one region of the Islamic world to another. So did its relationship with the state. In eleventh- and twelfth-century Nishapur, the patricians, who controlled local offices and identified themselves with the
city, exercised considerable autonomy and resisted any effort to force
them to become agents of the imperial government. In thirteenth- and
fourteenth-century Cairo or Damascus, these notables conferred legitimacy on an alien regime and buffered the local population from the more
extreme forms of exploitation, but found themselves rarely able to operate independently of the government and were co-opted and grew increasingly subservient to it over time.[2] As mediators between imperial,
often alien, regimes and local society, these elites ensured the stability of
civil society in the face of chronic political instability between the Ab-
basid and the Ottoman Empires and in later periods of Ottoman history.[3]
They were indispensable to the smooth functioning of the Islamic social
order.

The role of the notables emerges as a particularly important historiographical issue among Ottoman historians of the seventeenth through the
nineteenth centuries, the period of Ottoman decentralization and subsequent reform. What was happening to the notables was closely linked to
fundamental questions surrounding the transformation of Middle Eastern society in the early modern period, specifically, the restructuring of
the Ottoman state, the rise of nationalism and the emergence of classes.
An extensive literature exists on the notables, much of it concerned with

the "politics of notables."[4] In an influential article written thirty years ago, Albert Hourani defined the notables as "those who can play a certain political role as intermediaries between government and people, and—within certain limits—as leaders of the urban population."[5] Despite widespread agreement on the identification of these notables by their political function, however, differences persist among historians about who should be labeled a notable, whether the notables formed a cohesive political group, and the precise nature of the role they played. Some historians, like Halil Inalcik, use a more restricted definition of the notables: people of wealth who acquired provincial offices and revenue sources formerly reserved for imperial officials. The social background of these notables was similar to those identified as notables by Hourani: ulema, merchants, leaders of guilds, and former servants and soldiers of the Ottoman government.[6] But while Hourani says only that these individuals had access to political power, Inalcik concentrates on those who acquired official status and access to state resources and on the consequences of that for imperial administration. Herbert Bodman has a still more restrictive use of the term *notable* in the context of Aleppo. He referred to a general use of the term *a'yan* to include "that class of provincials who had acquired *iqta'ahs,* or 'benefices,' and had been able to pass this source of income on to their children." This group evolved into the a'yan in a more specific sense: those with landed interests serving on the provincial divan.[7] Bodman's notables are one subgroup of Hourani's, although he does not identify their social backgrounds. His definition is similar to Inalcik's in limiting the term to those who had an official position in provincial administration. The differences among these definitions of the notables grow in part out of whether these notables are viewed from the perspective of the imperial center or the provinces.

A precise and unambiguous identification of the notables remains elusive because the extent of their power and their relationship with the central government in Istanbul varied significantly from region to region and from decade to decade. Not surprisingly, the provinces of Rumelia, with a large non-Muslim population, sitting on the borders of Europe, and already developing extensive commercial contacts outside the empire, would produce a very different form of notable politics than Bursa, which was the second capital of the empire and was under the watchful eye of the imperial government. Even neighboring provinces, however, could be quite different. Aleppo never achieved the degree of autonomy from Istanbul that characterized Damascus under the rule of the 'Azm governors or Palestine under Jazzar Pasha. Nor was the relationship between the central government and the provincial notables characterized by a progressive weakening of control from Istanbul. Periods of greater provincial autonomy alternated with periods of greater central control, depending on the interplay between events and conditions in Istanbul and developments in the provinces. Karl Barbir, for example, identifies the seventeenth century as a time when the notables of Damascus first "tested their strength vis-à-vis the central authority and won important tax concessions." This was followed in the first half of the eighteenth century by a reassertion of central authority. After 1760 the imperial government was unable to maintain this degree of control, and the notables were able once again to enjoy considerable autonomy.[8] Attempts to generalize about the role of these notables are also hindered by the fact that they were not an "identifiable political unit," according to Philip Khoury. He argues that the notables of Damascus had different power bases and followings, forms of political activity, and relations with the Ottoman government and did not act together on political matters. Consequently, attempts to lump them together and analyze them as a single group run the risk of seriously distorting their interests and behavior.[9]

The need to be attentive to the complexities and dynamic nature of the relationship between the provinces and the central government, however, does not change the fact that the notables, as defined in functional terms, were identifiable and critical political actors in eighteenth- and nineteenth-century provincial society. An analysis of the composition and activities of these political elites is critical for understanding political change in the Ottoman state in the seventeenth and eighteenth centuries—the shifting balance of power between center and periphery, the degree of Ottoman control in what was supposedly the period of Ottoman decline, and a particular style of politics associated with this balance of political forces—and for understanding the restructuring of the state and the rise of nationalism in the nineteenth and early twentieth centuries.[10]

The historiography of the notables is also linked to other transformations in the Ottoman Empire in the nineteenth century, specifically the emergence of distinct social classes. For the province of Damascus, Khoury has shown how a politically divided and socially heterogeneous group of notables evolved into an integrated social class, based on their control of land and bureaucratic offices.[11] Batatu sees a similar process at work in Iraq. What had been complex, changing, and very localized systems of social stratification were transformed into a class system that was characterized by "the stabilization, expansion, and, eventually, extreme concentration of private property." The most important cause of this change was the integration of Iraq into the world economy.[12] Impressionistic evidence suggests a similar process in Aleppo in the late nineteenth century, although a detailed study still needs to be done.

Understanding the social processes that helped create a new class system by the end of the nineteenth century involves looking not just at the "politics of notables" but also at the system of social stratification *before* the emergence of these new classes. The term *notable* can also be used in a more general sense than it is in the historiography of notable politics to refer to those in Ottoman urban society whose role and importance in the city were determined by high social status and wealth, rather than their political role. This elite occupied the top layer of the social hierarchy. While there was considerable overlap between the political elite and the social elite, they were not identical. It is with the notables as a social elite that this study is primarily concerned.

The bases of high status in Ottoman provincial cities were broadly similar in important respects. At the same time, as Batatu has pointed out with reference to Iraq, the basis of social stratification was very localized. The relative weight given to different status markers varied from place to place. As a result, the composition of the elite and the degree of integration within it were not necessarily the same everywhere. It is important to recognize these differences and their implications for the way in which elites were affected by and responded to the changes of the nineteenth century.

In Aleppo, as in other cities, the stratification system was multifaceted. No single variable determined one's status. Social distinctions were made on the basis of religion, ethnicity, occupation, quarter, and ashraf status, and they helped shape an individual's identity and perception of his or her place in the social order.

Cutting across these status groups, however, were distinctions of wealth that linked people across these lines and that limited the extent to which these traditional status groups represented meaningful social groups. Bruce Masters makes this clear when discussing Aleppo merchants in the seventeenth and eighteenth centuries. He is primarily concerned with whether or not they were a class, and he concludes that they were not. Wealthy merchants remained part of a larger social and economic elite, rather than a distinct group united by common economic concerns.[13] The gaps between wealthy merchants and others involved in trade and commerce, like peddlers and retailers, were too great for common interests to develop.[14] While he argues that Ottoman society was vertically rather than horizontally organized, this discussion makes clear the limits of using traditional categories like occupation to understand social distinctions. Wealth and prestige, rather than common occupation, were more influential in determining social and economic connections. Marcus also stresses the centrality of wealth in determining social stratification. Aleppo was a "society with great contrasts of wealth." Although wealth by itself was not sufficient to place an individual in the upper stratum of society, "one's level of wealth was perhaps most important" in determining one's circumstances, opportunities, and social identity.[15] Wealth tended to coincide with other attributes of high status—certain occupations like religious and official careers, family background, access to political power, ashraf status—and, according to Marcus, it was leading figures in high status groups who formed the elite.

As in other societies in which group boundaries were not absolutely fixed by ascriptive status, sanctified by religion, or spelled out in law, high status in Aleppo derived from a number of criteria that could be combined in different ways. Where to draw the boundaries that separated this elite from the rest of the population remains a central question however. If some, but not all, ulema, merchants, Ottoman officials or their descendants, ashraf, power brokers, Sufi sheikhs, and families made up the upper stratum of Aleppo society, how do we determine which ones? If some, but not all, who had great wealth belonged to this group, how do we know where to draw the line? The best approach is to let the sources guide us. In the religious court archives, the most thorough source on local society, some people possessed family names. That these are family names and not simply *nisba*s (descriptive terms indicating occupation, place of origin, or some other personal characteristic) is made clear from the form: A name of an ancestor, place of origin, occupation, or some other distinctive characteristic together with the term -*zade* was the common form of family names in the Ottoman Empire, and family names in this form were used only by the upper class.[16] I would argue that the consistent use of these family names over several generations in official sources is clear evidence that the families were identifying themselves as members of the social notability and that the wider society recognized their "claim." If we begin with those people whom contemporary society identified as the social elite and then analyze who they were, rather than beginning with some preconceived categories, a clearer sense of who constituted the upper stratum of Aleppo society will emerge.

THE NOTABLES OF ALEPPO

When a family name is used as the marker of high status, Aleppo's social elite consisted of approximately 104 families between 1770 and 1840. A total of 178 families appeared in the religious court archives during this period, but 74 appear only once or twice and have been disregarded for purposes of this study. The information available on them suggests that they were not permanent residents of the city but were probably merchants or scholars residing temporarily in Aleppo. Of the rest, not all of these families were found in Aleppo throughout the seventy-year period covered by this study. Sixty-four were present throughout the period; the rest either disappeared from the sources or appeared for the first time at some point.[17] A fuller discussion of mobility into and out of this group and the significance of the mobility rate will appear later in the chapter.

These 104 families were a complex group. Because of the multiple attributes of status, some ambiguity and imprecision surround any definition of the group. Nonetheless, certain criteria of status are clear: Some combination of family background, wealth, occupation, political influence, and lifestyle plus a certain style and sense of proper deportment, characterized by dignity, decorum, and seriousness of purpose, was expected of this elite.[18] None of these alone was sufficient for high status, although it was also not necessary to possess all of them. Within each criterion, certain parameters defined who did or did not belong. Before examining each of these criteria in turn, three family biographies will be presented to illustrate more concretely the different ways in which attributes of status were combined, as well as the similarities and differences among families.

The Taha family was one of the most important families in Aleppo in the eighteenth century.[19] It traced its origins to a late-seventeenth-century *naqib al-ashraf* (head of the descendants of the prophet Muhammad), Mustafa (d. 1680), one of the leading figures in the city. Mustafa had been a qadi, serving for a time as qadi of Aleppo. According to the French consul d'Arvieux, he was very rich, highly respected, and extremely knowledgeable, especially about medicine, astrology, poetry, law, politics, and the history of his own country as well as foreign countries. He was also well connected in Istanbul through his relationship by marriage with the personal physician of Sultan Mehmet IV. He suffered from epileptic fits, and died during one of these at the age of fifty-five. Mustafa had four sons, from whom three distinct branches of the family had evolved by the second half of the eighteenth century. (The line of the fourth son had died out.) All three branches lived near each other in the quarter of Jallum.

Mustafa's male descendants all followed the ulema career path, with varying degrees of success. His son Yasin and Yasin's descendants served as naqib al-ashraf and mufti. Another son, 'Umar, not only served as naqib and *qa'immaqam* (deputy to the provincial governor) in the city but also became a qadi and was appointed to judgeships in Aleppo and elsewhere. He retired to Aleppo, built a large mausoleum, and set up a large waqf for his family, using properties he had accumulated over the years. 'Umar's nephew, Ahmad, son of his brother Taha, was also a qadi, serving in such important posts as Baghdad and Jerusalem. Ahmad had done well financially, accumulating large amounts of property, all of which he used to establish a large family endowment as well as to endow a *madrasa* (a college or higher school of religious learning) that he had built in Jallum, the Madrasa Ahmadiyya. This was one of the largest endowments created in the city and included a total of 113 pieces of property, much of it in Jallum.

Ahmad's wealth and power in the city were eclipsed, however, by his son Muhammad. The career of Muhammad Celebi Taha illustrates well the opportunities available to ambitious ulema for taking on new roles and functions and acquiring direct political power in the period of Ottoman decentralization. Muhammad, like his father, was trained as a religious scholar and reached the rank of qadi, although it is not clear that he ever served in that position. Until his death in 1786, he spent most of his time in Aleppo and operated from a power base that he had created for himself as naqib al-ashraf. European observers at that time saw him as the real power in the city, more powerful than the Ottoman governor. John Burckhardt claimed that Muhammad had been offered the governorship of Aleppo several times but had declined it, although there is no evidence to confirm this.[20] The Ottoman government seemed fully aware of the threat he posed: Muhammad spent a number of years between 1767 and 1786 in exile, usually in the aftermath of unrest in the city, for which he would be held responsible. That he was not permanently exiled reflected the influence and prestige of the Taha family and the hesitation on the part of a weakened Ottoman state to confront it directly.

Muhammad's power in the city was based in large part on his control of tax revenues and the agricultural surplus through tax farming. This control grew directly out of the changes in the Ottoman government and illustrates the extent to which well-placed ulema could take advantage of the situation. Like his father and great-uncle, Muhammad owned considerable property and also helped control even more extensive property that formed part of his father's waqf. But he had also expanded his investments to include the acquisition of tax farms, that is, villages for which he collected taxes, of which he controlled at least eighty-six. He was also owed large sums of money by many of these villages. Through tax farming and his role as moneylender, he effectively controlled the surplus from these villages and used this control to manipulate the grain markets in Aleppo.

When Muhammad died in 1786, most of his property was confiscated, although his sons managed to recover much of it. In particular they were able to profit from the large debts still owed by many villages to their father. Muhammad's brother ʿAli and his three sons all served as naqib, although they were never able to monopolize the office for long periods of time as Muhammad had. Muhammad's political power was inherited instead by one of his retainers, Ibrahim Agha (later Pasha). Because of Muhammad's activities, however, his branch of the family was in a position to take advantage of changes in the land laws during the Tanzimat period and become rural landowners as well as urban property owners. The mark that Muhammad left on the family was reflected in a name change in the mid–nineteenth century, as his descendants became known as Celebi Zade, a reference to one of his titles.

The Shaykhbandar family could also trace its origins to the seventeenth century, this time to an Ottoman governor, Muhammad Pasha Buyuni (governor in 1656), through one of his female descendants.[21] The family name, presumably a corruption of *shahbandar* (chief merchant), suggests that the paternal line was descended from merchants. It seems likely that some ancestor held that position at one time, although the title was not in use in Aleppo in the late eighteenth or early nineteenth century. By the second half of the eighteenth century, this lineage had three distinct but interconnected (through marriage) branches, the most prominent of which was the branch headed by Mustafa, residing in the quarter of Bayyada.

Despite its dual origins from merchant and 'askari[22] lines, the lineage had carried on the military-administrative tradition of its Ottoman ancestors. From the economic base of this family and the offices held by its members, it is possible to see the overlay of the old and new system of Ottoman land administration. The old *timar* (land grant given in return for military service) system had fallen into disuse in the seventeenth century as the Ottoman government had sought new ways to enhance revenues and as changing military technology had undercut the value of the old *sipahi* (cavalry) forces, whose salaries had been drawn from the timars. In place of this "feudal" form of land administration, the Ottomans had instituted a tax-farming system (*iltizam*), selling the rights to collect taxes to the highest bidder at annual auctions. In the early eighteenth century, these tax-collecting privileges were granted for life (*malikane*) in many cases, and increasingly these iltizams and malikanes were purchased by local notables. Nevertheless, the remnants of the timar system survived. Some lands were still designated as timar or *zi'am* (larger timar) lands. What percentage of the lands in the province of Aleppo fell into this category is not known, but the Shaykhbandar family still controlled lands called timar in the neighborhood of Latakiyya, and some family members were still referred to in the sources as *timariot* (holder of a timar). In addition, several members of the family held the title of *miralay,* a reference to the colonel who was in charge of sipahi forces from his own district. There is no evidence that they ever performed any military functions, however. Even during the Russian campaigns in the 1770s and again against Napoleon in 1799, when local forces were drafted to fight with the regular army, no mention was made of a Shaykhbandar leading these forces, although other local leaders were mentioned.

Although the old land system survived in places, or at least its terminology did, the government appeared not to exact any of the duties associated with a timar. Nevertheless, the sense of being part of the Ottoman ruling class seemed to persist in the Shaykhbandar family. Several members of the family held the offices of *mutasallim* (substitute for the governor in his absence) and *muhassil* (chief provincial financial officer). These were semiofficial positions, appointed either in Istanbul or by the Ottoman governor. In the first part of the eighteenth century, they went almost exclusively to local members of the old 'askari class or to retainers in the households of Ottoman officials. By the end of the eighteenth century, these offices were dominated by ambitious local notables. Mustafa Shaykhbandar was muhassil from 1779 to 1780 and mutasallim in 1778. He was followed in both offices by his son ʿAbd al-Qadir, who was mutasallim in 1781 and muhassil from 1780 to 1784. Before this time, other names occupying these positions were Kucuk ʿAli Agha and Khankarli, both old ʿaskari families, but after 1785 the names Shurayyif, Ibrahim Pasha, and Jabiri appear frequently. The only other times a Shaykhbandar appears are in 1812 and 1820, when Mustafa's second son, Darwish, was mutasallim.

What is significant here is not *that* the Shaykhbandars held these offices, but *when* they held them. In the early period, mutasallims and muhassils were chosen by virtue of their background. In 1812 and 1820, however, Darwish Shaykhbandar appears to have been chosen specifically for his loyalty to the Ottoman authorities. Both times he was appointed were years of unusual trouble in Aleppo. In 1812 the Ottoman government was trying to reassert its authority after several years of virtual Janissary rule in the city. Again in 1820 the government was trying to reestablish order after a bitter uprising that year. In both cases, it turned to the Shaykhbandar family for assistance, which suggests that they could be counted on for loyalty. This sense of belonging to the Ottoman tradition instilled a degree of loyalty to the Ottoman government not found in other segments of the elite.

The economic base of the family was drawn from its timar holdings, but the family was not content with that. They also took advantage of the opportunities afforded by the new tax-farming system and acquired several malikane in districts near their timar holdings. They also owned land near Latakiyya—*ciftlik*s (privately owned farms) devoted largely to the growing of tobacco. They were diversifying and consolidating their control of rural land, but they owned relatively little urban property. More than most of these families, their economic base remained in the countryside.

The Shurayyif family represents the third occupational category that made up the local elite: wealthy merchants engaged in international trade.[23] More recently established than the Taha or Shaykhbandar families, the Shurayyifs presented a classic case of an upwardly mobile merchant family. Originally from the Hijaz, the family claimed to belong to the Tamim tribe and therefore traced its descent to the first caliph, Abu Bakr. When the first Shurayyif settled in Aleppo is not known. It may have been 'Abd al-Wahhab (d. 1769) or his father, Muhammad. In either case, it was 'Abd al-Wahhab who established the family fortune through his involvement in international trade and moneylending. Having acquired his fortune, he assured his social position through marriages into two well-established families, the Zanabilis and the 'Imadis. Although not much is known about the former, his first wife, Rahma Zanabili, brought considerable property into the family. His second wife, Fatima 'Imadi, was the daughter of a distinguished 'alim who served for a time as naqib and who established a large waqf in 1720. Since the 'Imadi family had no surviving males, control of this waqf passed into the hands of Fatima 'Imadi's children. 'Abd al-Wahhab's position in Aleppine society was also ensured through the patronage of 'Uthman Pasha, the scion of an old Ottoman family residing in Aleppo who had served as its governor in 1737.

'Abd al-Wahhab had thirteen children by his two wives. In this second generation, the family continued to add to its wealth and began to diversify its economic base significantly. Several of 'Abd al-Wahhab's sons continued to be involved in long-distance trade, while others began to channel their wealth into urban and rural properties. Although investing in real estate was less lucrative than investing in commerce or moneylending, it was a decision in favor of economic stability, and accumulation of property seems to have been an essential step in the consolidation of position by upwardly mobile families. Most of 'Abd al-Wahhab's children invested in real estate. One in particular, 'Abd al-Qadir, became a major property owner. His brother 'Abd al-Rahman invested relatively little in urban property, but instead concentrated on gaining access to rural property, not by purchasing it but by acting as tax collector for malikane holders and *mutawalli* (administrator of a waqf) of some rural waqfs.

'Abd al-Rahman's sons, Isma'il and Nu'man, were active both in the urban real estate market and as tax farmers. Out of the urban property he accumulated, Isma'il established a large waqf to benefit both his and Nu'man's descendants. Nu'man and Isma'il were responsible not only for continuing to increase the family's wealth but also for establishing the family as an important political force in the city. In the early decades of the nineteenth century, they were two of the most influential men in Aleppo because of their acquisition of important political offices. Isma'il was muhassil from 1810 to 1811. Nu'man was naqib between 1816 and 1822, during a period when the power of the Janissaries had been undercut by the Ottoman governor and the ashraf faction subsequently represented a greater power in the city. During the time that Nu'man was

naqib, Isma'il became mutasallim, a position that he apparently acquired
through his brother's influence, since their enemies considered Nu'man
the power behind Isma'il. To acquire and retain these offices, the brothers also made use of their connections with important Ottoman officials
in Aleppo and Istanbul.

These connections, however, also made them vulnerable. Nu'man
had a close relationship with Governor Mustafa Pasha al-Bayluni. But
when Mustafa Pasha was replaced in 1822, the new governor, Bahram
Pasha, a rival of the former governor, arranged for the assassination of
Nu'man. The excuse given was that Nu'man had helped to instigate the
1819 uprising in Aleppo. In fact, the governor was irritated because
Nu'man had refused to lend him money, and his irritation was encouraged by Ahmad Bey Ibrahim Pasha, a rival of the Shurayyif brothers who
coveted the job of mutasallim. In 1822 Nu'man was assassinated, and
Isma'il lost the job of mutasallim to Ahmad Bey. Isma'il was able to make
a recovery from this setback, however, regaining the position of mutasallim and continuing in that office until he died in 1826.

Two of Nu'man's sons, Muhammad Sa'id and Yusif, continued to be
among the most powerful men in the city. Muhammad Sa'id, a member
of the ulema, first became active in city affairs in 1822, around the time
of his father's death. In 1829 he was muhassil and *amin bayt al-mal* (treasury official). However, his political career was cut short by his death in
1835 at the age of thirty-three. He left six sons, all of whom became beys
and pashas in later years.

The leading figure of the Shurayyif family in this generation was
Nu'man's oldest son, Yusif. Yusif was born in 1799 and also began making his mark in Aleppo about the time of his father's death in 1822. He
received the title of *ra'is al-bawabin* (honorific title given to provincial notables) in 1828, a mark of his distinction in the city, or at least of the Ottoman government's belief that it would find his support useful. During
this period he was also busy acquiring more wealth and was heavily involved in notable politics in the city. During the Egyptian occupation of
the city, he spent much of the time in exile, but he returned in 1839, and
for the next twenty-three years, until his death in 1862, he was one of the
most powerful men in the city. Yusif served as naqib and used the old
ashraf faction as a power base. He served on the newly created municipal
council, where he actively promoted the interests of the a'yan, and he
was several times entrusted with the command of irregular armies con-
scripted to subdue troublesome elements in the province, yet another in-

dication of the Ottoman governor's reliance on him. He was involved in
the 1850 rebellion in Aleppo, although his exact role in that was never
clarified. Throughout this time, he added to his malikanes and urban
properties and served as a tax farmer.

These three families, while different in social origins, occupations, political orientation, and economic base, were all "typical" families of the
social elite. They were associated with high-status occupations; they were
wealthy, and therefore able to maintain a certain lifestyle and standard of
living; they all claimed to be ashraf; and they all had political influence.
They provide a good starting point for looking more closely at the social
bases of elite status in Aleppo.

Certain occupations have always been highly regarded in Islamic societies, and the upper stratum of Ottoman provincial society was drawn
from families associated with these respected careers: religious learning,
mercantile activities, and service to the Ottoman state. This did not mean
that all males within the family practiced a particular occupation. Although there was a tendency for at least one son to follow in his father's
footsteps, sons in many families pursued different careers, so that occupational lines became blurred over time. For example, in the Taha family, most of the males were members of the ulema, but the Shurayyif
family included merchants, moneylenders, and ulema, and some individuals eventually became provincial officials. In some families no one followed the occupation with which the family was originally associated, although their prominence and status were derived in part from this earlier
association. Individuals from families descended from Ottoman officials
or soldiers who had established local roots, like the Shaykhbandars, rarely
had official positions in the Ottoman government, but the family's position in local society rested in part on the prestige of ancestors who had
served the state.

The occupational associations of 93 of the 104 families are known.
Thirty-four were ulema, 30 were merchants, and 21 were ʿaskari, including the 2 who were descended from the freed slaves of Mamluk officials.
Seven were both merchants and ulema, and 1 was both merchant and
ʿaskari.[24] One distinctive feature of Aleppo's notables was the predominance of merchant and ʿaskari families. Aleppo was first and foremost a
great mercantile center. While it produced some distinguished ulema and
had some important religious institutions, it never acquired a reputation
as a center of learning, and ulema families did not dominate the social
elite as they did in Damascus.[25] Aleppo was also a more Ottoman than

Arab city, with one foot in Anatolia. Its stronger ties to the capital were reflected in the relative importance of ʿaskari families.

Association with one of these occupations was not in itself enough to confer high social status, of course. There were many more ulema, merchants, and descendants of Ottoman soldiers living in Aleppo who were not part of the social elite. Within these occupational categories, what separated an upper-class religious leader from the mass of ulema, or a wholesale silk merchant from the retailer who sold the silk in his shop in the *madina* (city center), was wealth. Though, again, wealth by itself was not sufficient for high social status—although the "nouveau riche" were not scorned—wealth made it possible to acquire other attributes of high social status, something that was almost impossible to do without the financial means.

The economic power of these families was not grounded in a single form of wealth, such as land or merchant capital, that would link them together through shared economic interests. As indicated above, they were not a class. Instead what they had in common was the diversity of economic resources that they controlled. They had acquired their wealth in different ways: by engaging in commerce and moneylending, by appropriating rural surpluses as tax farmers and owners of rural property, and by controlling waqfs. Many also secured their wealth through investment in property, especially in the eighteenth century. In general, the wealthier the family, the more diversified the economic resources they controlled, or, the more diversified their economic resources, the wealthier they were—it is not clear what was cause and what was effect. Merchants invested in urban real estate, bid on tax farms, and set up waqfs, as well as being involved in regional and international trade. Ulema controlled religious endowments and bought houses and shops, but also bid on tax farms, lent money, and invested in commerce. That the richest families derived their wealth from a number of sources is evident in the three biographies above. When Mustafa Taha died in 1680, his estate, as recorded in the *mukhallafat* (records of inheritance) register, totaled 27,915.5 *qurush* (sometimes *ghurush;* basic Ottoman coinage, often translated as "piastre"), 51 percent of it derived from commercial goods, 16 percent from outstanding debts owed to him, 6 percent from animals and slaves, and 27 percent from household goods. Not included was the real estate he owned.[26] In the eighteenth century, the Taha family owned extensive urban property and controlled two large waqfs. Muhammad Taha became one of the biggest tax farmers in the city, as the ulema benefited from the changes in the way taxes were collected. From this position as tax farmer, he got into lucrative moneylending activities. The Shaykhbandar family owned rural properties, were tax collectors for others, and owned some urban property. They also periodically invested in commerce, although they were not themselves merchants. The Shurayyif family made its money from commerce, but had acquired urban and rural property through marriage and purchase, established large waqfs, and become tax farmers and moneylenders. Isma'il Shurayyif left to his grandsons an estate that included gold, silver, jewels, valuable furniture and textiles, money and grain collected from malikane property, and debts owed to him, valued at well over 70,000 qurush.[27] His nephew Yusif left an estate valued at 100,000 gold lira *'uthmani* (Ottoman coin; 1 'uthmani = 120 qurush in the mid–eighteenth century) when he died in 1862.[28] While these families often competed with each other for control of these resources, they also shared an interest in seeing that their access to these diverse resources was not threatened.

Because of the nature of the sources consulted, it is impossible to determine exactly how much wealth families or individuals from these families had. While inheritance registers list individual assets and liabilities at the time of death, three problems undermine their usefulness. Many of the mukhallafat registers from this period are missing; even if they were available, only some inheritances were recorded, since there was no legal requirement that the division of estates be registered with the qadi. Even when they were registered, some of the most lucrative sources of wealth, like income from tax farms and sometimes even real estate, were excluded from the inventory of assets. Nevertheless, because so many economic transactions were recorded in the court registers, it is possible to get a general impression of economic activities and wealth from the sources and of how the nature and extent of economic resources available to different families varied.

All of these families controlled significant resources compared to most of Aleppo's population, but gradations of wealth did occur. The immense wealth of Isma'il Shurayyif (see above) and of Muhammad Taha, whose yearly income from indebted villagers alone would have been at least 50,000 qurush, represented one end of the scale. The much more modest fortune of 'Abd al-Rahman ibn Mustafa Ubri—23,301 qurush—was typical of the other end of this scale.[29] Gradations of wealth also existed within families. To describe the family as wealthy did not mean that all family members were necessarily wealthy. Individual family members or branches might control few resources of their own. Whether they had access to family wealth or were aided by more well-to-do relatives depended on family relationships; in most cases, however, they could share the status of wealthier relations by virtue of their family connections.

Yet another ingredient of high social position was *sharif* (descendant of the Prophet; singular of *ashraf*) status. According to Hourani, what distinguished Aleppo's notables was their claim to descent from the Prophet.[30] The Ottomans, in their desire to be seen as protectors of the faith, had institutionalized the respect that had always been granted to Muhammad's descendants. The naqib al-ashraf of Istanbul was given an important role in court ceremonials, and ashraf throughout the empire were granted privileges such as personal inviolability, the right to be tried and punished by their own leaders, and exemption from certain taxes. The ashraf were therefore an important element in many Ottoman cities, but nowhere more so than in Aleppo. Here their numbers were very large, and some of the ashraf formed themselves into a political faction and became spokesmen for local interests. However, the very fact that the number of ashraf in Aleppo was so large, far in excess of the expected size of the ashraf population, meant that sharif status did not automatically confer high social status. Ashraf were found in all groups of the population. As Batatu found in Iraq, descent from the Prophet was not the basis for high social position; "if they [ashraf] mattered in the society, they mattered essentially on some other grounds."[31] The same was true for Aleppo.

While ashraf status alone did not give one a place among the city's social elite, almost all of these families (approximately 85 percent) did eventually acquire ashraf status.[32] All of the ulema families during this period were ashraf. Many of the merchant and 'askari families were not originally ashraf, but acquired ashraf status at some point, usually through marriage. Hajj Musa Amiri, one of Aleppo's wealthiest merchants in the middle of the eighteenth century, was not a sharif, but two of his wives were. Their status devolved on their children. The children of his other two wives married ashraf, so in the course of a couple of generations, the entire family had become ashraf. These ashraf from the upper ranks of Aleppo society were not usually involved in the political activities of the ashraf faction directly, with the exception of the naqib. The naqib al-ashraf was always a member of one of these upper-class families during this period. The Taha family dominated the post for most of the eighteenth century, but in the last decades of the century as well as in the first decades of the nineteenth century, Muhammad Trabulsi, Lutuf Bey ʿAdili, Ahmad Kawakibi, Mustafa and ʿAbd al-Qadir Jabiri, Muhammad and Taqi al-Din Qudsi, and Nuʿman Shurayyif challenged the Taha monopoly on this office. Some, though not all, of these naqibs used the ashraf faction as a political base for augmenting their personal power in the city. For most of the upper-class ashraf, however, the acquisition of ashraf status was important for the sake of social prestige rather than political power, part of the process of consolidating, rather than acquiring, high social status.

Family and occupational background and wealth were the basis of high social status and the sources of social power in Aleppo society. As Hourani has indicated, it was this social power that conferred on them leadership in local society and that made them valuable to the Ottoman authorities as mediators between the government and the local population.[33] This pivotal role gave them access to power. However, the way in which they gained this access, if and how they used it, and how important it was varied from family to family. For some, direct access to power was achieved through direct participation in provincial administration. By the second half of the eighteenth century, several offices, with direct or indirect administrative responsibilities, were open to the local population: mutasallim, muhassil, Hanafi mufti, and naqib al-ashraf. In addition, posts like *katib* (clerk) in the courts, while less significant, gave their holders direct access to the judicial administration, and katibs sometimes acted as deputies to the judges. More informal channels were also available to these families to exercise their influence and secure their wealth and position in the city. Many families maintained good connections in Istanbul, usually through patronage. For example, Muhammad Qudsi was from a prominent family in Urfa who settled in Aleppo around 1785. He quickly succeeded to the coveted offices of Hanafi mufti and naqib— usually reserved for well-established families like the Tahas and Kawakibis—because of his patrons in Istanbul, particularly the *walide sultane ketkudasi* (steward of the queen mother), Yusif Agha.[34] The loss of favor by the Shurayyif brothers and the rapid return to favor of Ismaʿil after Nuʿman's assassination show how significant patronage connections in Istanbul were in local politics. Other families had relatives in Istanbul who could cultivate friends at court. Yusif Jabiri, for example, settled in Istanbul and worked in the imperial bureaucracy after serving for many years as *raʾis al-kuttab* (chief clerk) in Aleppo.[35] It seems likely that his presence there had something to do with the growing power and favorable appointments received by his cousins—who were also his brothers-in-law—back in Aleppo. Finally, short of acquisition of offices and cultivation of connections in Istanbul, marriage of a son or daughter into the household of an Ottoman official was yet another channel for gaining influence in high places.

For some families, like the Shurayyifs, access to power was important for the opportunities it provided to gain additional wealth and to exercise greater authority in Aleppo itself. For others, the goal appears to have been one of serving the Ottoman state. This seems true for families like the Shaykhbandars and other ʿaskari families, who came from a tradition of service to the Ottoman state. Political divisions within Aleppo grew in part out of the different orientation of the families from different backgrounds. Still other families, however, seemed uninterested in getting involved in the political fury.

This is where the aʿyan as a political elite and as a social elite diverge. The political aʿyan would include individuals like the Janissary *aghawat* (commanders), some of the chief guild leaders, and some ashraf leaders because they exercised considerable political power and played an important mediating function between the government and the groups over whom they exercised control. Yet they lacked either the wealth or family and occupational connections or "culture" of those of high social status. Similarly, the social aʿyan would include families like the Amiris, who were well established in Aleppo and had the social power to exercise political influence but never chose to do so, at least in any obvious way.

Aleppo's notables, when the term is used, as in this context, to refer to a social elite, were similar to such elites in many other Ottoman provincial cities. At the same time, there were some significant differences between Aleppo and a city like Damascus. One difference was the relative importance of the different sources from which elite status was derived. The ulema of Aleppo played a less-dominant role in this group than they did in Damascus, and merchant and ʿaskari families were more prominent, as discussed above. A second characteristic that seemed to differentiate among elites in various places was the degree of homogeneity and social integration among these notables. In Damascus, according to Khoury, the ulema, aghawat, tax farmers, and merchants were socially differentiated from each other until at least the 1830s, a differentiation symbolized by the lack of marriages among these groups.[36] In Aleppo, on the other hand, there appears to have been a high degree of integration within this social elite. While these notable families came from somewhat different backgrounds, did not necessarily have the same kind of economic base, and were often on different sides of the fence in the political struggles that plagued Aleppo in the late eighteenth and early nineteenth centuries, they were essentially a homogeneous group in their social characteristics and lifestyles. This social homogeneity was reinforced by the high degree of social integration among them, visible in two ways, the first of which was marriage. These families were bound together by extensive and overlapping marriage networks, irrespective of occupation, family origins, degree of wealth, residence, or political connections. Each of these families was related to at least one other family. Many were directly connected to three or more families, and some to as many as eight or nine. To some extent this depended on how long the families had been established in Aleppo. Furthermore, the families were connected indirectly with an even larger circle of families through sharing common relatives by marriage. Marriage integrated them into a large network of kin and connections.[37]

The second visible expression of this integration was residential patterns. Almost all of these families lived in a handful of quarters in the center of town. Clear socioeconomic and political distinctions existed between the quarters inside and outside the city walls.[38] Most of the Christians of Aleppo lived outside the walls, as did many of the less "respectable" craftsmen, the Janissary aghawat and other military groups, and Kurdish and Turkish tribesmen and other recent rural migrants to the city. While the suburban quarters contained "many handsome homes," indicating the wealth of some of their residents, these people were, according to Russell, "less civilized than in the interior parts of the town."[39] The city inside the walls was not socioeconomically homogeneous, but its less well-off population included small shopkeepers and craftsmen and minor ulema and clerks, the more respectable part of the common people. The notable families, with only two exceptions, lived inside the city walls. Moreover, they were concentrated in only 16 of the 104 interior quarters and more than half of them lived in 1 of 7 quarters: Dakhil Bab al-Nasr, Frafira, Suwayqa ʿAli, Suwayqa Hatim, and Masabin, quarters to the northwest of the Citadel; Jallum to the south of the madina; and Bayyada to the east of the Citadel. Of the two families who lived outside the walls, the Tabbakhs were a relatively new family and by 1850 had moved into the city to the quarter of Dakhil Bab al-Nasr, and the Hatab family disappears from the sources. The geographical isolation and lack of other connections of the family suggests that it was rather marginal to

the group. The desirability of these few quarters as residences and the social importance attached to living in the right quarter is demonstrated by
the eagerness of upwardly mobile families, like the Tabbakhs and others,
to move from their old quarters into these neighborhoods. The social homogeneity of this elite and the degree of integration among the families
of high social status justify labeling them a distinctive socioeconomic
group, if not a class in the analytical sense of that word.

In the final analysis, high social status was tied to belonging to the
"right" family. Family name was not enough, as Marcus points out: "A
good family lineage was a social asset, but one not sufficient in itself . . .
live social connections were in many respects more essential than ancestral ties."[40] Families had to work at preserving their position in Aleppine
society. Downward mobility was a real threat; they could not rest on their
ancestral laurels. Nevertheless, social status that endured over time was
conferred on families, not on individuals. Without family connections,
wealth and power or sharif status could not be translated into social position. Here the historiography of the notables and the history of the family clearly intersect. Belonging to a notable lineage was evidence of high
social status; at the same time these lineages were kinship groups. The nature and significance of these lineages as kinship groups were intricately
tied to processes of social mobility and change in early modern Aleppo.
The next section will consider these notable lineages as kinship groups.

FAMILY AND LINEAGE

The Ottoman state of the classical period (1300–
1600) was structured to prevent the emergence of a hereditary aristocracy
that might challenge the ruling family. With a few exceptions, members
of the ruling class were unable to pass on position and status to their heirs.
When structural changes in the seventeenth century resulted in a more
decentralized state, and power increasingly devolved on the households
of provincial governors and of other Ottoman officials, these households
resembled "bureaucratic bodies" more than families, and ties of patronage and servitude were as important, if not more important, than kinship
ties, according to Haim Gerber.[41] He goes on to argue that kinship ties
were also not particularly important at any level in the central areas of the
Ottoman Empire. He attributes this to the proximity of these areas to the

capital, which afforded them greater security and implied a greater impact of the bureaucratic state, both of which reduced the need to rely on
family and kin to perform a variety of functions and services. In contrast,
greater significance was given to ties of kinship in the Arab provinces, and
Gerber specifically points to the absence of family names among Bursa's
elite and their presence in Aleppo as evidence of the differing importance
accorded to a sense of "blood."[42]

The difference Gerber is noting, however, may not reflect contrasts
between center and periphery or between Arab and Turkish parts of the
empire, but between the seventeenth and eighteenth centuries. Throughout the empire in the eighteenth century—not just in the provinces like
Aleppo and Iraq—elites were acquiring family names. Carter Findley
notes the eagerness on the part of the Ottoman ruling class to acquire
family names in the eighteenth century, with the -*zade* and -*oghlu* suffix
attached to a name or nisba being the usual form. Madeline Zilfi also
found that family names were common among the great *molla* (religious
leader, often specifically a qadi in the Ottoman context) families of Istanbul by the early eighteenth century, although such names were not always fixed, an indication of their recent acquisition.[43] Family names were
not unknown before the eighteenth century, but what appears to be different in this period was the conscious and consistent use of such names
among various elements of the elite and the way in which society and
state identified individuals as part of these family groups. I would argue
that the adoption of family names was more than an expression of a new
status consciousness; instead it reflected more fundamental changes in
Ottoman society and in the nature and role of family and kinship ties.
Zilfi's conclusions about the greater corporate stability of the great molla
families in Istanbul, a change reflected in their near monopoly of the most
important religious offices in the empire, would seem to support such an
argument.[44] So would Linda Schilcher's contention that the emergence of
the Damascus notability was a late-seventeenth-century development
linked to changes in the Ottoman state, but also linked to changes in the
structure and functions of the family, specifically the emergence of a more
patriarchal family.[45] This argument about the connection between the
use of family names and changes in the significance of kinship ties and the
conception of the family remains very tentative, particularly in the absence of more research on Ottoman families of this and earlier periods.
An examination of these Aleppine patrilineages as kinship groups can

perhaps begin a discussion of cultural perceptions of significant kin during this period and provide a baseline for looking more systematically at
concepts of kinship before and after this time.

Sharing a family name was an acknowledgment of a biological relationship, of connection with those of the same "blood" and descent. At
the same time, it represented a social construction of kinship. The fact
that individuals were descended from a common ancestor and shared certain genes only mattered if the individuals involved believed that it mattered. This "blood" family was a potentially large one, encompassing a
wide group of living relatives within a single generation and across generations. But the significance of this conception of the family and of
significant kin is that ties of kinship were not only with living relatives.
The acquisition of a family name conveyed a sense of "dynasty," of the
lineage extended backward and forward in time. The lineage included as
many ascending generations as genealogical memory preserved and all future generations. Having a family name was a public record of family status, but also a statement about passing that status on to future generations.
This was the largest kinship group, and the term *lineage* best captures the
nature of this kinship group, whose boundaries were drawn around all
those who shared a family name, no matter how distant the connection
or whether they lived together, married each other, or had economic interests in common.

When the boundaries of the kin group were drawn around all who
shared a family name, what did these lineages look like? They were first
and foremost patrilineal groups. Descent was traced through the male
line, and kinship was defined in terms of relationship among males, all
sharing a common ancestor. Females were also members of the lineage,
even after marriage, as reflected in their continued use of their natal family name. Children of female members of the lineage were in a somewhat
ambiguous situation vis-à-vis their mother's lineage. By the principle of
patrilineal descent, they would be members of their fathers' lineages.
Nevertheless, as will be discussed in later chapters, their tangible and intangible claims on their mothers' lineages were sometimes significant.
Moreover, the principle of patrilineal descent did not preclude the passing of the family name and line of descent through females. Several examples of this occurred among the Aleppo lineages. The Jabiris, a prominent ulema family that played a major political role in the city, got their
name from an Ottoman qadi, Jabir Halabi, who was the maternal grandfather of Musa Jabiri. The Rifaʿis, sheikhs of the Rifaʿi Sufi order in the

eighteenth and nineteenth centuries, were descendants of a wealthy sol-
dier, Shahin (d. 1695). He married a women of the Sayyad family, which
had provided Rifaʿi sheikhs for many years. The lack of male descendants
in the Sayyad family meant that the role of Rifaʿi sheikh went to her sons
and descendants.[46] In such cases, not only did the family name derive
from the maternal line, but social status, offices, and control of family
waqfs and other property were passed through the female. The Jabiris
and the Rifaʿis were not the only families in which this happened. The
Qabbad Bey, Nasir al-Din Bey, and Shaykhbandar families, whose high
status was linked to their descent from Ottoman governors, also traced
this connection through the female line.[47] Altogether at least ten families
owed their prominence, at least in part, to maternal ancestors. While this
usually occurred in families in which there were no sons in the direct line
and in a single generation, it underscores the flexibility of the kinship
system.

In contrast to many groups to whom the label *lineage* is applied,
Aleppo's lineages were not corporate groups. Islamic law does not recognize corporate groups, for the most part.[48] In Ottoman urban societies
this legal impediment, as well as other factors, largely discouraged the formation of such groups. No legal privileges or economic rights were tied
to lineage membership in Aleppo, in contrast to some tribal and peasant
societies in the Middle East in which one's access to land and other resources and rights to inheritance were determined by lineage membership, or in contrast to some medieval European societies in which the exercise of political rights and/or access to political office depended on
lineage membership. Wealth belonged to and was controlled by individuals, not by the lineage, and inheritance was determined by a person's relationship to the deceased, as laid down in the Islamic law of inheritance,
not lineage membership. There were two important consequences of this
lack of corporateness. One was the potential limit it placed on patriarchal
power.[49] Since the "patriarch," the senior male in the family, did not have
a legal monopoly on economic resources, his control over other family
members was not absolute. Secondly, it contributed to the flexible and
dynamic nature of these kin groups.

The flexible and shifting boundaries of these lineages are clear when
their size and structure is viewed over time. While the term *lineage* may
evoke images of very large and complex kin groups, Aleppo lineages, like
similar kinship groups elsewhere, varied considerably in size and structure, from multigenerational, widely extended groups of kin to small

groups that were little more than extended families. How far back the lineage could be traced and how prolifically individuals in the lineage re-produced affected the size and structure of the lineage within each gen-eration. To demonstrate this variation, Aleppo lineages have been clas-sified as small, medium, and large, based on the number of identifiable family members over a period of three full generations.[50] The largest lin-eages ranged in size from thirty-one (Jurbaji) to seventy (Amiri) mem-bers, with an average size of forty-eight members. The medium-sized ones ranged from fifteen to twenty-seven members, with an average of nineteen. Only twelve lineages totaled more than thirty members, with twenty-seven lineages in the middle category. That meant that over half of all lineages were quite small. This also meant, of course, that the num-ber of members of any single generation was also small. The largest doc-umented number of members in a single generation during this period—twenty-seven—occurred in the Taha family; the average per generation among even the largest lineages was only twelve. An average of three to five members per generation was much more common.

This predominance of smaller lineages underlines an important point about these families. Most did not continue to grow indefinitely, be-coming more and more complex over time. Instead, these lineages were in a continuous process of change, expanding and contracting according to rates of reproduction, age and gender distribution, mortality rates, and longevity of the individuals who belonged to the lineage. Some, like the Taha lineage (see genealogy in Appendix 2), produced several sons in each generation, most of whom had relatively large families. Under these circumstances, the lineage did continue to expand over three generations. More typical were lineages that remained stable in size or shrank over time, either temporarily or permanently. The Shaykhbandar lineage (see genealogy in Appendix 2) remained more or less stable demographically during this period. The Shurayyif family (see genealogy in Appendix 2) actually declined in numbers over time. 'Abd al-Wahhab fits our image of the lineage patriarch, fathering thirteen children by two wives. Yet in-stead of having a large number of grandchildren from this great brood, there were only twenty-one offspring in the following generation who belonged to the lineage (the children of his daughters are not included since they "belonged" to their fathers' families). Eleven of his thirteen children were sons, but four of them had no children. Of the seven sons who did, none had families approaching the size of their father's. In the next generation ('Abd al-Wahhab's grandchildren), twelve of the twenty-one offspring were females, and only five of the nine males are known to have children. With the exception of Nuʿman, who had eight children, none of the others had more than three. As a result, in the following generation there were only sixteen individuals. Even the Taha lineage, after growing for three generations, declined from twenty-five to ten members in a single generation. The ultimate fate for some of these lineages was extinction. A significant number did not survive, because there were no sons to carry on the patriline. The Arihawis, Batrunis, and Bakhshas in the late eighteenth century suffered this fate. Even when lineages did not end, few of them expanded indefinitely, since in most only a few males survived and produced offspring.

The relatively small size of most lineages and the fluctuation in their size from one generation to the next meant that the structure of the lineage was relatively simple. Almost half of these lineages included no relatives more distant than second cousins. When lineages did become more complex, and as they became further removed from the common ancestor, they often divided into distinct branches, sometimes every generation or every other generation and sometimes only once over several generations, depending on circumstances. The Taha family was divided into three distinct branches and the Shaykhbandar family into two by 1770. Over the next seventy years the more recently established Shurayyif family went through the same process, splitting into at least four distinct branches within two generations. Fourteen families had two branches, thirteen had either three or four; the rest did not appear to have distinct branches during this period. The most important factor in determining if and when lineages separated into distinct branches was probably size. Disputes over the control of wealth and property and how well brothers or cousins got along also played a role. So did an emerging gap between the wealth and power of different family members. The more successful ones would have wanted to preserve their wealth and position for their immediate offspring and not share it with the larger kin group.

The implications of this division into separate branches for kinship ties depended on whether active connections were maintained. In some families, like the Shaykhbandars, the two branches of the family lived in separate households and were economically independent of each other, but otherwise maintained close ties. In other words, they were distinct, but not completely independent, branches. If active kinship ties were not maintained, the feeling of being members of a common lineage was lost, even if the different branches continued to share the same family name.

Over time the identity of the common ancestor was lost, as was the genealogical relationship among the branches of the lineage. The only link
among them was the family name and sometimes proceeds from family
endowments. The branches for all practical purposes became separate lineages, even though they shared the same name. In other cases, separate
lineages were established intentionally. The deliberate choice to "secede"
from one's lineage and establish a new one was signaled in the adoption
of a new family name by one branch. For example, in the nineteenth
century, the descendants of Muhammad Taha adopted the family name
of Celebi, a reference to the title by which Muhammad had commonly
been known, while the rest of the lineage continued to use the Taha
name. Muhammad had been such a powerful and well-known figure in
the late eighteenth century that his descendants wanted to mark their distinguished lineage by adopting a new name.[51]

The emergence of distinct and often completely independent branches
of a lineage and their evolution into distinct families were not always
irreversible processes, however. Just as various factors led to the division of lineages into distinct branches over time, other circumstances
could result in a single line or a reintegration of two or more branches.
Some branches died out, leaving only one surviving branch. The long-
established Kawakibi family had two distinct branches in the eighteenth
century. The more illustrious of these two, the one that produced the
Hanafi muftis, Sufi sheikhs, and distinguished scholars, died out with the
death of Hasan Kawakibi in 1814. Hasan had only daughters. The bulk of
his personal property went to the offspring of his daughter who had married Mustafa Bey Ibrahim Pasha Zade. Those properties specifically associated with the lineage, especially control of the sixteenth-century waqf,
went to the surviving branch of the family. Marriages between cousins
could have a similar effect, reducing two branches to one if the bride had
no surviving male relatives in her branch. Cousin marriage could also
sometimes have the effect of merging two different lineages. The Shukri
and Trabulsi families had intermarried so often that the two lineages had
ceased to be distinct in many respects. With the death of the last male
Shukri without male heirs and the marriage of his sister to a Trabulsi
cousin, the Shukri lineage disappeared.

Both the "natural" limitations on family size and the tendency of
larger and more complex kin groups to evolve into separate lineages
played a role in keeping these lineages of moderate size. Another factor
was at work in this period as well: the rate of social mobility in Aleppo in

the eighteenth century. Many of the smaller lineages were families of upwardly mobile individuals, who, as they ascended the social ladder, brought only their immediate family with them. In other words, the relatively large number of smaller lineages is linked to processes of upward and downward mobility in eighteenth-century Aleppo.

Hourani refers to these notables as an "ancient bourgeoisie," a phrase conveying their sense of themselves as long-established families. The sense of family history and claim to a long and distinguished line of descent implied in acquiring and using a family name masks the fact that relatively few lineages went back very far. Both the Taha and Shaykhbandar families discussed above had been part of the upper stratum of Aleppo society for at least a hundred years, but they were unusual. Only 26 of the 104 families could trace their ancestors back a hundred years (roughly three to four generations); only 9 of these 26 could trace them back more than a hundred years.[52] Some families claimed longer lineages, such as the ʿAbd al-Baqi family, which traced its ancestors back to the Ayyubids, but the genealogical connections were lost and such claims could not be verified.[53]

More typical were the families like the Shurayyifs that had become established in the first half of the eighteenth century. More than three-quarters of these upper-class families had acquired their position in the preceding one or two generations and were still in the process of building dynasties and consolidating their position in Aleppo in the late eighteenth century. The shortness of genealogical memory was reflected in the failure to know the names of more distant ancestors and in the choice of family names. Most of these names were associated with recent ancestors. The gap between the sense of family tradition and longevity and the reality of short genealogies reflects the "nouveau riche" nature of many of these families. As upwardly mobile families, many were not interested in drawing attention to their rather humble origins, although some took pride in the "rags-to-riches" stories of their ancestors.

The true "ancient" families who could trace their ancestors back for many generations and who had historical verification of descent fall into three categories. The first were distinguished ulema families, like the Tahas, who were more likely than other families to have an accurate knowledge of more distant ancestors. In large part this was because they had the assistance of biographical dictionaries in preserving their family history, since these works largely recorded the lives of illustrious ulema. The advantage of a public record of their notable ancestors was compounded by the tendency to pass certain religious offices down within families. The Taha family was associated with the office of naqib al-ashraf from the seventeenth century; the Kawakibi family with the office of Hanafi mufti. This tendency was less pronounced in Aleppo than it was in Damascus; for example, in Damascus only three families provided almost all of the Hanafi muftis for 150 years, and their tenure in office was relatively long, while in Aleppo twelve families provided Hanafi muftis over the same 150 years, and they usually served for relatively short periods of time.[54] Nevertheless, certain families were seen as having a right to the office through long family association with it. Finally, those ulema families associated with the leadership of Sufi orders, like the Rifaʿis and the Kayyalis, could trace their ancestors back through many generations. Since these leadership positions were hereditary, preserving the knowledge of the order's sheikhs meant preserving the knowledge of one's ancestors.

A second category of families that were able to preserve longer genealogies were the descendants of high Ottoman officials. Many of these families had a strong Ottoman orientation and took pride in their ancestors' service to the state and their own quasi-official positions. Here, too, the lives of their ancestors were matters of historical record, sometimes in biographical dictionaries, but more often in official records supplemented by evidence of the official's activities in Aleppo. The ʿAdili family, descendants of a sixteenth-century governor, was constantly reminded of his role in the city by the presence of the beautiful ʿAdliyya Mosque. Other examples, like the Kucuk ʿAli Agha, descendants of a seventeenth-century Janissary commander, and the Shaykhbandar family, descendants of a seventeenth-century governor, could also point with pride to the importance of their ancestors.[55]

A final category of families that tended to keep the memory of their ancestors strong overlapped with, but was not identical to, the other two categories. These were families that were the beneficiaries of large waqfs and whose members needed to be able to validate their claims to the income or the post of waqf administrator. As the generations passed, the families grew larger, kinship connections became more complicated, and knowledge of the family genealogy became increasingly important. The extensive litigation involving the Ghawri family waqf in the late eighteenth century was caused by conflicting claims over rights to the income from the waqf; a successful claim was possible only if one knew and had proof of where one fit into the family genealogy.[56]

For families without such aids to memory, genealogical knowledge was often limited. Patronymic naming patterns helped determine the extent of such knowledge. Since names usually included both the father's and grandfather's names, knowledge of two ascending generations was preserved. But such a naming pattern also set a limit to knowledge of one's ancestors. Without strong reasons to preserve the memory of earlier generations or the means to do so, these memories faded, especially given the relatively short life spans of the time. Since life expectancy for people who survived childhood was only the mid-thirties, few people would have known their grandfathers much less anything about more remote ancestors.

The Aleppine lineages varied considerably in size and structure over time as they expanded or contracted with changing circumstances. Some of these lineages were wealthier, more powerful, and more prominent than others; such distinctions also existed within lineages. Some had been established in Aleppo for centuries, others only for a generation. New families joined the ranks of this elite in the late eighteenth and early nineteenth centuries. Nevertheless, belonging to one of these lineages was a marker of high social status; they provided a sense of social identity, of being a part of the elite, and of having a family history.

The consideration of these lineages as kinship groups, and what this can tell us about the functions and perceptions of the family in eighteenth-century Aleppo, underscores the extent to which the history of the family and the history of individual families, taken collectively, are closely linked to fundamental questions about the timing and process of social change in Ottoman society. The next section will explore in greater depth what the history of these lineages can tell us about processes of social mobility and elite integration in Aleppo.

SOCIAL MOBILITY
AND SOCIAL INTEGRATION

The fact that a large number of upper-class families rose to prominence in the eighteenth century does not mean that upward social mobility was common. Socially ambitious individuals and families of humble origins did not find assimilation into the upper levels of Aleppo society easy to achieve. As Marcus has pointed out, the obstacles to upward mobility in this society were formidable and impossible

for most people to overcome.[57] Some of the "new" families originating
in the early eighteenth century and later had a definite advantage. These
were families that had not risen from humble origins, but had moved to
Aleppo from other places where they were part of the local elite. They
therefore brought with them the wealth and status that made assimilation
relatively easy. Given the connections between the major urban centers
of the Middle East, the commercial, scholarly, and administrative networks among imperial and local elites, and the extent of geographic mobility, some of these families were undoubtedly already known to people
in Aleppo. Families like the Jazmatis from North Africa, possibly the
Amiris and Qurnas from Basra, and the Qudsis from Urfa were new to
Aleppo, but they were already distinguished families whose integration
into the elite represented lateral rather than upward mobility.

Considerable upward mobility did occur in the first half of the eighteenth century, however. Mobility into the elite was achieved by the traditional methods found in premodern and early modern Islamic society:
education, marriage, patronage, and the accumulation of wealth. A religious education and membership in the ulema were theoretically open to
all male Muslims, and obtaining a religious education could be a major
step toward upward mobility from the lower classes. It not only conferred
some prestige in itself, but it also allowed an opportunity to make a reputation as a scholar and to associate with prominent members of the ulema
who were themselves among the notables of the city—both opportunities that could provide connections that would help in bettering one's position. Even at times in the history of the Islamic world when social mobility was very limited, as in eleventh-century Nishapur, some "new
blood" was permitted into the upper class through this means of assimilation.[58] Education was the means by which the founder of the Tabbakh
family, Hasan (d. 1731), achieved an important position in Aleppo. As the
family name suggests, his father, 'Ali, was a cook who had made a fortune leasing utensils for use on festive occasions and who therefore was
able to provide a childhood of luxury for his son Hasan and an education
that allowed him to enter the ranks of the ulema. Hasan became a distinguished 'alim, and through his wealth and personal stature, assured his
children a position of prominence in Aleppine society.[59]

A number of upwardly mobile families during this period used patronage networks to facilitate their rise in Aleppo society. Without the
right family background, and even sometimes with it, career and social
advancement were difficult without the help of a patron. By the eigh-

teenth century, patronage was an indispensable feature in the distribution of favors and political, military, and religious posts at all levels of government. The most common form of patronage grew out of the large households—modeled after the sultan's inner and outer service—established by top government officials and commanders of the army as well as wealthy and powerful notables. Favored retainers in the households were rewarded with offices, gifts, and wealth, and their careers were furthered. After leaving the household, they usually maintained connections with the patron that could be extremely useful to both parties.

The most striking example of the importance of patronage in facilitating upward mobility in eighteenth-century Aleppo involved Ibrahim Pasha and his family. The family's position in the city was the result of the wealth, prestige, and power that Ibrahim Pasha, its founder, had acquired from serving as an Ottoman governor, but his achievement of high office was directly due to the wealth he had accumulated and the connections he was able to make as a trusted retainer in the household of Muhammad Taha. Little is known about his life before he became connected with Muhammad Taha, but his nisba, "Qataraghasi," suggests that he or a recent ancestor had been connected with the caravan trade and might have been of Turkish background. After Muhammad's death in 1786, Ibrahim Agha (as he was then) began his meteoric rise, serving as muhassil and then mutasallim of Aleppo from 1788 to 1798. In 1799 he was appointed governor of Damascus, and he served as governor of Damascus, Aleppo, Tripoli, and Diyarbekir off and on between 1802 and 1808. At that point he retired or was forced to retire from politics.[60]

Patronage relationships could also develop between a powerful individual and people outside the household, as in the case of Hasan Mudarris and the Yakin family. Hasan Mudarris's growing prominence in the city was the result of the patronage of the Yakin family, who gave him the post of *mudarris* (professor) in the 'Uthmaniyya Mosque, of which they served as mutawallis. In return for wealth and other forms of payment, the patrons would provide protection for their clients, help them in times of need, and further their careers. In addition to material payment, the patron also got from this relationship the benefit of having clients, which enhanced his prestige, demonstrated his generosity and his ability to help others, and increased his power by providing him with ready-made supporters when he needed them.

Marriage was also commonly used to achieve upward mobility, for it allowed a wealthy person who had not yet acquired other attributes of high social status to be easily assimilated into the notables through connections with a distinguished family. Marriages between a wealthy man of humble social origins and a woman from a distinguished family were the most visible examples of marriage as a vehicle of social mobility. The greater importance of the woman's family was reflected in the use of the family name from the maternal line. As indicated above, the social prominence of the Rifa'i and Jabiri families came from such marriages, and their family names were connected to maternal ancestors. It is not clear if marrying a daughter into an elite family offered similar opportunities for upward mobility. Upper-class males were more likely to marry outside their social group than their sisters. However, because these women are more difficult to identify, since they did not have family names, the consequences of these marriages are harder to see. We do not know if marrying a daughter into a wealthy and prestigious family improved only the status of the female or allowed her natal family to climb the social ladder as well.

Education, patronage, and/or marriage were not sufficient to achieve upward mobility, however. The accumulation of wealth at some point in the process was essential. Although wealth itself was not sufficient to guarantee familial prestige and influence, the other avenues to social mobility were largely closed without it. Making an advantageous marriage or acquiring a religious education and the right appointments afterward depended on having access to substantial resources. Acquiring a patron was the only way of achieving mobility without first accumulating wealth; in fact, the backing of the right patron could be a means of acquiring wealth. Nevertheless, even patronage was usually a means of acquiring status and access to power, *after* sufficient wealth had been acquired.

However entry into the upper stratum of society was achieved in eighteenth-century Aleppo, the result of this process was a relatively large number of new families moving into this group in the early eighteenth century and still consolidating their position in the latter part of the century. The key question is how significant this rate of mobility was. Two interpretations are possible. One is that this rate of mobility was "normal." That is, at any given time more than half of upper-class families had only achieved this status in the last generation or two. Demographic realities, geographic mobility, and the economic and political pressures that could ruin a family meant that most families may only have survived or been able to retain their high status for a few generations, to be replaced by other upwardly mobile families. Therefore a fairly constant turnover among the elite occurred.

This high turnover among the elite may have been particularly characteristic of major commercial centers like Aleppo where a large number of merchant families were found among the elite. Merchant families may have been able to rise fairly rapidly in the social hierarchy of Aleppo, as did the Arihawi family, whose founder, Niʿmat Allah, went from small peddler to wealthy long-distance merchant in a relatively short time.[61] At the same time they may have been less able to establish lineages that survived over a long period. Bruce Masters gives the names of what appear to be merchant dynasties in the seventeenth and early eighteenth centuries: Shammali, ibn al-Misht, ibn al-Laqab, al-Samirli, as well as the Arihawi family.[62] Of these, only the Laqab family was still important in the late eighteenth century. The Shammali family appears only twice in the sources and then disappears completely. The Arihawi family had died out by the end of the century. There is no mention of the other two.[63] While such evidence is hardly conclusive, it suggests that merchant dynasties may not have been particularly long-lived. In order to test the validity of the hypothesis that high turnover among the elite was "normal," it would be necessary to go backward and forward in time and attempt to calculate the rate of upward mobility and lineage longevity, a task that must await further research.

The other possible interpretation is that the rate of mobility into elite status in the first half of the eighteenth century was unusually high and that it was a significant indicator of important social changes taking place during this century. If we look at the backgrounds of those families who first became prominent in the early eighteenth century, some suggestive points emerge. About half of the "new" families whose origins are known were merchant families. Some were merchants who had moved to Aleppo from other regions; others were residents of the city who were able to overcome the usual barriers to social mobility. The fact that so many new families, and most of the families who were especially wealthy and prominent later in the century, were merchant families is testimony to the continued commercial vitality of the city in the first half of the eighteenth century. Rags-to-riches stories similar to that of Niʿmat Allah Arihawi mentioned above must have been occurring in the first half of the eighteenth century, although it is the results rather than the process that is visible later. If merchants were attracted from elsewhere to settle in Aleppo, and if the poor but ambitious were able to get rich, the opportunities to make money must have been there. Moreover, this evidence also indicates that Muslims, as well as minorities, had access to and were taking advantage of these opportunities.

This evidence on social mobility is consistent with Masters's analysis of developments within the Aleppine economy between 1600 and 1750. Structural changes were occurring in the world and regional economies that in the long run benefited minority merchants at the expense of Muslim merchants. In particular, as trade with Europe grew in volume and became an increasingly large share of the city's external commerce, Greek Orthodox and Melkite merchants with close contacts with the Europeans were reaping much of the profit. Nevertheless, in the first half of the eighteenth century, despite the end of the silk trade with Iran, Muslims were still enjoying the benefits of a healthy commercial economy. They continued to dominate the trade with India. Although there are no statistics that would allow us to quantify the volume of this trade, impressionistic evidence suggests that it was brisk and lucrative during this period.[64] Wealth was also being generated in other ways, and opportunities for accumulating riches were not restricted to commerce. Tax farming and moneylending were both more readily available and potentially more lucrative because of the financial needs and fiscal policies of the Ottoman state. Merchants were investing in a variety of areas, not just commerce; people other than merchants were investing in commerce and moneylending. While the "new" families were predominantly of merchant origins, new ulema and 'askari families were also being established, an indication that these financial opportunities were not restricted to merchants. Others were taking advantage of them as well. The redevelopment of parts of the madina, much of it in conjunction with the endowments of Ahmad Taha, 'Uthman Pasha, and Hajj Musa Amiri, was a visible sign of a thriving economy. Taken together, the conditions were right for relatively rapid social mobility in the first half of the eighteenth century. This evidence would support the second interpretation—that the rate of mobility into the elite in the first half of the eighteenth century was unusually high.

The rapid mobility of the first half of the century slowed markedly in the second half. By the end of the eighteenth century, many of the above-mentioned opportunities had dried up as a result of changes in the economy and political problems in the city as well as in the empire as a whole. Only seven new families appear in the sources by the end of the century who had not appeared twenty years before. Nine more new families had appeared by 1840. This seventy-year period was a clear contrast to the previous seventy years.

Coupled with the relatively few new families who were assimilated into this group during this period was the disappearance of a relatively large number of families who had been prominent in Aleppo earlier. Almost one-fourth of the notable families of the 1770s had disappeared from the sources by 1840. This attrition was partially the result of "natural causes," as some of these families died out. By the law of averages a certain percentage would simply not continue to reproduce themselves in the male line. One example was the Bakhsha family, descendants of a Khalwati sheikh of Amasya (d. 1523). The sheikh's grandson, a prominent religious dignitary in Istanbul in the seventeenth century, was invited by a group of Aleppo ulema to become a sheikh of the Zawiya Ikhlasiyya in Bayyada, a position held by the male line until the last one died in 1792.[65] The Muwahibi family, Qadiri sheikhs, suffered a similar fate.[66] In both cases the offices and honors associated with them passed to unrelated members of the same order. The Arihawi family mentioned above also succumbed to demographic misfortune. Ni'mat Allah's great-grandsons had no surviving male children. In families in which there were no surviving males to carry on the family name, females sometimes carried family offices, wealth, and "honor" as they were absorbed into other families—the Durkli family became part of the Yakin, the Shukri part of the Trabulsi, and the 'Imadi part of the Shurayyif.[67]

Although demographic attrition was always at work, the number of families that died out, especially in the early decades of the nineteenth century, seems unusually high and was undoubtedly connected to the time of troubles that Aleppo experienced. The worsening of factional conflict, the revolt of 1819, the massive earthquake of 1822 and its aftershocks, and the cholera epidemic shortly after took a major toll on Aleppo's population. Ruth Roded talks about the decimation of the ranks of the scholarly community that resulted and the efforts to encourage ulema from other parts of the empire to make their careers in Aleppo.[68] The decline in the number of religious leaders and in the population as a whole was paralleled by the decline in the number of upper-class families.

Worsening economic and political conditions affected population size in another way as well. Just as people had been attracted to Aleppo in the early eighteenth century when economic opportunities abounded, they left the city when times were difficult. Some names disappear from the sources because the families left the city. Individuals and families leaving the city for political reasons or because of economic ruin or, on a more positive note, to seek fortune or career opportunities elsewhere was nothing new. One noteworthy seventeenth-century example was the Janbuladh family. After his involvement in an uprising against Ottoman authorities in 1603, ʿAli Pasha Janbuladh decided that Aleppo was no longer a healthy place to be. When invited by Amir Bashir to reside on Mount Lebanon, he reestablished his family there in the early seventeenth century. His large palace in the quarter of Bahsita was still known as "saray Junbaladh" (Junbaladh Palace) in the eighteenth century, although the family had long ago left the city.[69] Leaving the city to settle permanently in other regions became more frequent in the unsettled conditions of the early nineteenth century.

Even when families did not leave the city, downward mobility followed political disfavor and economic ruin. Several examples exist of families whose mounting debts caused them to sell off most or all of their property. In at least one case, that of the Trabulsis, the cause was political. Muhammad Trabulsi happened to be naqib in 1770 when a major ashraf uprising occurred. Although he was not an instigator of the trouble, he was held responsible by the Ottoman authorities, and most of his economic assets were confiscated.[70] More often, however, these losses were due to economic causes. In times of economic change like the late eighteenth and early nineteenth centuries, the number of such economic failures undoubtedly increased.

Despite the upward and downward mobility of this period and the political and economic difficulties that affected the city after the turn of the nineteenth century, the overall result was a remarkable continuity among the families who already belonged to the upper class in 1770, especially among those families who rose to prominence in the early eighteenth century. Over two-thirds of the families were still the same in 1840 as in 1770. This continuity in the upper class continued through the rest of the Ottoman period. A relatively high percentage of the families prominent at the beginning of the nineteenth century were still upper-class families until after the Second World War, when the social and political transformation of Syrian society after independence undercut their economic base and political power. If the names of elite families from the early nineteenth century are compared to the list of notable families in the early twentieth century, most are still the same. In his 1923 survey of the quarters of Aleppo, Kamil al-Ghazzi mentioned prominent families who resided in each quarter. Altogether he mentioned sixty-nine different families. Fifty-three of them (three-fourths) were the same families who were part of the elite in the early nineteenth century.[71] Some families or branches of families changed their names. In a couple of cases, family names changed when the acquisition of the name was fairly new and not yet fixed. One example of this was the lineage established by Ibrahim Pasha Qataraghasi at the end of the eighteenth century. The family was sometimes known as Ibrahim Pasha Zade and sometimes as Qataraghasi Zade in the early nineteenth century and only became fixed as the latter at a later date. A change in family name might also occur to reflect a major event or development in the life of the family that conferred new importance or status on it and was symbolized in the use of a new name. For example, ʿAbd al-Rahman Siyyaf's family played host to Ahmad Jazzar Pasha in 1788. During his visit Siyyaf's son ʿAbd Allah was born. In later years the Siyyaf lineage came to be called Jazzar.[72] New family names sometime appeared when lineages evolved into two distinct branches, as happened when the descendants of Muhammad Celebi Taha Zade came to be known as Celebi Zade.[73] About two dozen new families had been assimilated into this class in the second half of the nineteenth century; a number of families had disappeared completely. The rest of the elite, however, was made up of the descendants of the same families who had dominated Aleppo society between 1770 and 1840.

Ruth Roded has examined the elites of Aleppo and other Syrian cities in the late Ottoman period to try to explain this continuity. She points to the ability of old elites to adapt successfully to changing circumstances— for example, by sending their sons to Ottoman schools and into new careers in the bureaucracy and army—and to innovate within traditional structures. "New upstarts" were found in all these cities, but they were largely assimilated into the existing elites and did not change the nature of this group. The continuity in families was more striking than the changes.[74]

What this evidence from Aleppo suggests is that there was greater continuity among the elite from the eighteenth to the twentieth century than between the seventeenth and the eighteenth centuries, despite the great changes that affected Aleppo as well as other parts of the Middle East during this period. Further research would be needed to reach a definite conclusion, but it confirms other evidence about the ability of existing elites to take advantage of Ottoman reforms and new world economic

order to consolidate and enhance their positions. It also draws attention
to the extent and importance of changes taking place in the Ottoman
Empire in the seventeenth and eighteenth centuries *before* the full impact
of European expansion was felt. The need to further our understanding
of the internal roots and dynamics of change is made clear.

CONCLUSION

At the apex of Aleppo society in the late eigh-
teenth and early nineteenth centuries was a group of elite families, de-
riving their social power from a variety of sources and sometimes competing with each other for control of economic resources and political
power, but at the same time socially homogeneous and well integrated
through ties of kinship, marriage, and residence. This group was a visible
and dominant force in the life of Aleppo in the eighteenth and nineteenth
centuries. Many of them had only relatively recently risen to social
prominence, but in the course of the eighteenth century were able to
consolidate their position. By the early nineteenth century, their success
in establishing themselves at the top of the social hierarchy and the decreased opportunities for social mobility made this elite a more stable
group. The integration of the group through close networks of marriage
and residential ties, their common economic interests, and less permeable
social boundaries marked the early stages in the process of class formation
that would accelerate with the social and economic transformations of
the nineteenth century.

Central to their own sense of identity and to their success in perpetuating their social power was a strong sense of family. One set of kinship
ties was to all other members of the patriline—those who shared the
same family name. But how important was the lineage beyond providing
this social identity and position within the social hierarchy? In the next
chapters we will look at the other family "circles" of the notables—those
created by residence, marriage, and inheritance.

Two

FAMILY AND HOUSEHOLD

T he large houses of Aleppo's upper class dominated the quarters of Frafira and Dakhil Bab al-Nasr, Suwayqa 'Ali and Suwayqa Hatim, Bayyada and Masabin. Less visible in the urban landscape than the tower houses and palaces of the Florentine patricians, these houses were nevertheless easily identifiable to the residents of the quarter and the city. Observers of this society, both European and Middle Eastern, have described the households that occupied these mansions as large families encompassing several generations and various degrees of kinship—in effect entire lineages—whose residency spanned decades, even centuries. Included as well were slaves, retainers, and dependents. William Goode claims that the houses of the merchant and landowning elite of Aleppo in the 1920s contained forty to fifty family members.[1] It is usually assumed that elite households in previous centuries were at least this large, if not larger. They were large not only in comparison to households today, but also in comparison to households of other classes at the time, since only the wealthy could afford to maintain such households. Moreover, the size and structure of these households and the complex ties of kinship, service, and patronage within them served purposes that were presumably important to these families: patriarchal control, joint economic ventures, the accumulation and preservation of wealth, the concentration of political power, and the protection of family honor.

This chapter will examine these upper-class households.[2] Family and household were not coterminous. Households were larger and more inclusive than the family, often incorporating many members who were not kin. At the same time, family members had important ties to relatives outside the household. However, for most people the most frequent and intimate ties of kinship were with members of the same household. Precise answers to many of the questions that historians usually ask about households are elusive, in the absence of evidence like census data that would provide lists of household residents and their relationship to the head of household. We cannot know, for example, how many people lived in each household, their relationship to the household head, and the proportion of kin to non-kin. What we can extract from the sources is evidence about the formation and stability of households that allows us to see patterns in this process and to draw some conclusions about the kinds of households in which these notables lived. The sources also provide us a picture of what these notables themselves perceived as the ideal household. The following discussion will focus on the kinds of households in which these notables lived, the relationship between actual households and cultural ideals, and the connections between household patterns and the distribution of power and authority within the household.

CULTURAL IDEALS AND
SPATIAL ARRANGEMENTS

The large courtyard houses of Aleppo's notables were a symbolic and physical embodiment of the family's presence in the city. The connection between the family home and the family's history was reflected in the way in which houses were often identified in the court records by the name of a particular family. Numerous references are made in the court records to, for example, the "Dar Asadi Zade" (House of Asadi) or the "Dar Qurna Zade." Families were also identified with the quarters in which these houses were located. Some families had been resident in a quarter for many generations. The Kawakibi family, for example, had, and still has, a large house in the quarter of Jallum, in which at least some family members had lived for generations. A family mosque and mausoleum dating from the sixteenth century documented the historical connection between the family and the quarter. The symbolic importance of this identification with house and quarter is even further emphasized in its persistence in many cases long after the family has died out, left the city, or moved to other quarters.

The symbolic and tangible association between house and family was reinforced by cultural ideals about the household that were widely held throughout Aleppine society. These ideals are most clearly expressed in the arrangements associated with the establishment of family endowments. Family endowments gave the endower the freedom to decide how the property that constituted the endowment would be used by family members in the future, unlike the inheritance system, which gave the legator little choice as to how property was distributed among his or her heirs. Therefore, how an endowment was set up expressed the endower's vision of his family's future. Since these endowments often included quite specific dispositions for the family residence and who would be part of the household in future generations, they reflected an endower's view of the ideal household.

Of the 468 waqfs registered in the religious court archives between 1770 and 1840, 199 were family endowments. Seventy-nine of these included the endower's residence as part of the endowment and specified who was to live in it. In all cases, the endower continued to occupy the house until his or her death. In 68 of these 79 cases, the house was then left to the endower's children; in the other 11, it went to siblings or the children of siblings of the endower. In 52 of these cases, the house was left equally to all children, although in some cases daughters were to be excluded if they married. In only 2 cases were females excluded entirely. Even when women were excluded after marriage, they often had the right to return and reclaim their share of the household if they later became widowed or divorced, and in some cases, their male descendants had the right to live in the household as well. Following the death of the first generation of beneficiaries, the house was to be a residence for all of their children and future generations, with the same restrictions that applied with regard to the original beneficiaries, such as the exclusion of females. Clearly the endower envisioned that his or her male descendants, with their families, would continue to live in the house provided. What is particularly interesting in these arrangements is that they also left the door open to female descendants. The provisions that defined female rights to the endowment were undoubtedly inserted to ensure that women who never married or who were left alone as a result of death of a spouse or divorce had a claim on their natal family, but the provisions also left open the possibility that descendants of females as well those of males had residential rights.

The ideological preference for large extended-family households expressed in these documents was more than just a legal formula. The *waqfiyya* (document setting conditions of an endowment) was a binding legal document whose provisions could not be overturned without considerable difficulty. Descendants of the endower who felt that they were being denied their right to live in a house could, and on occasion did, bring suit to claim that right. Even if the realities of household patterns and the contingencies of family life meant that such households rarely existed beyond a generation or two, dictating one's after-death wishes for the household in such a legally binding way was nevertheless a clear statement of the endower's vision of the ideal family and of his or her expectation that these conditions would be carried out.[3]

The vision of the family and of the living arrangements for future generations expressed in these documents was not the only factor that would seem to predispose these families to form large and complex households. Their existence was also facilitated by the physical structure of the traditional Syrian house. In many parts of the world, there were upper limits on the size of the household, even among the wealthy, simply because space became a problem as the family expanded. The Syrian house, however, was infinitely expandable in theory because of its courtyard plan. A typical upper-class house consisted of connecting courtyards with rooms or alcoves opening off each one, as well as a kitchen, other offices, stables, and sometimes a bath and a *qanaq* (reception room), often shared between two related families. In Aleppo, such houses were usually only one story, although there was sometimes a *masif* (literally, "summer place"), a room for sleeping on hot summer nights located on the roof.[4] The size of the house was determined by the number of courtyards that were linked together. The smaller elite houses had at least two courtyards, but a house could be expanded with relatively little structural change by adding more courtyards, connecting them to the original house with the construction of a corridor or by knocking out a wall. Courtyards could be joined together or separated into discrete households as the size, needs, and circumstances of the family changed. The homes of many of these upper-class families were essentially family compounds composed of several connecting courtyards. The Jazmati family, for example, occupied five adjacent houses, known collectively as the "dur Jazmati Zade," in the Suwayqa Hatim quarter. The Khanlarli home in Frafira, the Ghawri home in Bayyada, and the Qurna home in Bustan were all extended in this fashion at one time.

The modular construction of these houses was not the only feature that made it theoretically possible to accommodate a large number of people. The unspecified use of space also played a role. The layout of these houses allowed for the separation of public and private space. Separate courtyards—the *dar al-uta* for the reception of visitors and occupied only by male members of the household if male guests were present, and the *dar al-haram* for the family and off-limits to males from outside the family—defined the distinction between public and private space. This reflected cultural values about the privacy of family life and the need to protect females from public view, although it was only the well-to-do who could afford this luxury. In contrast to houses of wealthy Europeans, where rooms opened off each other—before new ideas about privacy in the eighteenth century changed the design of houses significantly—the rooms in the Middle Eastern courtyard house were not connected to each other but instead opened off the courtyard, a communal space. Within this overall division of space, however, there was little functional differentiation. Eating, sleeping, and daily living took place in the same room or rooms. Benches, used for sitting during the day, were beds at night. Not having to provide a separate bedroom for each individual or separate eating and "living" rooms made possible the accommodation of larger numbers of people.[5]

The image of the large multigenerational family cohabiting in the family compound—evoked by cultural preference for such households, by the identification of families with particular houses, and by the way houses were constructed—obscured a much more complex reality, however. To understand this reality, it is necessary to determine more about the processes of household formation and change and to consider their implications for family structure and family relationships.

OTTOMAN HOUSEHOLDS IN COMPARATIVE PERSPECTIVE

Much of the thinking about household structure in the past has been shaped by the work of European family historians. The issue of household structure has been one of the most widely discussed, and hotly debated, in the historiography of the European family. The debate was sparked by Peter Laslett's rejection of the long-held view that families in pre-industrial societies had been large and complex domestic groups, including not just the conjugal family but numerous relatives. Using English data from the seventeenth century, Laslett argued that households in the past were small and nuclear, and he therefore re-

jected the argument that the emergence of the nuclear family went hand
in hand with industrialization.[6] Laslett's conclusions have been justly criti-
cized both on methodological grounds and on the uniqueness of the English case. Nevertheless, the discussion generated by his thesis has inspired
sophisticated work on household structure and formation and their wider
significance. Historians working with Laslett at Cambridge have developed a classification scheme that recognizes how widely households in
the past varied and makes it possible to discuss households from a comparative perspective. The key variables used to compare different types of
household formation are (1) the composition of the household at any
point in time (who actually lived together), (2) the age of marriage of
males and females, and (3) the timing of fission (at what point, if at all,
did the household split into two or more households). At least four distinct "European" household patterns have been identified, while household patterns in other parts of the world have been lumped together as a
single "non-European" type, because of the lack of research on historical
patterns of household formation in these areas.[7]

Thanks to the recent research on Middle Eastern households—notably by Alan Duben on Turkish households in the nineteenth and early
twentieth centuries and by Ken Cuno on Egyptian rural households in
the nineteenth century—we are beginning to accumulate the evidence
that allows us to move beyond the undifferentiated "non-European"
household, to see variations in household patterns in the Middle East in
the past, and to identify the variables that determine these patterns. Alan
Duben has concluded that in the nineteenth century the household system in Turkey outside the urban areas was a joint family one, characterized by a household that consisted of an older married couple, one or
more sons with their wives and children, and unmarried sons and daughters. Associated with this household type was an early age of marriage
for both males and females. As sons remained in the father's house,
daughters-in-law moved in, replacing daughters who married and moved
out. Households broke up and new ones were formed after the death of
the head of the household, not the marriage of sons, and the division of
property coincided with the breakup of the household. Households therefore went from simple to complex or extended, then back to simple. Consequently they were relatively small, except for the stage between the marriage of the first son and the death of the head of household, a stage that
was in any case fairly short, given normal life expectancy.[8] Having shown
that Turkish households were small and simple, except at one phase of the

domestic cycle, and that statistically joint households represented only one-third of all households, Duben is faced with the problem of reconciling this with his conclusion that Turkish household structure can be characterized as joint. He argues that the percentage of households of this type at any one time is less important than the fact that the cycle includes such a phase. That makes it distinct from other family types.[9]

Work by Justin McCarthy suggests similar conclusions about household patterns in small towns and rural areas of the Ottoman Empire. In a study of Black Sea Turks in the 1840s, McCarthy also found evidence of the joint family. He does not directly address the question of the domestic cycle, since he is looking at one point in time, but his conclusion about the prevalence of the extended family with a statistical occurrence of 33–34 percent seems to fit the process of household formation and change proposed by Duben.[10] However, one town that McCarthy studied followed a different pattern. In Vize, males moved out of the father's household after marriage, and therefore simple households were the norm, not just a stage of the joint household domestic cycle. Why this difference existed is not clear. However, it is suggestive that one town out of the three McCarthy studied had a different pattern of household formation. It seems very possible that other small towns and villages also had a different household system, so at least two different patterns of household formation coexisted in the rural areas and small towns. Further research is needed to determine if this was true and what the causes of these differences might be.

Ken Cuno has also found evidence of a joint family household system in the Egyptian Delta in the nineteenth century. Using the census data that first became available in the 1840s in Egypt, he finds simple family households more common at any given time. Yet, like Duben, he argues that a joint family household system existed because many of these simple households were in the process of becoming joint households. Most people spent at least some of their lives in joint households, and at any given time the majority of people lived in joint households, although the majority of households were not joint.[11] Because Cuno is looking at specific villages, he is able to present a more nuanced and detailed picture of the households in these villages than is Duben, and he is able to identify variables that affected their formation and stability. He found a number of significant correlations that can explain the similarities and some of the differences among households. One is the correlation between landholding and joint family household. Many people in these villages did not

own land or have tenancy rights, and their households were less likely to
be joint family households. Similarly, there is a high correlation between
class and joint family households. Rural notables were more likely to
form larger, more complex, and more durable joint family households
than other groups.[12] Finally, he suggests that levels of prosperity can affect household formation. By looking at one village at two different
points in the nineteenth century, he finds that there were many more
simple family households when times were bad.[13]

This research on Egyptian and Turkish rural households shows a broad
similarity in the tendency of landholding groups to form joint family
households. However, there are some differences in the kind of joint family households and in the durability of these households from one region
to another. The basic difference between the two regions was the economic relationship among males after the death of the father. In the
Turkish areas, property was divided and new simple households were set
up each generation; the domestic cycle was a simple one in which households moved from simple to joint to simple.

By contrast, joint ownership of property could persist in Egypt over
several generations, presumably with coresidence. Cuno finds evidence
of a more complex domestic cycle that included six stages. *Stage one* is the
nuclear family; *stage two* is the joint family of father and mother and married sons and their families; *stage three* would begin after the death of the
father, with two or more brothers and their families continuing to share
the same house; *stage four* would occur after the death of one brother, so
that uncles and nephews and their families are living together; in *stage five*
the household would consist of cousins, all males of the older generation
having died; and *stage six* would again be simple families, as the cousins
split up into separate households.[14] While joint households could experience fission after stage two (i.e., following the death of the household
head, as Duben found in Turkey), they could also continue through some
or all of the other stages. Some joint households were fathers and their
married sons, but others consisted of brothers living together or uncles
and nephews. All were joint households, but they involved quite different household types and life experiences for family members. The differences in the household patterns between Turkish areas of the Ottoman
Empire and Egypt could well be connected to the availability of land.
Land was scarce in Egypt relative to the population, despite the reclama-
tion of new lands in the nineteenth century. Strategies to retain land and
work it jointly were often necessary to survive and prosper. On the other

hand, land was plentiful in Anatolia, and new lands could be acquired to round out holdings that were divided between or among brothers.[15]

Differences in patterns of household formation may also have reflected differences in rural class structure and in the nature and rate of changes in land tenure and land laws between Egypt and the Turkish areas of the empire during the nineteenth century. Cuno has shown that joint households, especially those that were maintained for several generations, were associated particularly with rural notables, who had an interest in maintaining joint households in order to prevent the division of property through inheritance, and who used their power in the Egyptian Assembly to write laws to increase the power of the household head and preserve undivided property at the expense of the interests of individual family members.[16] Further research on the connection between the class structure of rural society, changes in land tenure and the law, and household formation is needed to determine how important these differences between Turkey and Egypt were.

How did urban households fit into this picture? Much of what determined rural household formation was the family's relationship to the land and need to ensure the family's economic survival (or prosperity). Different considerations would have affected household formation in urban areas. Duben and his collaborator, Cem Behar, have looked at Istanbul households between 1880 and 1940. They found that Istanbul households were quite different from the joint household system found in the countryside—they see the contrast as so great that they refer to this as a "dichotomous society."[17] In Istanbul, both men and women married late; the average age of marriage for men was thirty, for women, twenty-one. Moreover, newly married couples usually set up their own households rather than live with parents. If they did live with parents, they were as likely to live with the wife's family as the husband's. Sixty percent of the population lived either in simple family households or without family. Extended- or multiple-family households made up only 28 percent of the population. Households were not only simple but also small. The mean number of family members per household was 3.6. Class did have some effect on household size and structure, not surprisingly. The elite were more likely to live in complex and somewhat larger households. However, even elite households were not very large on the average (4.6 family members per household), and only 21 percent of elite households were multiple-family households.[18]

The obvious reason for these differences between the late-nineteenth-

century Istanbul household and the others would appear to be that the
social transformations of the nineteenth century had gone further in Istanbul than in other places. In other words, Istanbul was unique, different from other urban areas as well as from rural areas and probably different from early-nineteenth-century Istanbul as well. This is the position
taken by Duben and Behar.[19] However, the obvious answer might not be
the correct answer. It is possible that urban household formation in the
past was different from that in rural areas throughout the empire and
that it was more similar to late-nineteenth-century Istanbul than to rural
areas. Haim Gerber, drawing on his extensive work on Bursa in the seventeenth century, argues that "the nuclear family was much more widespread in the past than commonly realized," at least in the core areas of
the Ottoman Empire.[20]

Gerber's evidence for this conclusion comes from his study of 2,300
estates of individuals in Bursa. An analysis of these estates reveals, according to Gerber, that families were typically small; that life expectancy
was low and that therefore many men did not live long enough to see
their own children marry and to head multigenerational households; that
grown sons were often economically active and accumulated their own
property before the death of their fathers, a circumstance that suggests
that they were economically independent of their parents and may have
resided in households separate from them; and that there is no evidence
of brothers keeping property together for a long time. While Gerber does
not have the statistical evidence available to Duben and Behar at the end
of the nineteenth century, the patterns he cites would suggest household
and family size not unlike Istanbul at a later date. As discussed in Chapter 1, Gerber believes that greater security closer to the capital, the nature
of Ottoman/Islamic law, and the bureaucratic nature of the Ottoman
state reduced the importance of kinship ties in the core areas of the empire; small families and simple households would be consistent with less
emphasis on kinship.[21]

This research on Ottoman households is only beginning, and it is too
early to draw any definite conclusions. However, it does underscore the
danger of assuming that all Middle Eastern households were the same, and
it provides a comparative context for examining households in other parts
of the empire and at different times. Gerber's argument suggests that urban households outside the core areas of the empire might be quite different from those in Bursa and Istanbul, and Duben and Behar emphasize
the uniqueness of the Istanbul case. The next part of the chapter will look

at Aleppo's upper-class households to see how elite households in a major provincial city at an earlier period compare to what we are finding out about households in other regions of the Middle East in the past. What kinds of households did this elite form and what factors determined that? Did these upper-class Aleppo households more closely resemble those in seventeenth-century Bursa, nineteenth-century Istanbul, or nineteenth-century Egypt? At the same time, an examination of these households provides an opportunity to look at the relationship between the ideal of the large extended-family household and the reality of actual household arrangements.

FAMILY SIZE, HOUSEHOLD STRUCTURE, AND THE DOMESTIC CYCLE IN ALEPPO

The dynamics of household formation in the past were complex, whether one is considering urban or rural families, rich or poor. Various factors—cultural, economic, political, familial, personality—came to bear in different ways on the decisions that were made about household arrangements. One inescapable factor, however, was family demography. The size of the family around which the household was centered and the constraints of mortality could overshadow other considerations. Before looking at patterns of household formation in Aleppo, it is necessary to consider the issue of family size.

It is impossible to provide anything other than an estimate of family size in Aleppo because reliable statistical sources are lacking before the end of the nineteenth century. Birth records of any kind do not exist for the premodern or early modern Middle East. Instead, historians have relied on inheritance records (mukhallafat) to estimate family size, in effect counting how many children were alive at the death of one or both parents.[22] Using this methodology for Aleppo, it appears that family size among the population as a whole was small. The average number of children per conjugal family was only 3.3.[23] That number is consistent with what other historians using this methodology have found. Gerber estimated that the average Bursa family in the seventeenth century had 2.15 children. Tucker arrives at a figure of 3.3 for Nablus in the eighteenth and nineteenth centuries. These figures on the number of children per family are also consistent with the estimates of household size used by Ot-

toman historians working with cadastral surveys and census data. Omer
Barkan used a coefficient of 5 (i.e., two adults and three children) to
determine the population of the Ottoman Empire in the sixteenth century from the cadastral surveys of households. Although McCarthy and
Duben suggest slightly higher numbers for household size for rural areas
(6.5 and 5.3 – 6.5 respectively) in the nineteenth and early twentieth centuries, their figures reflect the existence of joint family households rather
than significant differences in the size of the individual conjugal families
making up the households. The number of children per couple would
still be between two and three.[24] Other contemporary evidence about
family size in Aleppo confirms what is found in the archives. Henri Guys,
who served as French consul in Aleppo in the early decades of the nineteenth century, indicated that Muslim families were small, usually consisting of the father, mother, and two or three children. Sometimes the
mother, aunt, or sister of the husband or wife resided with the family.[25]

When class is taken into consideration, average family size does not
change significantly. Elite families also had relatively few surviving children. There were families with many children, of course. ʿAbd al-Wahhab Shurayyif (13 children) and Hajj Musa Amiri (11) were two noted
examples, but both had more than one wife. Hajj Musa had four, as well
as several concubines; ʿAbd al-Wahhab extended his reproductive years
by marrying a second, much younger, wife, probably after the death of
his first wife. Nevertheless, these large families were rare. The average
number of children per conjugal family among these upper-class families
was 3.6, only slightly higher than the average overall. Since these calcu-
lations are based on family reconstruction for the upper class—a more
thorough, though not complete, record than the inheritance registers for
the population as a whole—the difference may be due simply to different methods of computation. While upper-class *households* may have been
significantly larger than those of other classes (an issue that will be discussed below), the number of surviving children per conjugal family was
not class-specific. Although the standard of living was higher and health
and sanitary conditions presumably better among the elite, the consequences of this were only marginal. Upper classes were subject to the
same life-threatening diseases as others. Infant mortality was high, and
life expectancy, even for those who survived childhood, was only the
mid-thirties, though some people did live to an older age. Judith Tucker
has commented on the particular risks that women were subjected to

through childbearing.[26] The prevalence of widows with young children, however, suggests that men fared only marginally better.

While a high mortality rate was the most important factor in limiting family size, other factors may have played a role in keeping family size small. Limits on fertility may also have been significant. Short life expectancies meant that people died in the midst of their reproductive years, and that affected fertility rates. Other "natural" limits on fertility, such as age of marriage, percentage of individuals who married, normal lactation periods, and fecundity, undoubtedly had some impact, although there is relatively little evidence about these points.[27] It is also possible that fertility was limited by artificial as well as natural means. Basim Musallam has argued persuasively that the knowledge and practice of contraception was common at least among some of the population, notably the urban middle and upper classes. He believes that the demographic depression in Syria and Egypt from the fourteenth to the nineteenth centuries was consistent with both high mortality and relatively low fertility, produced in part by a conscious effort to control births. He points to medieval sources that explicitly draw a connection between smaller families and a better quality of life. This recognition led at least some families to limit their offspring in times of difficulty when they wanted to minimize the problems created by hardship and preserve as much as possible their lifestyles.[28] Without direct evidence from Aleppo, it is impossible to test Musallam's hypothesis, but it remains an interesting one that deserves some consideration.

The relatively small size of most upper-class families has somewhat contradictory implications for household formation. On the one hand, it meant that joint family households were feasible; that is, in most cases families were not so large that they were forced to divide up because of inadequate space within a house to accommodate everyone. Many of their residences were sufficiently large to house parents, sons and their families, and unmarried daughters. On the other hand, high mortality rates—the most important cause of smaller families—and short life expectancies often precluded the formation of multigenerational and multiple-family households. The joint household of father, mother, and grown sons with their families was too often disrupted by the death of one or both of the parents during the minority of the children or the failure of children to survive to adulthood. If the fathers died during the minority of their children, this implied either female-headed households or women and minor children being incorporated into the households of relatives. It also meant that married brothers would not spend part of their lives together in a joint family household ruled by their father, but might immediately set up separate households on obtaining their majority and taking possession of their inheritance. The way in which mortality disrupted the normal process of household formation could have resulted in a low percentage of joint households, despite a preference for this.

So what kinds of households were found among Aleppo's elite families? At first glance, what is most striking about upper-class households was their diversity. While the majority of families experienced a similar process of household formation and fission as children grew to maturity, married, had children of their own, and parents died, the family members who shared the household, the timing of fission, the reconfiguration of households after fission, and the relationship among these new households differed considerably. In some of these families, separation into discrete households occurred every generation and soon after the death of the head of the family; in others it could be delayed long after the father's death, sometimes through an entire generation. In some cases, each son formed a separate household; in others, two brothers might remain together while others moved out. The different family groups might live side by side after the division or they might be widely scattered through several quarters. Underlying this diversity was one similarity. Most of these households could be labeled "joint family" households, if by that we mean, following Duben, that the domestic cycle could and often did include a joint phase, and if we keep in mind that the label "joint family" can be applied to households that actually differed from each other in significant ways.

Before examining the different kinds of households among the elite, it would be useful to look at the households of one lineage over several generations. The Jabiri family was one of the most prominent families in Aleppo during this period and well into the twentieth century. Descendants of an Ottoman qadi whose daughter had married a man of humble social origins, members of this family had become important ulema by the second half of the eighteenth century. In 1760 the head of the family was Ahmad Jabiri, who lived in the quarter of ʿAynayn in the western suburbs of the city and owned considerable property there. In 1765, about five years before his death, Ahmad created a waqf from this property, including the family home, which was to be a residence for his descendants. Nevertheless, before he died, three of his sons had moved into new houses in different quarters of the city. (The fourth son, As'ad, pre-deceased his father, and it is not clear where he lived.) Taha had moved to Frafira. Yusif, who had served as mudarris in the new madrasa, the Iskandariyya in 'Aynayn (which suggests that he still lived in that quarter for some part of his adult life), had moved his family to Masabin, although he spent most of his time in Istanbul, where he had taken a post as clerk in the imperial divan. Mustafa had moved to Suwayqa 'Ali.[29] Part of the explanation for the choices of residence of these Jabiri brothers lies in the desire of upwardly mobile and ambitious men to move from the suburbs into the "aristocratic" quarters of the city. But it also reflects the natural process of household fission that most families underwent.

In the last decades of the eighteenth century, the wealth and power of the family increased, especially in Mustafa's branch of the family. Mustafa and his brother Taha were officials of the religious courts, often serving as deputies to the qadi. Mustafa used this position as a stepping stone to more important offices, Hanafi mufti and naqib al-ashraf, in which he was succeeded by one of his sons, 'Abd Allah. His other son, 'Abd al-Qadir, was also a court official and then muhassil. These Jabiri brothers, 'Abd Allah and 'Abd al-Qadir, were among the most powerful men in Aleppo in the first decades of the nineteenth century and were heavily involved in the factional politics of that time. The household patterns in this branch of the family were different from those of the previous generation. Mustafa and his sons lived together until Mustafa died, and then the sons continued to maintain a joint household until 'Abd Allah's death in 1821. Their political successes were closely linked to their joint efforts. Between them they shared some of the most important local religious offices: mufti, ra'is al-kuttab, *na'ib* (deputy judge) of the court, and naqib al-ashraf. 'Abd Allah also became a qadi, serving for a time in Izmir, thereby expanding the brothers' links to the imperial religious establishment. Back in Aleppo 'Abd al-Qadir became mutasallim for a time. Their success was also a product of their wealth, which they invested in extensive property.[30] After the death of 'Abd Allah and that of 'Abd al-Qadir a few years later, some of their sons and daughters continued to live together in the household in Suwayqa 'Ali, although how many is not clear. What *is* known is that some of the sons set up their own households. 'Abd al-Qadir's son 'Arif had moved to Dar Imamli in Frafira, and his cousin Ahmad, 'Abd Allah's son, bought the Jundi family home in Masabin.[31]

The households of Yusif Jabiri and his descendants were different. Although he had spent considerable time in Egypt, and moved permanently to Istanbul a few years before his death because of official appointments with the Ottoman government, his family (one son and two daughters) remained in Aleppo. When Yusif died, his son and one daughter had come of age, although how long before his death is not clear; the other daughter predeceased him. The son, Muhammad, married his uncle Mustafa's daughter Sharaf, and they lived in the house in Masabin. Muhammad's mother and his sister Fatima apparently lived with them; there is no indication that the latter ever married. Both his mother and Fatima died before Muhammad. Muhammad and Sharaf had one surviving child, Yusif, who had come of age by the time of Muhammad's death, sometime before 1792. Yusif lived in the family home until his death (1819) with his wife, five children, and his mother. Two of his five children, a son and a daughter, died after Yusif but before they reached their majority, and another had predeceased him. The two surviving children, both sons, were presumably still living in the family home with their mother and grandmother in 1840.[32] By this time, one son, Talib, was already married to Habiba Ikhlas and had a minor son. So this branch of the family lived in a simple or extended-family household, rather than a joint family household, throughout most of this period. Within this one lineage, then, there were different types of households and different patterns of household formation. This diversity within one lineage reflects the diversity in the group as a whole.

Perhaps the best way to conceptualize elite households in Aleppo is along a continuum of household types. The parameters of the continuum were set by the norm of the joint family household; within those parameters, households ranged from simple households to large multiple-family households that remained undivided over several generations. Where households fell on this continuum reflected the particular stage of the domestic cycle the family had reached. Household patterns among the elite in Aleppo are best understood within the context of the more complex domestic cycle proposed by Lee and Gjerde and used by Cuno to analyze Egyptian households. The key difference between this model and the simpler domestic cycle described by Duben is the timing of the breakup of households, which may, but does not necessarily, occur after the death of the father (end of stage two). At any time among Aleppo's upper class, there were joint households that included father and married sons (stage two); grown brothers and their families (stage three); and uncles and nephews (stage four), as seen in the Jabiri. Most of these households experienced fission at some point, but it could be at any of a number of points in the family's domestic history (usually but not always, after the death of key males). There were also households that remained undivided throughout this period as well as simple households that may or may not have been in the process of becoming joint households. The exact timing of the division of households is hard to see in the sources. We know that households split up; we do not know exactly when this occurred. Circumstantial evidence is available, however, and allows us to get some sense of this process.[33] A closer look at the different types of upper-class households can shed light on the process of household formation and fission and some of the factors that determined it.

Joint households composed of father and married sons represented the norm in terms of people's expectations; that is, sons would remain in their father's household after they married. Because it was the norm, clear evidence of this type of household is harder to see, since people would tend to take it for granted, although Alexander Russell, a British physician living in Aleppo in the mid–eighteenth century, did specifically mention this type of household in his history of Aleppo. The actual number of such households was probably smaller than the norms might lead us to expect, however, since the death of the father before his sons came of age and married often prevented this type of household from coming into existence. Some sons, especially those who were economically active and financially independent of their fathers, may also have set up their own households before the death of their fathers, though it is not clear whether their financial independence meant that they had also set up their own households.[34]

After the death of the father, some of these joint households would break up within a relatively short time, assuming that there was more than one surviving son. Each son would then set up his own household, as was true among the sons of Ahmad Jabiri, and as was the pattern Duben found among Turkish rural households. Other households did not experience fission after the death of the household head, and at that point these joint households consisted of brothers and their families (stage three). Some households of this type stayed together until the death of one of the brothers, but others were not permanent arrangements. Whether these household arrangements were considered temporary or permanent depended on what factors influenced the decision that brothers remain together. Although the sources rarely give any explicit reasons that might explain it, circumstantial evidence suggests two reasons why brothers might choose to maintain a joint household for some years after

their father's death, but without the expectation that this would become
a permanent arrangement. One was the presence of minor children in the
household. The need to provide for custody and support of these minors
and to manage their inheritances may have encouraged households to
remain intact until these children reached their majority. The second
factor was mentioned by Russell, an intimate of many Aleppine households. According to him, households split up not at the death of the patriarch, but rather at the death of the matriarch. He made this observation as a way of acknowledging how much authority and control
the mother had.[35] Russell's observation is echoed by the early twentieth-
century sociologist Daghestani, who also noted the correlation between the death of the mother and the breakup of the household among
upper-class urban families.[36] There is no direct evidence from the religious court archives to refute or confirm this, but piecing together
indirect evidence suggests that this could have been a factor in some
cases. For example, 'Abd al-Wahhab Shurayyif died in 1765, and his wife
Fatima died in 1770. It was after her death that 'Abd al-Wahhab's household broke up, although some of his older sons had already moved out.[37]
If the death of the mother rather than the death of the father marked the
point of household fission in these cases, it suggests that the dynamics of
household formation and fission did not necessarily revolve only around
the life cycle of males. This has important implications for the position
and role of women in the family—a point to be considered later in the
chapter—and for the way we think about the nature of these patriarchal
households.

When households shared by brothers and their families after the death
of their parents remained together until the death of one or the other of
the brothers, there were usually special circumstances involved. The most
visible examples of households of this type were those in which the
household was also important as a stepping stone for the politically ambitious. These households would become a core around which to orga-
nize a political base. For those provincial notables who aspired to be part
of the ruling class or simply to wield political power, household formation was affected by the ambitions and insecurities generated by the nature of the Ottoman system. On the simplest level, a large household was
a sign of status and a way of imitating the ruling class. At the same time,
the chaotic political situation, the factional rivalries, and the shifting balance of power meant that the most reliable political base lay in those to
whom one had personal ties of kinship, patronage, or ownership.

A household that was a political unit as well as a domestic and economic unit affected the nature of household structure and the process of household formation in a number of ways. The household would necessarily have been larger, as dictated by status and especially by the need for more people to look after the interests of the household head. With the family as the core, the size of the household would have been augmented through marriage, clientage, slavery, and possibly adoption. Furthermore, the number of non-kin within the household would probably have been proportionally greater than in other households. The number of kin had an upper limit imposed by biological constraints; patron–client relationships could be expanded indefinitely with the proper incentives. Nevertheless, since kin formed the core of the household, ensuring the continuation of the joint family household over time was very important. The advantages of cooperation offset any advantages gained from breaking up into separate households and separate economic units. In Aleppo, the impact of political ambitions on household formation is most visible in three pairs of brothers, each of different origins and each pursuing diverse paths to political power, but all forces to be reckoned with in the early nineteenth century.

The household of Mustafa Jabiri and his sons ʿAbd Allah and ʿAbd al-Qadir, discussed above, was a prime example of the household as both domestic group and political unit. Similarly, Nuʿman and Ismaʿil, sons of ʿAbd al-Rahman Shurayyif, were political allies and business partners and shared a household throughout their lives. Details of the origins and history of the Shurayyif family are found in the family biography in Chapter 1. Nuʿman and Ismaʿil emerged as the most prominent members of the family in the early nineteenth century. Like the Jabiri brothers, they shared offices between them, Nuʿman becoming naqib al-ashraf and Ismaʿil, mutasallim. The Shurayyif family, like the Jabiris, had undergone the "natural" process of fission in the previous generation, when ʿAbd al-Rahman had stayed in his father's house and bought his other siblings out, but Nuʿman and Ismaʿil continued to live together after the death of their father and to operate as a team, both economically and politically. The continued close relationship was expressed in the virtual merging of their two families reflected in the waqfs of Ismaʿil, set up after Nuʿman's assassination in 1822. The beneficiaries of the endowment were his children and Nuʿman's equally.[38]

The great rivals to the Shurayyif brothers and the ones responsible for the assassination of Nuʿman were two sons of Ibrahim Pasha, Ahmad and

Muhammad. Ibrahim Pasha had turned his local power into a springboard to acquire appointments to governorships outside of Aleppo. His efforts were short-lived, however, as were his attempts to gain similar appointments for his sons. But Ahmad and Muhammad remained politically active on the local level, and much of their power rested on their links to various factions in Istanbul. In this area the value of cooperation was important. Muhammad apparently spent most of his time in Aleppo, while Ahmad cultivated their connections in Istanbul. These connections ultimately did not save them. The vulnerability of the politically ambitious, especially at a time when such major changes were occurring in the capital, became painfully apparent when they were both ordered killed.[39]

After the death of one of the brothers in this type of joint household, some split up into separate households, while others remained together, creating households composed of uncles and nephews (stage four) and, after the death of the other brother or brothers, of cousins (stage five). In the examples mentioned above, the Jabiri household appeared to have split up after 'Abd Allah's death in 1821, or at least some of his grown sons moved out of their uncle's house at that time. On the other hand, Nu'man Shurayyif's children remained with their uncle Isma'il in a household that also included their paternal aunt and her daughter. After Isma'il's death in 1826 in Damascus, his surviving heirs, two minor grandsons, remained in the household of their cousins and guardians Yusif and Muhammad Sa'id, Nu'man's sons.

Households that consisted of uncles and nephews or of cousins were not common, however; most had experienced fission before they reached this point. However, a few households apparently remained undivided throughout the seventy years covered by this study and were consequently very complex households of grandparents and great-grandchildren, great-uncles and great-aunts, and cousins to the second degree. These were large families with several males in each generation; therefore their households were large, multiple-family ones that most nearly approached the ideal of the patrilineal and patriarchal household. This apparently was the pattern followed by three wealthy merchant families, the Jazmatis, Miris, and Amiris, during all or most of this period. The Jazmati family were all descendants of Khalil Jazmati (d. 1738), who came to Aleppo from Tlecem in the early eighteenth century. Khalil's son, Ahmad (d. 1778), had ten children (six sons and four daughters). Each son had children, including Khalil, who had eleven; altogether Ahmad's six sons produced twenty offspring, although not all survived childhood. In the next

generation, there were seventeen offspring. According to the sources, the
entire family lived throughout this period in what was called the "dur
Jazmati Zade" in Suwayqa Hatim, a complex of five adjoining houses.
This tight-knit arrangement did not preclude family feuds, as several
intrafamilial lawsuits appear in the court records. Nevertheless, they apparently did not create enough bad feeling to break up the household.

The descendants of Hajj Musa Amiri also remained in his home in
Suwayqa ʿAli. Hajj Musa had thirteen children, seven sons and six daughters. Altogether his sons produced twenty children and their sons twenty-
one, although as in the Jazmati case, not all of them survived infancy and
childhood.

The Miri family, which was much smaller than either the Jabiri or
Amiri family, lived in Bab Qinnisrin. Two brothers, Ismaʿil and Hasan
Miri, had six children between them: Hasan had a son and a daughter and
Ismaʿil, a son and three daughters. Two of Ismaʿil's daughters married
their cousins, so remained in the household. Hasan's son, ʿAbd Allah, had
eight children; his cousin ʿAbd al-Wahhab had three. ʿAbd Allah died in
1769, heavily in debt, and ʿAbd al-Wahhab became head of the extended
family. The next generation produced few male children, and they had
no surviving male children, so the family died out.

It is probably no coincidence that all three families who followed this
pattern were merchant families. Not all merchant families maintained
these kinds of households, but the fact that two of the wealthiest, most
prominent, and most successful among them (the Jazmatis and Amiris)
did, suggests that pursuing their commercial undertakings successfully
was facilitated by maintaining close family relationships. André Raymond has suggested that this was true for Cairo, where a tight-knit family could offset the disadvantages of a lack of corporate structure in large
commercial enterprises.[40] At the same time, the Miri case shows that this
might also have been an appropriate strategy for families who had run
into financial difficulties. Like the Amiris and the Jazmatis, the Miris were
a prominent merchant family. However, ʿAbd Allah Miri had died with
a heavy burden of debt.[41] It is possible that the decision to maintain a
single household was designed to cope with the financial difficulties that
the family was facing; in other words, they needed to manage resources
very carefully to escape the ruin that such indebtedness threatened.

While the joint family household, which could take on a number of
different forms, was the preferred and probably predominant type among
Aleppo's elite, simple households did exist. Most, and perhaps all, of these

households may have been in the process of becoming joint households (stage one of the domestic cycle). In reality these households might never evolve into joint households because of the early death of the father or the failure of the family to have more than one surviving son. This could happen over several generations in some families or branches of families, as it did in the case of Yusif Jabiri's family. Given the realities of early modern society with its high mortality rates, such a situation was not uncommon. In these cases, there was only one surviving son, and the death of the father coincided fairly closely with the coming of age and marriage of the son. At any time, therefore, there was only one male head of household, his wife (or wives), their children, and perhaps some female relatives, such as the husband's mother or unmarried sisters.

The large patriarchal and undivided household may have been the ideal to which many families aspired, and the joint family household may have been predominant, at least in the sense that most families experienced a joint family stage in the course of the domestic cycle. Nevertheless, the reality was that at any given time a diversity of households—diverse in both size and structure—were found among the upper class. Over the course of the domestic cycle and over generations, households and families changed, and individuals were likely to find themselves living in different kinds of households with a different group of family members at different points in their lives. Many factors shaped this process. Some of these have already been mentioned, such as the presence of minor children or political ambitions. The two most important were undoubtedly the consistent constraint of mortality, most apparent in the relatively small size of families and the early death of parents, and the relationship between family size and the nature and extent of family resources. If families were small, with no more than one or two surviving males over several generations, and family resources were extensive, there may have been no fission for long periods of time. The resources were adequate to sustain all family members, so fission was unnecessary, unless there were pressing noneconomic reasons. At the opposite end of the scale, large families, even among the wealthy, could put sufficient pressure on family resources to necessitate division of the household before the death of the patriarch. For example, if there were numerous daughters for whom dowries had to be found, resources could be strained. A sudden crisis of a political or financial nature, both of which were not uncommon in the unsettled circumstances of the late eighteenth and early nineteenth centuries, could also sharply limit family funds. Therefore, older sons might leave and set up their own households, especially if they were already economically active. Even if this did not happen, financial pressures could lead to an earlier division of property and household fission than might otherwise have occurred. Furthermore, a larger family could limit the choice of residence after household fission, making it less likely that the residence could simply be divided to accommodate everyone, and therefore requiring family branches to be more widely scattered. Ultimately, the timing of fission and therefore the nature of the household were inseparable from decisions about the devolution of property and capital. At what point did family members want to divide up the family patrimony? This critical question will be considered in Chapters 4 and 5.

Despite the importance of demographic, economic, and political factors, household formation and fission were not simply a mechanical response to cultural norms nor a product of them nor merely an economic process. They were also influenced by the specific interests and goals of the families, the personalities of their members, and the dynamics between them. Purely personal factors undoubtedly played a significant role, in addition to other factors already discussed. Family feuds over inheritance, control of waqfs, guardianship of children, and personal possessions appear regularly in the legal records. The sources do not always tell us whether the repercussions of these cases led to permanent rupture within or among households or prompted early breakup of the household. At a later date, Daghestani remarks on the inability of brothers to get along as a reason for the breakup of households, and this was undoubtedly true in this earlier period as well.[42] Then, too, some family members may simply have wanted to be on their own, perhaps out from under the shadow of a dominant father. Many of these upper-class men were economically successful and independent long before their father's deaths. They may well have desired the status and authority that accompanied having their own household.

The difference in the timing of fission from one household to the next or even from one generation to the next in the same household meant that the life experiences of individuals could vary considerably. While some would spend most of their lives in simple family households, with only a very short time as part of a multiple-family household, others might live all of their lives in complex households. All these households might fall into the same general category as defined by household structure and the phases of the domestic cycle, but the differences in timing of

fission resulted in very different kinds of households and experiences for
the people who lived in them.

Just as the timing of fission varied, so did the meaning of fission. In
other words, although separate households were formed, the actual physical arrangements involved in the breakup of the household varied, with
important consequences for the relationship among families after division
into discrete households. In some families, the houses themselves were
simply divided up among the new households. Here is where the physical structure of the traditional urban house played a significant role in
shaping family structure. Since it was relatively easy to divide up these
courtyard houses into physically distinct units, it presented the simplest
solution to the pressures for fission, assuming that the size of the house
and the number of new households were compatible. During the period
under study, the Khankarli house in Frafira, the Qurna house in Bustan,
and the Ghawri house in Bayyada were divided up in this fashion. All had
been expanded at some time in the past and were commodious enough
to accommodate several separate households.[43] In some cases when this
happened, the different households continued to maintain a common reception area and entrance, known as the "qanaq." Such was the case with
the Shaykhbandar brothers, ʿAbd al-Qadir and Muhammad Darwish.
Each brother maintained separate living quarters for his family but jointly
owned and used the "qanaq Shaykhbandar Zade."[44] These arrangements
suggest that the division into separate households was seen as temporary
and the boundaries between them permeable. This would fit well with
the ideological preference for joint family households.

More commonly, however, fission into separate households meant
that one son and his immediate family continued to occupy the family
home while others moved out. The evidence for this process comes
largely from the efforts through the courts to maintain the residence as an
intact unit in the hands of one of the heirs. Various strategies were used.
In some cases property was divided up in such a way that the residence
was passed on to one heir, while the other heirs took their share of the
estate in other pieces of property. In other cases the family residence was
left jointly to the heirs, but one heir, who was to occupy the house,
bought out the others. For example, ʿAbd al-Rahman Shurayyif bought
his father's home from the rest of the heirs. ʿAbd al-Wahhab Shurayyif,
mentioned above, lived in the quarter of Dakhil Bab al-Nasr. At his death
in 1765, at least some of his thirteen children as well as his wife Fatima
ʿImadi were still living in the family home. A few years later, however,

the family home was occupied by his son 'Abd al-Rahman and his family. Another son, Abu Bakr, was already deceased, but had been living in Frafira before his death. 'Abd al-Rahman himself had lived in Frafira for some time before his purchase of the family home from his father's other heirs. Ahmad was living in the 'Imadi family home by virtue of his right to the 'Imadi family waqf through his mother. Hafsa had moved to the home of her husband, 'Abd al-Rahman Khankarli. Six of the children had died without heirs and perhaps without ever marrying, since no spouses are mentioned.[45]

The newly created households sometimes moved into houses within the same quarter and sometimes into new quarters. What dictated the choice is not clear from the sources, but it was probably largely determined by the availability of real estate. By the late eighteenth century, unlike earlier periods, there was little vacant land available in the central quarters favored by the notables.[46] Houses within these quarters were much sought after and did not change hands often, as can be seen from the geographical distribution of sales of house properties. Relatively few involved the large houses in the central quarters. When such houses or parts of them sold, many of the sales occurred among family members; the property was not in fact being sold on the open market. Large family homes remained in the family, for the most part. Therefore, when a new household was looking for a house, the choices would have been fairly limited.

As a result, although some families occupied several houses in a single quarter, like the Kucuk 'Ali Agha in Saha Bizza, other families such as the Jabiris were scattered among different quarters as a result of the domestic cycle process. The Taha family was closely associated with the quarter of Jallum, where both 'Umar and his nephew Ahmad had built religious monuments. Most members of both branches of the family continued to live in this quarter, but the most prominent member of the family, Ahmad's son Muhammad, had a large home in the quarter of Jabil.[47] The Kawakibi family was also closely associated with Jallum, but its most powerful figure was living in Bandara by 1790, in a house he had acquired by inheritance from his mother. It later became a residence for one branch of the Ibrahim Pasha family, after the home was inherited by Hasan Kawakibi's daughter Hibbat Allah, the wife of Mustafa Ibrahim Pasha.[48] Ibrahim Pasha's other sons lived in Frafira, although one of them rented the saray of 'Uthman Pasha in Dakhil Bab al-Nasr for several years.

The relationship among households after division influenced the soli-

darity of the lineage and the nature of kinship ties. When related households continued to be neighbors, as happened when families continued
to live side by side or in the same quarter, the division into separate
households probably had little effect on the strength of kinship ties. Physical proximity presumably encouraged frequent interaction among these
households. Although families lived in separate households and were economically independent of each other, boundaries between households
were permeable. When brothers or cousins set up new households in
different quarters, the establishment of these households may also have
marked the emergence of distinct family branches, in contrast to some of
the previous examples in which household arrangements after fission appeared to be temporary and close association among households was
maintained.

Regardless of the personal wishes of individuals or the societal expectations for how families should live together, actual household formation was affected by so many different factors that *which* family members shared a household varied considerably from family to family and
from generation to generation. It is difficult to talk about a "typical"
upper-class household. Nevertheless, elite households in Aleppo were
clearly different from households in late-nineteenth-century Istanbul or
eighteenth-century Europe. They seem similar in many ways to households of rural notables in nineteenth-century Egypt, a fact that suggests
that class, rather than location, was the key variable in distinguishing different kinds of household formation. However, the fact that this urban
elite was not a landowning class during this period also accounts for some
of the differences among them as well.

Support for the importance of class in household formation comes
from what seem to be the differences between these households and those
of other classes, although until we know more about households of the
rest of the population, no firm conclusions are possible. The joint phase
of the domestic cycle was undoubtedly longer among the upper class.
Even though the amount of time that passed between the death of the
household head and the breakup of the family varied considerably, and
though individuals lived in different types of households and indeed in
different households in the course of their lives, those from the upper
class spent longer periods in larger and more complex households than
did members of other classes. Even after the breakup of a joint family
household, ties between the newly formed households remained close
in many cases. By contrast, the more modest resources of other classes

would encourage early fission. While there is some evidence to suggest that households of urban artisans and craftsmen were economic as well as residential units and followed the process of household formation in rural areas, this was probably not true for the poorer among them. In these families, sons would be forced to go off to work for others, and the lack of common economic bonds or a patrimony would make the connection of a common residence unlikely. Furthermore, their living arrangements would discourage this. Among the lower classes of Aleppine society, families were lucky to occupy a single room off a courtyard, much less a small house. The lack of space and privacy would not encourage long-term coresidence by an extended family.[49]

This discussion of Aleppo's upper-class households has thus far centered on the family that formed the center of such households, since it was the history of the family that determined the dynamics of household formation and fission. However, these households also included slaves, servants, and retainers, who could play a very important role in the household and form close relationships with family members. Non-kin in the household will be considered next.

NON-KIN IN THE HOUSEHOLD

The presence of non-kin in the household in significant numbers was a common feature of upper-class households. Many of these dependents were slaves; others were resident servants who worked for wages and retainers linked to the household head or other family members through ties of clientage or long-standing family connections. Unfortunately, the sources available for Aleppo in this period are not very helpful for learning about these household members. Some literary sources, in the form of descriptions by visitors or foreign residents, comment on the large size of some households, including the large number of dependents. However, such evidence is not necessarily reliable. Duben and Behar point out the discrepancy that existed between what people in late-nineteenth-century Istanbul said about the size of elite households, including the large number of retainers, servants, and slaves, and what the census figures actually show: that at the end of the nineteenth century in Istanbul, elite households had relatively few servants or slaves.[50] Other kinds of evidence, such as the religious court records, do not have data that allow us to estimate how many non-kin

resided on average in these elite households or to know how many were
slaves, servants, or retainers. Only when census data that include household lists become available, beginning in Egypt and some parts of the Ottoman Empire in the middle decades of the nineteenth century, can we
start to answer these questions with any certainty. Based on the fragmentary evidence that does exist, however, it is possible to make a few impressionistic observations about non-kin in these households.

The first observation is that the number of resident non-kin varied
considerably even within this one class. Not surprisingly, wealthier
households were more likely to expand the size of their households
through patron–client relationships and the purchase of slaves, just as they
more often maintained complex households for longer periods of time.
Not only could they afford to do so, but they often had specific needs and
interests that encouraged the inclusion of many dependents. For example,
merchants engaged in international and regional commerce would have
needed the services of agents and brokers throughout their trading networks; employing people who were members of their own households to
act for them would help guarantee that their interests were protected.
Similarly, politically ambitious household heads depended on the support
of reliable allies in the factional struggles of this period, and allies who
were also members of their households would ensure their loyalty and
commitment. Other members of this class who did not have such political or economic motivations were less likely to maintain establishments
on the same scale.

A second observation is that even the wealthiest and most powerful
households in Aleppo did not approach the size of the grandee households of Istanbul and Cairo or even of the households of some Syrian notables like the ʿAzms of Damascus. Carter Findley cites a figure of several
hundred as the size that some ruling-class households could reach in this
period.[51] Households of some Mamluk beys in Cairo were on a similar
scale. Admittedly, many of the members of these households did not actually live in the residence of the household head; that is, they were members of the household by virtue of ties of patronage rather than as residents of the household. Nevertheless, a significant percentage of these
"household" members would have been residents as well.[52] A comparison of the size of houses in these different cities provides convincing evidence on this point, even in the absence of reliable figures on household
size. According to Abdel-Nour, no houses in Aleppo reached the size of
two thousand square meters, as some Damascus houses did, an indication

of the smaller size of households of the elite in Aleppo even compared to Damascus.[53] For some of Aleppo's notables, their households were also their political base, and this had an impact on the size and structure of the household, as indicated above, including, undoubtedly, the number of non-kin who were members of the household. However, they were not able to build up the large households that allowed the ruling class or the Mamluk beys in the autonomous province of Egypt to play the political role that they did. The limited degree of autonomy that the province of Aleppo had, even when central authority was at its weakest, did not leave these notables the room to maneuver or the access to the resources required to build political or military households that could rival the power of Ottoman officials. The smaller size of their households reflected the differences in political dynamics.

Whether servants, slaves, or retainers, most of these non-kin dependents undoubtedly performed various kinds of domestic tasks. In the largest, wealthiest, and most powerful households, however, there was a more articulated division of labor, and opportunities existed for dependents to hold positions of considerable influence and responsibility and therefore to have a correspondingly high status within the household. Some managed the household, handled financial affairs, and served as secretaries. Outside the household they were used as tax collectors for malikanes and overseers of property and endowments as well as agents and brokers. Such positions as these provided the non-kin opportunities to get rich and become prominent figures in Aleppo in their own right. The most famous example of a household retainer in Aleppo during this period was Ibrahim Agha Qataraghasi, later Ibrahim Pasha, who began his career in the household of Muhammad Taha in the 1770s and 1780s, when the latter's power in Aleppo was at its height (see Taha family biography and comments on this patronage relationship in Chapter 1). We know little about Ibrahim Agha's background before he was employed by Muhammad Taha. Ibrahim Agha began accumulating wealth while serving as tax collector for Muhammad Taha, who held the tax farms for many provincial villages. After Muhammad's death, Ibrahim became a powerful figure in city and provincial affairs.[54]

The status of non-kin within the household, and their relationship with the family, probably depended in large part on their roles. We know that the position of servants and slaves in the household varied historically from one region to another and on the basis of function. According to Duben, servants or resident laborers were not considered part of the *hane* (household) by traditional villagers in rural Turkish society in the early twentieth century. In their eyes, one not only had to reside in the household and contribute economically, but also had to be a kinsman. However, Duben noted that certain groups of resident servants, particularly concubines and nannies, were considered part of the family in urban areas at the end of the nineteenth century and were given certain rights of female family members, such as dowries.[55] Further investigation will clarify the extent to which these variations were due to role or to contrasts between urban and rural areas or to the decline in the institution of slavery and the lessening importance of servants in a changed economy between the end of the nineteenth century and the 1940s.

In the case of eighteenth- and nineteenth-century Aleppo, the sources do provide some evidence about the relationship between kin and non-kin in the household for one category of non-kin: slaves or freed slaves identifiable through their masters. This can give us some insight into whether relationships between family members and this category of dependents were intimate and informal, resulting in close ties that essentially erased the distinction between kin and non-kin, or were more formal and distant, preserving the hierarchy implicit in the relationship.

Slavery was a legal and legitimate institution within Islamic society. In accepting slavery as a legitimate institution, Islamic law also assumed the responsibility for regulating that institution. The underlying principle on which regulations governing conditions of servitude were based was the recognition of a slave as fully human and in most cases as a fellow practitioner of the faith, while also acknowledging his or her status as property. Needless to say, a certain tension existed between these dual attributes of a slave, a tension that could be exploited by the owner. To attempt to lessen the ambiguity in this situation, slaves were guaranteed certain rights that were protected by the courts.

The complex position of slaves and the varied roles they played in Islamic societies, as well as the rights accorded them, helped shape the attitudes toward them and the treatment they received. Tucker's research has suggested that physical mistreatment of household slaves was uncommon enough to cause a woman to report her husband's brother to the courts for mistreating slaves.[56] Moreover, there seems to have been little of the "upstairs, downstairs" distinction so characteristic of nineteenth-century European households. Like master-servant relationships of an early period in European history, free and informal relations existed between master and slave. Certain categories of slaves lived among the family, eating with them and participating in their activities and conversations, as well as waiting on them. Even in the great houses of the ruling class in Istanbul, servants sat down to eat with their masters.[57]

If distinctions of status were not emphasized on a day-to-day basis, the overall position of household slaves was determined by their roles and the rights granted to them. The evidence from Aleppo is impressionistic, but it seems to bear out what has been found to be the case in other parts of the Islamic world: that a quasi-familial relationship existed between master and slave.

There are no estimates of the number of slaves there might have been in Aleppo during this period. Cairo, for which somewhat reliable figures are available, may provide a general point of comparison, however. In the two-year period from 1838 to 1840, there were roughly 30,000 slaves (5 percent of the population) in Egypt; about half of those were in Cairo and the vast majority were domestic slaves.[58] It seems unquestionable that the total number in Aleppo was much smaller, since Aleppo was about half the size of Cairo. It is also probable that the percentage of slaves in Aleppo relative to the total population was smaller, as Aleppo had fewer of the grandee households characteristic of the Mamluk amirs of an earlier period or of Muhammad ʿAli and his followers during this period. In addition, John Bowring commented on the relatively small number of slaves, black or white, in Syria by the 1830s. He attributed this to the ready availability of domestic servants that lessened the need for slaves as domestic labor. There was also a decline in the number of white slaves imported from the Caucasus because of unsettled conditions there. The limited supply meant that the price of such slaves had become very expensive.[59] The other point that the Cairo figures show is the overwhelming preponderance of female slaves, almost six times as many females as males. A similar disproportion would have existed in Aleppo.[60]

Female slaves performed a variety of functions within the household, but we know most about those who were concubines, so this discussion will focus on them.[61] Concubinage was a legal institution in Islamic society. Men were given sexual access to an unlimited number of female slaves. The only restriction was that those female slaves must be his own slaves, not, for example, his wife's. Therefore, a man did not automatically have access to all female slaves in the household. As a legal institution, concubinage granted men the enjoyment of their female slaves, but also put them under certain obligations to their concubines, who had clearly defined rights. The most significant of these concerned the children borne by the concubine and the way in which childbearing affected her status. Children of concubines were considered free and equal to other offspring of the man in question. Once a concubine had had a child, she was granted *umm al-walad* (literally, mother of the child) status. As a result, she could no longer be sold, pawned, or given away; all her future children were free; and she was freed on her master's death, if not previously manumitted.[62] The important status of a concubine who bore children within the household was evident as well in the cases in which she ended up married to her owner. While a man was not supposed to marry his own slave, some did, as was clear in several court cases in which a deceased man's relatives challenged the woman's position as legal wife. One example of this was a suit brought by Khadija, a former slave of Isma'il Pasha, against Isma'il's daughters, daughter-in-law, and grandson, claiming that they had refused to turn over to her her rightful share of Isma'il's estate. She said that she had been Isma'il's concubine and bore him children; after that he had freed her and married her. The defendants responded that she had a son by Isma'il, but that he had never married her and therefore she was not entitled to a wife's share of his estate. Khadija, however, was able to produce witnesses to the marriage, and the judge ruled in her favor.[63] The legal formalities were observed by the owner manumitting the slave before marrying her.

The high status of some female slaves was also apparent in other kinds of marriages arranged for them by their owners. Female slaves were sometimes married to other slaves, but more often they were married to a relative of the owner or to someone outside the household. For example, 'Abd al-Wahhab Taha had freed his slave a year before his death and had then married her to 'Abd al-Qadir Ghannam.[64] In these marriages, the slave woman was treated much like a daughter. She was usually manumitted before the marriage, and she was often given gifts of money or clothing to take with her to the marriage. Marrying female slaves, that is, former concubines, to relatives or men outside the household served a similar purpose to the marriages of daughters; it reinforced existing kinship ties or made alliances with other families. This practice of marrying slave women to others with whom one wanted to create or maintain strong ties was a time-honored way that the Ottoman sultan bestowed favor on his subordinates. Members of the ruling class and provincial elite followed his example and used it as a way of sealing patronage and other kinds of relationships.

From the perspective of the men who married former slaves, there was at least one other advantage to this kind of marriage, in addition to the connections it provided. According to Russell:

> *Among people of rank, as well as the rich merchants, there are many who marry a slave in preference to a free woman; choosing to forego the pecuniary, and indeed all advantages of alliance, rather than submit to the conditions on which such females are obtained. A woman of birth, conscious of family consequence, is apt to be haughty and petulant, and her relations sometimes make it one of the marriage articles, that the husband shall not take another to his bed.*[65]

The positions of great responsibility and high status that some male dependents could hold in these households was discussed above. Many of these positions were given to male slaves whose close ties to the family and honored place in the household were apparent in a number of ways. The most important reward for loyal service was manumission. Most male slaves were probably freed at some point. Once freed, former slaves of the notable families accumulated property, set up endowments for the benefit of their owners' families, and were legators and legatees of these families. A particularly noteworthy example was Sulayman, freed slave of Isma'il Shurayyif, who became a very wealthy man. Often a freed slave's property was then bequeathed to the former owner or his descendants. This in itself was not necessarily significant, since it was required by Islamic law. Of greater significance in reflecting on the quasi-familial relationship were the religious endowments. Freed slaves did create waqfs from their accumulated property, and these were usually set up to benefit the master's family. In addition, it was freed slaves rather than collateral branches of the family who acquired rights to family endowments if the original line of the endower died out. Finally, one interesting error in the sources may in fact reveal just how much some freed slaves were considered family members. Sulayman Agha, mentioned above, was clearly identified as the freed slave of Isma'il Shurayyif between 1835 and 1838. However, a couple of years later, he is called Sulayman Shurayyif, making him appear to be a kinsman, with no reference to the master-slave relationship.[66]

Further evidence of close ties with slaves or former slaves was the practice of marrying daughters to these slaves after they were freed. Theoretically, for a woman to marry a slave or former slave would be prohibited by Islamic law, since she would be marrying a social inferior, but such marriages did occur. One took place between Ruqayya, a daughter of the wealthy merchant Hajj Musa Amiri, and Salih, a freed slave of her father's. This marriage was the subject of a lawsuit that gives some insights into how such unions were viewed by those involved and by the courts. The marriage took place several years after Hajj Musa's death. When the contract was signed, Hajj Musa's cousin, ʿAbd al-Qadir, brought suit to prevent the consummation of the marriage, on the grounds that he and Hajj Musa had previously arranged a marriage between Ruqayya and his son Mustafa and that the marriage to her father's former slave was unsuitable. The judge dismissed his suit, after getting a fatwa from the mufti. He denied ʿAbd al-Qadir's request that the marriage be forbidden, since he was not the legal representative of his absent son and since there was no evidence of the earlier arranged marriage. Moreover, claiming that the marriage was unsuitable was not a valid argument because her guardians had approved of the marriage.[67] In other words, the marriage of a free woman to a former slave was not automatically unsuitable. Hajj Musa was not the only wealthy Aleppine to marry a daughter to a freed slave. Suitability was determined by the family, and the close relationship between the family and slave or former slave was underscored in these marriages. Afaf Marsot found a similar practice among the Sharaibis, a merchant dynasty in Cairo.[68] In addition to reflecting the close ties and quasi-familial relationships between masters and some trusted slaves, these marriages of daughters to freed slaves had one of the practical advantages of cousin marriage that will be discussed in the next chapter: They helped to maintain an undivided patrimony. The daughter's share of the family wealth would stay within the family.

Although the presence of non-kin in the household, as well as their role in it and their relationship to family members, is not easy to see with the available sources, the evidence that does exist suggests that slaves at least were an integral and valued part of the household. They performed a variety of functions inside and outside the household, serving the family and promoting its interests. Indeed some evidence seems to suggest that the line between kin and non-kin, master and slave, within the household was not strictly drawn. Whether this was also true with non-kin in the household who were not slaves is impossible to know with any certainty. It probably depended on how long they had lived in the household, what prior connections there might have been, and what roles and functions they performed. Minimally, circumstantial evidence suggests a free and easy relationship between the family and its dependents that would encourage close ties.

HOUSEHOLD STRUCTURE AND PATRIARCHAL AUTHORITY

The relationship between the nature of the family and the system of gender relations that characterized early modern Ottoman urban society is one of the major themes of this study. The work already done on women, gender, and family in the early modern Middle East has begun to challenge the model of "classical patriarchy" and to identify what Judith Tucker calls a "modified" patriarchy in which the absolute power of the male head of the family is limited in significant ways. Tucker has focused on the multiple kinship relationships in which women were involved, including lifelong relationships with their natal families, as important protection for women in their husband's households: "The ongoing involvement and interest of a number of family members diffused her husband's control and protected her against an overly imperious, or neglectful and abusive husband."[69] Nelly Hanna and others have emphasized the role of the Islamic courts in providing women with a place to take their grievances: "Therefore, the courts played an intermediary role in the family . . . they provided a horizontal relation between family members and an institution outside the house, which could counterbalance the otherwise vertical relations between the head of the household and the rest of the family."[70] Work by many scholars on women and the courts has shown the extent to which women throughout the Ottoman Empire and Egypt used the courts to impose conditions on their marriages, to claim their rights, and to bring suit against men in their own families who were violating these rights. These cases underscore women's willingness to use the courts, their confidence that they would receive justice at court, and the extent to which the qadis protected women's rights and upheld their claims.

I would argue that household patterns found among the elite in Aleppo suggest yet another way in which the inequality in gender relations was modified. In the model of classical patriarchy that Deniz Kandiyoti lays out, the patrilocal, patrilineal extended household is the key to the "reproduction of the patriarchal system." She acknowledges that this type of household was not always realized in practice because of demographic and economic constraints, but argues that it was a "powerful cultural ideal."[71] Upper-class families presumably came closest to the family of "classical patriarchy."[72] This group had the resources to make the formation of such households feasible and had more at stake in terms of wealth, power, and status, so it is assumed that they would tightly control family members in the interests of the greater good of the family. However, the evidence from Aleppo reveals that even among the elite there were different types of households. While this was a multiple-family household system in which residence was usually patrilocal, the different forms these households took, as described above, had important implications for the experiences of individuals and for the hierarchies of power and authority within the household.

Some households did closely resemble the model of classical patriarchy, with all lineage members or one branch of the lineage residing together in the family compound for several generations and maintaining an undivided patrimony, under the control of a strong patriarch. Even in the impersonal and formulaic court records, the strong personalities and personal wealth and power of some men come through. Some of them were long-lived and dominated family affairs in the public sphere over the span of their adult lives. Many of their activities were clearly directed toward looking after the interests of their families: accumulating large amounts of property; establishing family waqfs to provide for the future; arranging the marriages of children, siblings, and nieces and nephews; and taking unmarried relatives under their wing. These households, as discussed above, were usually merchant households or political households. But not all political or merchant households followed this pattern, because their continuation also depended on having a succession of powerful household heads.[73] One branch of the Shurayyifs, which has been mentioned frequently, is a good example. 'Abd al-Rahman was succeeded by his two sons, Isma'il and Nu'man. After their deaths, the mantle passed to Yusif, son of Nu'man and nephew of Isma'il and a dominant figure in Aleppine politics from the mid-1820s until his death in 1861 (see Shurayyif family biography in Chapter 1). In Yusif's household lived his children, several siblings and their families, his uncle Isma'il's two grandsons, and his aunt Nafisa and her unmarried children.[74] In households such as these, the authority of the household head over others was undoubtedly very strong. In the absence of a dominant personality to head the household in each generation, the chances that the prototypical patriarchal household would remain intact were small, even when other factors would seem to favor its continuation.

In the other kinds of households described earlier, the authority of the household head could be limited by a number of factors. Cuno has shown how household structure affected the authority of the household head in Egypt. In households composed of brothers or of uncles and nephews, authority was more diffuse than in households composed of fathers and sons, because in the former each male adult had equal legal right to resources.[75] The exception to this shared authority would be situations in which there were one or two dominant personalities, as in the Shurayyif case.

Another factor that could affect the authority of the household head was age. The reality of short life expectancy meant that few were headed by venerable patriarchs for long periods of time. Duben has estimated that the life expectancy for males who reached the age of twenty was only thirty-six.[76] Even if they began producing sons as early as fifteen and had their first grandson at thirty, the period during which they would have headed a complex household was very short. There is no evidence from Aleppo that allows us to estimate life expectancy, but there are numerous cases related to inheritance that suggest a similar pattern: household heads who died not long after the death of their fathers, the division of family property, and the setting up of their own households, and who died when their children were still minors or young adults. This pattern meant that many households were headed by young men. After the death of the father in a joint family household consisting of fathers and married sons, the household would either break up into separate households, each a simple or possibly extended household headed by a young man, or the brothers would remain together. In many of these households, the mother would still be alive, so that the authority of the new heads of household would have been affected both by their age and by the authority their mothers would continue to exercise within the household. The tendency for households to break up resulted in the changing and flexible nature of household structure over the course of the domestic cycle; the size and composition of the household changed often. Short life expectancies meant greater instability within the households and shorter periods of joint family structure characterized by a paterfamilias surrounded by sons and their wives and grandchildren, the type of household in which the father's control and authority was greatest, at least in theory.

Another constraint on the authority of the household head was generational tension: the desire on the part of the older generation to remain firmly in control of patrimony and household and the desire of the younger generation to claim their share of the patrimony and have some independence. While scholars have concentrated on the strict control to which women, especially in their sexually active years, were subjected, the activities of younger males were often rigidly controlled as well. The classic example is the Ottoman princes of the early modern period. They were denied any political role and confined to the palace, and strict control was exercised over their access to women and their production of offspring. Their mothers were largely responsible for exercising this control. The extent to which their activities were restricted reflected recurring fears on the part of the older generation that the younger one would try to supplant it and the determination of the older generation to prevent this from happening.[77] This generational tension was replayed in less exalted circles as well. Martha Mundy has noted the refusal of some family heads in Yemen to allow younger males to have access to their share of inheritance as a way of controlling their activities.[78] Ken Cuno has shown that legislation to enhance the authority of the head of household in the nineteenth century was partially a response to efforts by younger males to leave the household and take their share of jointly owned property with them.[79] In both cases, the need of these household heads to assert their right to control family property and family members and prevent any challenge to their power was an indication that their authority and power were indeed being challenged.

In Aleppo, challenges to family heads desiring to keep household and patrimony together occurred regularly, usually in the form of individuals asking that inheritances be settled so that they could claim their share. Sometimes these claims were settled without opposition, but they could also result in lengthy litigation, such as a case in which Yusif Shurayyif's second cousins, for whom he had served as guardian during their minority and who had inherited a large fortune from their grandfather, demanded that Yusif release their inheritance.[80] Many of these cases were settled in favor of the younger generation who were asking for their share of the patrimony. Moreover, there were many sons of long-lived and powerful men who were already well-established in careers and economically active and independent long before their father's death or "retirement." Sons of prominent members of the ulema were already working their way into important positions while their fathers also held offices.

Sons of wealthy merchants were engaged in commercial ventures of their own. Some were acquiring personal fortunes long before they acquired access to family resources through inheritance. The fact that they were able to do so reflected economic conditions that allowed them to make fortunes independently. There was no sense that these men were being forced to wait in the wings until their fathers died. The authority of the head of the family over adult males who were economically active, financially independent, politically influential, and pursuing their own careers was clearly limited.

Women did not have the same opportunities that males did to escape from or challenge patriarchal authority. Nevertheless, the fluidity of these households and the diffusion of authority in many of them created openings for females to have some control over their own lives and to impose limits on the arbitrary exercise of power by the male head of the household. The maneuvering room they had, the strategies they used, and the degree of their autonomy varied over the course of their life cycles. The most privileged women in the household and those with the greatest autonomy were the older women who had produced sons. The mothers of the oldest or most important sons gained prestige and even power within the household as their sons grew to maturity and they aged. The mother of the sultan in Istanbul was the outstanding example of this pattern. The mothers of the Ottoman princes rose out of the ranks of ordinary concubines to exercise great power, especially during the "sultanate of women" in the sixteenth and seventeenth centuries. As mothers of possible future sultans, they served as political tutors for their sons, especially after the princes were confined to the palace and no longer served as provincial governors. They were closely involved in promoting their sons' interests and seeing that one did become sultan. Those women who did become *walide sultans* (queen mothers) not only ruled over the enormous imperial household but also exercised sovereignty in a variety of publicly visible ways and at times were the most powerful figures in the empire.[81]

On a less exalted level, this was a pattern repeated in families throughout the empire. Alexander Russell's comment on the role of the matriarch in Aleppine households in keeping households together after the death of the patriarch reflects the authority that these women wielded in the household. Other sources put emphasis on the strong personalities, administrative skills in controlling the households, and the leverage of upper-class women who brought considerable property to a marriage and sealed political alliances. Afaf Marsot has argued that upper-class women

moved easily into public positions of authority requiring management
skills after they left the harem in the twentieth century because they were
so accustomed to organizing and running large households.[82] Powerful
matriarchs who controlled considerable wealth and exercised real authority inside and sometimes outside the household are clearly visible in
the Aleppo sources. Sharaf Jabiri was one. The sister of ʿAbd Allah and
ʿAbd al-Qadir Jabiri and a wealthy woman in her own right, she set up
for her grandchildren one of the largest endowments founded by a
woman during this time.[83] When ʿAbd Allah Miri died, with an estate
much encumbered by debt, it was his sister to whom he had entrusted
responsibility for protecting the interests of his minor children and ensuring that the property he left them was not swallowed up by these
debts.[84] The extensive endowments of the ʿUthmaniyya Mosque were
overseen for many decades by a succession of women from ʿUthman
Pasha's family, first his sister, then his niece and her daughters.[85] All of
these women were assuming major family obligations, usually reserved
for senior males, and in all three cases there were senior males who could
have assumed these roles. These women were overseeing extensive property and wealth, taking on primary responsibility for the family as a
whole, and in the case of the women of ʿUthman Pasha's family, representing the family in a public role.

Kandiyoti has argued that the existence of these matriarchal figures
highlights the extent of female subordination. Allowing older women to
have this authority helped internalize the patriarchal system among its
victims and therefore helped to reproduce it.[86] Leslie Peirce, however,
understands the position of these matriarchs in another way—as a reflection of the degree to which the hierarchy of age was more important than
the hierarchy of gender. In describing the household of the Ottoman
royal family, she argues that "the most important distinction with regard
to the distribution of power within the household appears to have been
based not on a simple male/female dichotomy, but rather on other di-
chotomies stemming from the interaction of commonly accepted views
about sexuality and authority. Chief among these was a generational distinction."[87] The same was true in other households. This is not to deny
the significance of gender inequality within the household, but rather to
see it intersecting with the generational hierarchy in ways that worked to
women's advantage. To a large extent the life cycles of males and females
were parallel.

Younger women were also not completely powerless and helpless. In addition to connections outside the household that worked for them, short life expectancies and the tendency of households to break up after the death of the household head meant that many of these young women became the senior woman in a new household headed by her husband at a fairly young age. Moreover, our limited glimpses of women's activities that would appear to be directly related to their place in the family hierarchy suggest that women were not powerless or completely subservient unless or until they assumed the role of family matriarch. The significant role that women of various ages and positions played in the guardianship of children is one indication. Women were assigned not just the responsibility of raising and nurturing children in their early years, but also that of managing the property of minor children who were left fatherless until they came of age.[88] Another indication is the willingness of women to take male members of their family to court. They, like men, sometimes challenged the authority of the older generation or challenged the dominance of males of their own generation, such as brothers.

There is no question that cultural ideals and social norms bestowed great power on males, especially older men who headed households. The ability of women and even younger and weaker males to exercise some control over their own lives and to have some meaningful role in matters that affected them and those close to them could never be taken for granted. Yet it is also important to recognize that there were limits on the power that even the most tyrannical men could wield—limits imposed by factors outside their control and sometimes by the resistance of family members to abuses of their authority. This made the distribution of power within the household less lopsided than it might otherwise have been.

CONCLUSION

The households of the Aleppine urban elite appear to fit what was probably a fairly widespread household pattern in the Middle East among the well-to-do in the eighteenth and nineteenth centuries. These households, however, only fit the model in a general way. Actual households were diverse and changeable and responded to the particular circumstances of the families. Moreover, two fundamental facts shaped upper-class, as well as lower-class, households, irrespective of ideological preferences or other family goals: (1) the regular breakup of households in many families over the course of the domestic cycle and (2) the consistent constraint of mortality. These two facts meant that even upper-class families—those in the best position to do so—were only able to achieve the cultural ideal of the large and complex household for limited periods of time, if at all. Most upper-class individuals lived some part of their lives in a complex household, but there was great variation in the length of time involved. This reality had important implications for hierarchies of power and authority within the household as well as for understanding which kin "counted" most. The household was the family "circle" with the greatest impact on the individual. Ties among family members who shared the same household were likely to be the strongest because of the daily interaction and the dependence and close emotional ties following from that. The household included a fairly small group of kin and one that changed. Moreover, the non-kin who shared the residence could compete with ties to family members.

It is important, however, not to overestimate the importance of the household in defining the "kin who count." As Duben and Behar noticed in Istanbul, "households are embedded to varying degrees in a large weave of kinship relations and are often fluid and not easily demarcatable social units."[89] Relations to kin outside the household were very important. The next chapter will look at marriage and the relationships among households and families connected by these marriages.

Three

MARRIAGE BONDS AND MARRIAGE PARTNERS

Lineage and household were two of the family circles to which individuals belonged, although the intensity of ties to each varied considerably. Both of these structures reflected the patrilineal basis of kinship ties. Lineage membership was by agnatic tie. Household formation was determined by the life cycle of dominant males, as least in theory if not always in practice, and residence was usually patrilocal. The male-centered nature of these basic kinship groups raises the question of the significance of marriage and of the ties of kinship created by marriage. Since marriage was not the engine of the domestic cycle, and since the conjugal family was subordinate to the extended family in many respects, what was the significance of the marriage tie? It has been argued that marriage was not viewed as a permanent relationship, since divorce was relatively easy, at least for men, and the threat or reality of polygyny and concubinage precluded strong and enduring ties between spouses.[1] In this view, the relationship between husband and wife appeared to be less significant than the relationship of either husband or wife to other relatives; conjugal ties took second place to consanguine ones. As a result, kinship ties created by marriage were less significant than agnatic ones.

Yet while the conjugal relationship and affinal ties are assumed to be overshadowed by the patrilineal kinship system, the importance of marriage in Islamic societies is undeniable. Marriage was a religiously sanctioned and socially mandated state for adults. Marriage was also an important strategy for achieving familial goals—from basic survival and reproduction to consolidation of vast family fortunes and political power.

The importance of marriage as a social strategy was particularly true for the elite. Marriage was fundamentally a relationship between families rather than between individuals. Considerations of property, status, and honor meant that much was at stake in contracting a marriage and creating a relationship between families.

This chapter will examine the complexities and seeming contradictions that surround marriage among Aleppo's upper class, focusing on marriage practices and patterns and what they reveal about the importance of the conjugal tie; the permanence of marriage; and the impact of marriage on family dynamics, gender relations, and social structure. The first sections of the chapter will address the making of marriages, the economic exchange involved, polygyny, and divorce and how they might have affected the bond between husband and wife and the gender system. The remaining sections of the chapter will examine marriage patterns. Who married whom and why affected the strength of the marriage bond and the position of women within their husbands' households. Moreover, the choices of suitable marriage partners made by families provide important evidence about the boundaries of the effective family and of the social group to which these families belonged. Endogamous marriages, permitted by law and custom and practiced to some extent by these families, highlight kinship ties worth reinforcing, that is, those with the kin who count. Exogamous marriages offer insights into relationships between families and how the families perceived themselves and their interests.

THE MARRIAGE BOND

Marriage is a legal contract, not a religious sacrament, in Islamic societies. However, religion and religious law shape the institution of marriage in important ways. Islamic law spells out the rights and obligations of husband and wife, many of which deal with the economics of marriage and the guardianship of children. The Koran and Hadith both stress the importance of marriage and are explicit in their disapproval of celibacy. In the past, marriage was seen as necessary in order to live a good Muslim life, and it was assumed that everyone would marry. These attitudes were codified in Islamic law and found expression as well in medieval writings on the married state.

Because it was a contract, certain legal formalities were followed in getting married. In eighteenth-century Aleppo, representatives of the bride and groom met at the court in front of witnesses and drew up a contract. The contract stated the amount of the mahr and any other conditions either party wanted to impose. The sheikh in attendance gave his blessing, the contract was signed and sealed and then presented to the qadi, who granted the license, placing it either on the back of the contract or on a separate sheet of paper. If either party belonged to the ashraf, the naqib also affixed his seal.[2]

The signing of the contract was the culmination of what could be a lengthy process of choosing a suitable spouse. Selecting a bride was in the hands of women, except in cases in which the bride was selected from within the family or a closely related one and would therefore already be known to the family. In a society in which women were secluded, the role of women in critical decisions about marriage was crucial. It was through women's networks that information about marriageable girls was available. Contact with women from other harems in the baths and gardens, on ceremonial occasions, and through visiting provided opportunities for finding out about suitable brides. Female peddlers who visited the harems were also a source of information.[3] Women often initiated marriage arrangements, and even in cases where they did not, they would still be responsible for "vetting" the potential bride.

The way in which marriages were arranged and contracts drawn up and signed underscores the extent to which marriage was fundamentally a relationship between families, at least for the elite. Strict family control was exercised over marriage choices. Although much of the literature has focused on family control of the marriage of daughters, the family was also concerned about marriages of sons. Both sons and daughters could be married as minors. Even when they reached their majority, sons and daughters of marriageable age often had little say in the choice of a partner, and they did not expect otherwise. However, Islamic law does place some limitations on parents' and guardians' power to arrange marriages of females. Some of the schools of Islamic law, such as the Hanafi, the dominant school in Aleppo, did not allow females to repudiate marriages made for them while they were still minors, but other schools did give them this right. On the other hand, Hanafi law allowed a woman more control of her own marriage once she came of age. At that time she could arrange her own marriage or could refuse a marriage if she objected to the chosen groom. Maliki law, by contrast, requires the consent of the woman's guardian, even after she has reached her majority.[4] These differences in legal interpretation did give women some room to negotiate in marriage matters, but how often women were able to take advantage of this flexibility is difficult to determine, given the scarcity of the evidence. The few court cases that deal with this issue suggest that certain women had some say in the choice of a marriage partner. One such case involved a girl named Layla Qatanji, who had married Hasan Ikhlas, the younger brother of her mother's second husband. Her guardians, three brothers who were first cousins to her deceased father and presumably her closest male relatives on her father's side, brought suit against Layla and Hasan, arguing that the marriage was invalid because she had married without the approval of her guardians and that she was still a minor and therefore incapable of making a rational decision about a marriage partner. The judge upheld the right of the guardians to prevent the marriage, but the way in which the case is framed suggests that the girl had attempted to take an active role in the choice of her spouse.[5] A second case involved a woman who had been married as a minor to ʿAbd al-Rahman Biri. When she came of age two years later, she married someone else, not knowing of the marriage during her minority arranged by her *wali* (guardian), who was her brother. In effect she repudiated the marriage made for her by her guardian while she was a minor, an action not permitted by Hanafi law in theory. She argued that she had not known of the earlier contract that her brother had arranged, and she also claimed that the size of the mahr was unsuitable. The judge ruled in her favor, once the issue of repaying the mahr was settled, and let the marriage that she had arranged stand.[6] The number of cases dealing with these issues is too few to be able to draw any conclusions, but they do suggest that at least some women attempted to exert influence on the choice of spouse and to act independently of male guardians in this matter.

Family control over marriage was facilitated by the expectation that individuals would marry at a young age. Alexander Russell said that Aleppo parents began thinking about their children's marriages while they were still infants.[7] Just how young they were when married is a key question. Much attention has focused on the practice of marrying girls who were still minors. Two issues need to be considered in assessing this practice and its significance in the lives of females. The first is how often it occurred. In the absence of marriage contracts that would have stated whether or not a bride was a minor, it is not clear how often minor girls were married off in Aleppo. In eighteenth- and nineteenth-century Nablus, less than 20 percent of marriages involved minor girls, most from

the upper and middle classes.[8] Other similarities in marriage practices between Aleppo's and Nablus's upper classes suggest that the rate of minor
marriages in Aleppo might have been comparable. The second issue is
what the marriage of a minor actually meant. When evidence of minor
girls being married appears in the Aleppo sources, it is clear from the context that the marriage was purely a formality until the girl came of age,
in much the same way that the European aristocracy betrothed their children while still in the cradle. As in the case above, the girl was not even
aware that a marriage contract had been signed until she had come of age
and was ready to make another marriage.[9] Whether marrying off girls as
minors was or was not common, most females were probably married
soon after coming of age; this could be as young as eleven and presumably coincided with the age of puberty.[10] Many males married early as
well. According to Russell, mothers in particular were anxious for sons
to marry soon after they reached puberty (usually around thirteen or
fourteen) and began pressuring them to do so.[11]

From the perspective of the late twentieth century, marrying in the
early teens seems very young and is viewed very negatively. Yet age at
marriage must be understood in its cultural and historical context. Young
age at marriage was the norm in most societies in the past, with the exception of Western Europe. The age at which people married was linked
both to cultural concepts of adulthood and childhood and to social conditions. Concepts of adulthood and childhood vary significantly from
culture to culture and have changed over time, as work by a number
of European historians has made clear.[12] Research on the life cycle in
Middle Eastern societies in the past is just beginning. As we learn more
about the stages of childhood, the transition to adulthood, the expectations about behavior and responsibilities at different stages, and how these
all varied by gender, we will be in a better position to understand the
significance of a particular age of marriage.[13] The evidence available now
indicates that for eighteenth- and nineteenth-century Syrians adulthood
essentially began at puberty. This was the time when they assumed control of their own property, entered into business contracts, and undertook
the full responsibilities of adults. It was therefore not a question of "children" marrying, but rather of young adults entering the "normal" married status of adults. Moreover, young age of marriage was not only desirable, but also feasible for them. There were no structural or financial
pressures to discourage the early marriage, at least among the well-to-do.
Couples usually lived with the husband's family after marriage, and mar-

riage did not involve the dissolution of the household or any financial outlay beyond the mahr. The connection between age of marriage, household structure, and economic conditions is made clear by the case of late-nineteenth-century Istanbul, where marriage was often delayed. Most young married couples set up their own households, and the economic conditions of the time made that a costly process. As a result, age of marriage of both males and females was relatively high.[14] This suggests that age of marriage among those who were not well-to-do in Aleppo and other places at an earlier period was also higher than for the elite. Constraints of space and money would often have necessitated that newly married couples set up their own households rather than live with parents and therefore would have led to delays in marriage.

The lack of choice of spouse and the young age of marriage are often cited as two of the features of the marriage system that worked to the disadvantage of females and contributed to their subordination. For most brides, marriage meant moving into a new household and being separated from all that was familiar to them, except when they married closely related cousins. There is no doubt that the situation of a young bride in her husband's family's household could be difficult. She had to adjust to a new status and a new set of relationships and had to prove her fertility, especially her ability to bear sons, as did young brides in many cultures. Within the harem hierarchy, she was near the bottom. Yet we need to be careful not to overestimate the difficulties these young women faced. It seems likely that in the close social world of Aleppo's elite, many young women would have been entering households already familiar to them from frequent visiting and the friendships developed with other girls in their childhoods and that they would already know a great deal about their spouse. We are well aware of the lines of communication that women in the segregated social setting of the urban Middle East were able to develop, their awareness of outside events, and their ability to control information. The conversation and gossiping that went on among females as they visited each other and met at the baths would have included much information about other households and the people who occupied them, information that would have been passed on to the prospective bride. Even if she had never met her husband before, she may well have known his mother, sisters, aunts, or female cousins and have learned quite a lot about her new husband from them.

Moreover, females were not completely powerless in setting the conditions of the marriage. Islamic law allows conditions to be imposed in the marriage contract. How often women in Aleppo exercised this option is unknown, although Russell conveys the impression that it was quite common for upper-class women to restrict their husband's options to marry a second wife. Where contracts have survived in large numbers, as in Cairo, there is ample evidence that at least some women used marriage contracts to give themselves more mobility and restrict the mobility of their husbands, to prohibit husbands from taking another wife, to determine the place of residence after marriage, to arrange for a clothing allowance, and to provide for the support of children from a previous marriage.[15]

A critical part of the arrangements about marriage involved the economic exchange that occurred. This was not a dowry given to the bride by her parents nor was it bridewealth paid by the groom's family to the bride's family. By law this payment, called the mahr, was a dower given by the groom to the bride, and it had a symbolic and practical importance for the relationship between husband and wife. Symbolically, the groom's endowing the bride with part of his wealth avoided the pre-Islamic custom of the groom paying for the bride. At the same time, it implicitly recognized the importance of the bond that was being formed between individuals. Practically, the dower had the potential to be an important way for women to gain access to property. However, its practical value to the women as well its symbolic importance depended on actual social practices. There has been considerable divergence between the law and social practice historically and from one region of the Middle East to another, so assessing the dower's role and significance requires careful attention to context and practice.[16]

In Aleppo in the eighteenth and nineteenth centuries, social practice appears to have largely conformed to the law. The dower went to the bride and belonged to her absolutely. It was usually used to buy jewelry and clothing. If the bride's family were wealthy, her father added a sum to the mahr and, if sufficiently large, it would also be used to purchase household goods.[17] These items also remained the property of the bride. The dower was usually paid in two installments. One part, the *mahr muqaddam* (prompt dower) was paid at the time of the marriage; the rest, the *mahr mu'akhkhira* (delayed or deferred dower), remained in the pocket of the husband until he died or until he divorced his wife. This delayed mahr was not forgotten by the wife. The sum still owed to the woman was always cited in divorce cases and was considered the first obligation against a husband's estate in the event of his death. Women did not hesitate, if necessary, to sue their former husbands (if divorced) or his heirs (if deceased) to recover the mahr still owed to them.

Since women did get control of the dower in Aleppo, it was one way in which they gained access to property. These payment arrangements, however, meant that the point in their lives when they were able to control the resources varied. For those women who received most of the dower payment up front or those who were widowed or divorced relatively soon after marriage, the period during which they had full control of this capital was longer. For the majority of women, however, one-third to one-fifth of the dower was "deferred," so their access to property that was nominally theirs was restricted, and the immediate value of the mahr to them was reduced. However, the deferred dower represented some insurance in the event that a woman was left on her own, a trade-off that probably seemed advantageous, especially since by law women bore none of the costs of setting up or maintaining the household. The timing of payment of the dower, therefore, emphasized its function of providing some long-term economic security for women. Their right to this sum was potentially more important than immediate control.[18]

The importance of the dower as a means of access to property and as a way of providing some economic security to women ultimately depended on its value. Determining the value of dower payments in Aleppo during this period is problematic. The lack of surviving marriage contracts in the Aleppo court records means that evidence about the mahr comes primarily from three kinds of information in the sources: divorce cases, inheritance settlements, and litigation arising from failure to pay the mahr.[19] While providing considerable information on mahr, this evidence presents certain methodological difficulties. In all cases the sum mentioned is the deferred mahr, the amount not paid to the bride at the time of the marriage. This latter sum usually represented one-third to one-fifth of the total, but not always. For example, in one incident, the total mahr was 1,325 qurush, 1,300 of which was turned over to the bride at the time of the marriage.[20] Therefore, because of the imprecise nature of the evidence, it is possible to provide only a range of the sums paid.

The size of the deferred dower in the last decades of the eighteenth century ranged from 150 to 500 qurush, with the average around 200 qurush. The total mahr therefore ranged from 450 to 2,500 qurush, averaging between 600 and 1,000 qurush. By the second and third decade of the nineteenth century, the delayed mahr ranged in size from 25 qurush to 3,000 qurush. The average was around 500 qurush, making the average total payments between 1,500 and 2,500 qurush. The increased size of these payments reflected the sharp rise in overall prices in the early decades of the nineteenth century. The size of the mahr was not absolutely determined by wealth and social class. The two largest dowers were paid by men who appear to be craftsmen; that is, the nisbas following their names appear to refer to their actual occupation, and there are no titles to suggest a different status.[21] The amount of mahr paid by upper-class families was significantly higher than the lowest dowers recorded, but in general tended to be around the average paid by people from other classes; only a few were much higher.

While these figures are not very precise, they provide some sense of the economic significance of this marriage obligation, both for the men who had to pay it and for the women who received it. When the size of the mahr is compared to other significant financial outlays, it becomes clear that the mahr was not an insignificant sum. For most people outside the elite, their residence represented their single largest financial asset. In the late eighteenth century, average house prices ranged from 50 qurush in the poorer quarters to 5,000 qurush in the wealthier districts surrounding the madina and the Citadel. By the second quarter of the nineteenth century, this average had risen by 50 percent as a result of price inflation. A comparison of average house prices with average mahr payments for different social groups in both periods shows that providing the dower was as expensive as buying a house, for many classes of the population. For the wealthy, the expense of the mahr was not insignificant, but it was less costly than a house, and both mahr and house would have represented a smaller percentage of total assets. For the less well-to-do, the mahr represented a significant part of total wealth. The economic significance of the mahr is also apparent in the inheritance records. The mahr could be as high as 50 percent of a woman's total estate, although it averaged around a fifth. In general, the wealthier the woman, the less significant the mahr in terms of total assets. Similarly, the delayed mahr owed to his wife could represent a significant percentage of a man's estate.

Because the mahr was sufficiently large and belonged to the wife, whether she had control of it from the beginning or a claim to it to be activated later, it did represent some economic security for her, both in the event of divorce or death of the husband and also in the event of his financial ruin. One observer remarked on the importance of this inviolability of the wife's property during periods of political insecurity or economic instability when a man might be vulnerable to having his property confiscated or losing it through bad investment.[22] The wife had a buffer against such economic disaster.

Once the marriage took place, what kinds of ties developed between spouses in these arranged marriages between usually young adults? The relationship between husband and wife is almost impossible to uncover, given the nature of our sources. In particular, answers to the critical questions of what expectations husbands and wives themselves had of these marriages, whether they were seen as anything more than a legal and sexual bond with reproduction as their main purpose, and whether ties of affection and love developed within them remain elusive. However, some observations about the nature of this relationship are in order.

The first is that marriage was not primarily an economic partnership among the upper class. Among many groups in Middle Eastern societies, marriage definitely was an economic partnership. Peasant households were units of production, with husband and wife (or wives) both performing tasks essential to that production and to the economic survival of the family. In the cities, craftsmen and their wives were less likely to work together, with the men in their workshops and the women doing piece work at home or performing services outside, but joint economic activities by husbands and wives were not unknown. For example, two couples in which the wives were sisters were partners for four years in weaving and selling the *alaja* (striped silk) cloth.[23] Even when spouses did not work together, the economic contribution of each was essential to the well-being of the household. Among families of "modest substance," some wives also became involved in husbands' businesses through lending money, and husbands and wives occasionally bought and sold property together. Property jointly owned by husbands and wives appeared in 6 percent of all transactions in Aleppo.

Among the elite, however, joint economic activities were exceptional. On rare occasions married couples owned property together, and a few set up joint endowments, but the infrequency of such cases emphasizes how unusual it was. Elite women lent and borrowed money and invested in commercial ventures, but not with their husbands. Conjugal ties among this group were not primarily economic ones. Both the nature of the legal system—the lack of community property—and the actual way that property and other economic assets were handled prevented marriage in most cases from turning into an economic partnership.

But what about affective relations? Love was not the basis on which marriages were made, of course. The transition from arranged marriages to those in which females and males had some choice was one of the important milestones in the transformation of marriage and family relationships and in the process of renegotiating gender relations that begins in parts of the Middle East in the nineteenth century. Beth Baron has pinpointed the emergence of marriages in which women had some say about choice of husband as occurring in the early twentieth century among Cairo's upper and middle classes.[24] Duben and Behar examine at length the discussion about the relationship between love and marriage in late-nineteenth- and early-twentieth-century Istanbul. As more and more people came to accept the idea that love was an appropriate basis for marriage, the feelings of the prospective bride and groom were taken into account, although arranged marriages remained common well into the 1920s and 1930s.[25] By the early twentieth century, Syrian girls were regularly consulted about their parents' choice of a husband, according to Daghestani.[26] At what point this became a common practice among the urban upper classes in Syria has still to be determined.

Although love was not the reason for which marriages were made before this transition, this does not mean that marriages were devoid of ties of affection. Unfortunately, the question of affective relations between spouses remains largely unanswered. Close emotional bonds seem unlikely to develop in a society where the social worlds of men and women were largely separate. The social segregation mandated by the gender system prevented anything resembling companionate marriage until a later period. Women's closest ties would therefore be with their natal families, the women of their households, and their children. It is easy to assume that spouses remained virtual strangers to each other throughout their married lives, with little affection between them. But it is necessary to be very cautious in drawing such conclusions. There is circumstantial evidence that close emotional bonds between spouses were not unknown. In one of the few sources that can shed some light on this issue before the modern or early modern period—letters from the Geniza collection— Shlomo Goitein found that love between spouses was frequently mentioned. He concludes by saying that "I do not attempt to prove the obvious, namely, that love was present in the Geniza world just as it is in our own. . . . When Geniza husbands speak of love, we should take them seriously. They were not people from another planet."[27]

The lives and relationships of members of the Ottoman royal family are also revealing in this respect. Since the personal was at the same time very political in this family, their sexual and emotional lives are better

known than those of nonroyal families. The relationships between several
sultans and their favorites were much like marriages, even though, except
in the case of Sulayman and Hurrem, they never married. Leslie Peirce
has carefully documented these enduring and intense emotional ties and
the attitudes of contemporaries toward them. The reaction to Sulayman's
marriage to Hurrem was largely negative, but it grew out of a sense that
the sultan should not be so intimate with, nor dependent upon, a single
person who could exercise undue influence on him, rather than from disapproval or shock at this evidence of strong love between a man and a
woman who were husband and wife.[28]

This question of the emotional ties between husbands and wives in
Middle Eastern societies is not a new one. It was in the minds of Europeans living in Aleppo in the eighteenth century. Russell struggled with
this problem of marital happiness, and it is interesting to see what his conclusions were. On the one hand, Middle Eastern marriage lacked what
he considered some of marriage's best features. Men and women did not
eat together; a husband's friends never saw his wife or wives and therefore missed their civilizing influence. Nevertheless, Russell concludes
that marriages were not less happy than those in other countries. Women
were "treated with civility, from which tenderness is not wholly absent."
He goes on to suggest that arranged marriages do not lead to a "greater
proportion of domestic unhappiness" than in countries where individuals are free to choose their own spouses.

> *The matrimonial conjunction of opposite tempers is not*
> *confined to Turkey; nor does there seem to be in fact a*
> *greater proportion of domestic unhappiness, fairly*
> *imputable to that cause, than what may be found in*
> *countries where both sexes enjoy the inestimable privi-*
> *lege of free choice, grounded on previous intimacy.*[29]

POLYGYNY, DIVORCE, AND DEATH

The strength of the marriage bond and the na-
ture of the relationship between husband and wife were also affected by
expectations about the permanence of marriage. The issue of the permanence or impermanence of marriage is inseparable from certain features

of marriage in Islamic law, notably polygyny and the relative ease of divorce for men. One of the basic features of the marriage system in Islamic societies was the sanctioning of polygyny. The legal permissibility of polygyny and its consequences for the status of women have sparked some of the most heated debates about the Middle Eastern family. Critics of the practice have argued that it is degrading to women and a sign of their low status. They present a picture of polygynous households dominated by the rivalries and jealousies of the harem. Apologists, on the other hand, see the practice of polygyny as a way of providing for women in difficult times, under social conditions where women did not have the means to support themselves outside the family context. They emphasize the cooperation and mutual support that existed among fellow wives and claim that the image of the strife-ridden harem is a product of extrapolating Western attitudes and feelings to a different cultural context. While there is undoubtedly some truth in both of these views, understanding the role of polygyny and its social consequences involves delving into some complex and often emotional issues that are not easy to resolve, especially when dealing with the past, for which evidence about both the rate of polygyny and how it was perceived is fragmentary.

The impact of polygyny on the relationship between husband and wife and on the position of women depended in part on how frequently it occurred. Outsiders visiting or residing in Syria in the eighteenth and nineteenth centuries often commented on the infrequency of polygynous marriages. Alexander Russell said that, the legal sanction of polygyny notwithstanding, few men in Aleppo had more than one wife. Expense was often cited as a reason. Large harems were usually the prerogative of wealthier and older men. Alan Duben reached the same conclusion about the role of class in determining the frequency of polygyny in the Turkish parts of the empire later in the nineteenth century. Men in most classes simply could not afford it, nor could young men of the upper class.[30] John Bowring observed that polygyny was rare in the villages in the mountains and along the desert borders of Syria.[31]

Efforts by scholars to calculate rates of polygyny historically appear to support these impressions, although such studies are few in number and difficult to compare because of the different methodologies used to determine these rates. Haim Gerber calculated the rates of polygyny in seventeenth-century Bursa by using the estates of males to determine how many men had more than one wife at the time of their deaths. Out of a sample of 2,000 men, he found that only twenty (1 percent) had more than one wife when they died.[32] Gerber acknowledges the problems with this method of determining rates of polygyny—in particular the possibility that some of these men had other wives who had predeceased them—but he argues that the rate of polygynous marriages would have been low, even allowing for some undercounting. Tucker, using the same methodology for determining rates of polygyny as Gerber, also found few examples of men who were survived by more than one wife in eighteenth- and nineteenth-century Nablus, although she noted that men of the elite were more likely to have more than one wife.[33]

In the nineteenth century, more detailed and reliable evidence about polygyny becomes available for much of the Ottoman Empire in the form of census data. Using these data for Egypt, Ken Cuno found that 10 percent of households in the Delta village of Badaway and 5 percent in Damas were polygynous. Almost all of the polygynous households were landholding households, and most were multiple-family households. Interestingly, he found that in most of these households, only one man was involved in a polygynous marriage.[34] At the end of the nineteenth century, Duben and Behar calculated the rate of polygyny in Istanbul and found that it was less than 3 percent of all marriages. When these aggregate data were broken down by wealth and occupation, there was some differential in rates by class. About 11 percent of the marriages of religious leaders and upper-level bureaucrats, for example, were polygynous. Duben and Behar argue that there is no reason to think that these low rates were new, that is, the result of changing attitudes after exposure to Western cultural attitudes. They also believe that *successive monogamy* may be a more accurate term than *polygyny* for what occurred in Istanbul. Most polygynous marriages occurred when a man took a much younger wife after many years of marriage to one woman. Because of his age, the man often did not survive his second marriage by many years. In other words, even those individuals involved in polygynous marriages only spent a relatively short period of time in such a marriage.[35] Duben and Behar also found that people's perceptions of the rate of polygyny had little to do with the statistical reality—they thought it was much higher than it actually was.[36] This gap between perception and reality in Istanbul warns us that statements by contemporaries about the many wives that wealthy men had need to be used cautiously.

As suggested by the evidence on Nablus and Istanbul and by Russell's comments, rates of polygyny were at least in part a function of class. Men of wealth and consequence could afford to have more than one wife; a large harem, including several wives and concubines, was a sign of status, a way of emulating the sultan, and a means of extending the patrimonial household through multiple ties of marriage. At the same time, while wealth undoubtedly played a role in determining whether or not a man took more than one wife, class linkages were not absolute. Rates of polygyny were affected by other variables as well. Justin McCarthy found high rates of polygyny among Black Sea Turks in the middle of the nineteenth century. Out-migration by males was very high, and polygyny became a "demographic remedy for a lack of males." Polygyny allowed a replenishment of the population despite a drop in the number of young males. It also helped to solve the problem of having a large number of unmarried women left behind and the threat they were believed to pose to family honor.[37] Cuno also noted that wealth was not always the determining factor. While he noted that many polygynous marriages did occur among rural notables, he also argued that the need for labor could encourage polygyny even among those who were not as well-off.[38] Just as polygynous marriages were not restricted to the wealthy, the rates among the upper class could vary as well, depending on the circumstances. The Shiuk were a wealthy rural tribal group that settled in northern Syria in the late nineteenth century. In the first generation after they became settled on the land, they were concerned with expanding their alliances through marriage with other landed lineages and with reinforcing family solidarity through cousin marriages. In effect, polygyny allowed them to make endogamous and exogamous marriages simultaneously. As their position became well established, "out-marriage" became less important, and rates of polygyny dropped.[39] Class was undoubtedly an important factor in determining whether polygyny occurred, but not the only one, and it did not always operate in the same way.

The data on polygyny in Aleppo largely confirm what has been found in Nablus, Bursa, Istanbul, and other places. The rates of polygyny in Aleppo for the population as a whole, as determined by using a methodology similar to that of Gerber and Tucker, were low. Out of a sample of the estates of 270 males who had at least one surviving spouse, only 6 percent had more than one wife. Less than 1 percent had more than two wives. As was also true in other places, polygyny was more common among the upper class. To determine the rate of polygyny among the upper class, it is not necessary to rely only on using the estates of males to determine polygynous marriages, since family reconstruction provides evidence about marriages throughout the lifetimes of individuals. The marriages of 414 males from the upper-class families are known. Forty-nine (11 percent) of these had more than one wife. However, we do not always know if they had more than one wife at the same time. In some cases, circumstantial evidence suggests that the man may have married the second wife after the death or divorce of his first wife. For example, 'Abd al-Wahhab Shurayyif had two wives, Fatima Zanabili and Fatima 'Imadi. Fatima Zanabili was his first wife and the mother of seven of his sons, the oldest of whom was almost thirty by the time 'Abd al-Wahhab died in 1769. Fatima 'Imadi's children by him were much younger, only minors at the time of his death, so she was clearly a much younger wife by whom he had a second family. It is possible, although not certain, that he married her after the death of his first wife. Even if we assume that all men with more than one wife were involved in polygynous marriages, the rate is comparable to what Tucker found for Nablus's elite and what Duben and Behar found among religious leaders and higher-level bureaucrats in late-nineteenth- and early-twentieth-century Istanbul.[40] This rate is considerably lower, however, than the rates that Aswad found among the Shuik during the period in which they were pursuing a dual-marriage strategy.

Although rates of polygyny were higher among the elite in Aleppo than among other groups, as was also true elsewhere, the absolute number of occurrences was low enough to suggest that sharing a husband with a second or third wife was not a common experience for most elite women. Moreover, polygynous marriages were concentrated in a small number of families. A few wealthy merchants and a few men with political ambitions accounted for a large percentage of such marriages. Hajj Musa Amiri, who had four wives and several concubines, and several of his sons together accounted for 13 percent of such marriages. Other wealthy merchants who had more than one wife were Abu Bakr Ghannam and his wife's nephew, also called Abu Bakr Ghannam; Hasan Hamawi; Mustafa Jazmati; and three men of the Qurna family. Two factors may explain this pattern. One is that the wealthiest individuals, at least in terms of disposable cash, were the big merchants. They were therefore in a position to support more than one wife, and being able to multiply the number of useful alliances through more than one marriage could be beneficial in accumulating additional capital and connections that might facilitate future business activities. Similar considerations were probably at work among politically ambitious individuals. Mustafa, 'Abd Allah, and 'Abd al-Qadir Jabiri; Muhammad Qudsi; and Nu'man Shurayyif—all of whom figure prominently in the political history of this period—represent a significant percentage of the individuals with more than one wife. The diverse connections that one man could form through having several wives could be very important to his political success. For example, Muhammad Qudsi married a woman from a prominent local Ottoman family as well as a woman from Istanbul, where he had important political connections that needed to be consolidated. Just as larger households were found among those with political ambitions for both pragmatic and status reasons, multiple marriages were one of the ways of augmenting the size of the household and increasing the number of loyal supporters. The concentration of polygynous marriages among a relatively few families and at particular times in the families' histories suggests that among the wealthy, powerful, and socially prominent in Aleppo, as among the Shuik, polygyny was a social strategy used at times to accomplish specific goals rather than an option routinely chosen if one could afford it.

The relative lack of polygynous marriages does not mean that men had only one sexual partner at a time, of course, since sexual access to female slaves was allowed. Nor does it tell us what the attitudes toward polygyny were, especially among women. Since women's own voices on the subject during this time are silent, trying to determine these attitudes is very difficult. Nevertheless, some suggestive evidence about women's perceptions of polygyny comes from places where marriage contracts have survived in significant numbers, especially for seventeenth- and eighteenth-century Cairo. In many of these contracts, women have exercised their right to place conditions on these marriages; if their husbands did not abide by these conditions, the women had the right to divorce them without financial penalty. One of the more frequently evoked conditions was prohibiting the husband from taking a second wife.[41] The need to insert such a condition suggests that women were very concerned about the possibility of their husband taking a second wife, which in turn implies that they saw the threat of a husband's taking another wife as real and that they were not willing to live within a polygynous household. Many of the women who exercised the option to include such conditions were making second marriages and might be imposing these conditions based on prior experience with marriage.[42] Although hardly conclusive, this evidence is the best we have about women's perceptions of polygyny, and it would seem to confirm that they did see it as a real and undesirable possibility. At the same time, it also shows the willingness of many women to take advantage of the legal rights available to them and to take an active role in negotiating some control over their marriages.

Unfortunately, the lack of surviving marriage contracts for Aleppo means there is no comparable evidence on which to judge whether this concern existed there as well. There are also no cases of divorce in which the reason cited was the taking of a second wife. Russell asserts, however, that the prohibition against taking a second wife was often inserted in the marriage contracts with which he was familiar.[43] It seems likely, then, that women in Aleppo shared the view of their sisters in Cairo that polygyny was a threat and also that they were willing to take steps to prevent it.

The ease of divorce for men has also been cited as an important factor in weakening bonds between husband and wife and undermining the position of women. Under Islamic law, husbands could divorce their wives by repudiating them unilaterally. There were certain legal formalities that had to be observed, including a waiting period to see whether the wife was pregnant and the requirement that it be a triple repudiation. There was also a financial disincentive in most cases. Unless a husband could prove that his wife was at fault, he had to hand over the remainder of his wife's dower if he divorced her. Nevertheless, the procedure was remarkably easy, not even requiring a court appearance. Women's access to divorce, on the other hand, was much more limited, and they did have to go through formal legal channels to terminate a marriage. They had to appear before the judge and to have a legally justified cause for ending the marriage, and they ran the risk of incurring financial penalties. This inequality was not limited to the conditions under which a divorce could be obtained, but also extended to the fundamental economic insecurity that a woman could face when left without support. As is true today, the lot of a divorced woman without considerable financial resources or the support of her family was not a happy one.

Still, the inequalities may not have been as great in practice as this summary of divorce law suggests. For example, Russell asserted that all divorces, including unilateral repudiation by men, went through certain formalities in court or at least had to be conducted publicly in eighteenth-century Aleppo.[44] Recent research has also shown that women in the Ottoman Empire had more options for getting out of an unwanted marriage than was previously thought. The usual way for women to end a marriage was through a form of divorce known as *khulʿ*. A woman requested repudiation by her husband, but in return for her freedom, she had to forfeit her remaining dower and often pay an additional sum to her husband to get his cooperation. Some women had other options, however, that allowed them to avoid the financial burden of a khul‘ divorce and even to claim some of their dower from their husbands. In Nablus, for example, Tucker found two other arrangements that did not penalize women as much: a decree of formal separation (*fashk*) and an annulment before the marriage was consummated.[45] In addition, women could divorce their husbands under certain circumstances without financial loss. If a husband violated the conditions of a marriage contract, his wife could divorce him and recover her mahr as well as demand support at least for a certain period of time. Moreover, women were able to use the different interpretations of legitimate causes for divorce by the different law schools to broaden the grounds for divorce. The Hanafi school only allows divorce in case of impotence, but the Hanbali and Shafi‘i also include nonsupport in what they allow. In Cairo, Hanafi judges would allow Hanbali and Shafi‘i to rule on divorce cases, in effect giving women the "best deal."[46] In the final analysis, the fact that women could use the law and the courts was important. The legal inequality between men and women remained, but it was modified to some extent by the flexible nature of the legal system.[47]

As was true with polygyny, the impact of divorce on the relationship between husband and wife and on the position of women within a marriage depended in part on its frequency; just because divorce was easy did not necessarily mean that it was common. Unfortunately, it is almost impossible to determine how common divorce was in Aleppo during this time. Russell argues that the divorce rate was low, largely for financial reasons—it was too expensive[48]—but it is impossible to verify this observation from the court records. Most of the divorce cases recorded in the archives were cases of khul‘ divorce. While these cases are not uncommon, there is no way to know from them how many marriages ended in divorce, especially since this was only one form that divorce could take. Cases of *talaq* (divorce initiated by husband) almost never surface. Even the khul‘ cases are not very informative; they are largely formulaic and provide few insights into the reasons for, or the consequences of, the breakup of these marriages. One trend, however, is apparent in these cases in the early decades of the nineteenth century: a growing number of women divorced their husbands because of desertion. This probably reflected the social impact of the worsening political and economic conditions in the city. In a commercial city with a high degree of geographic mobility, there would always be examples of men leaving and never returning. The economic decline and political instability of the early nineteenth century undoubtedly intensified the problem and contributed to the resulting social dislocation.

Elite families, with greater economic resources and family support, were relatively immune from these consequences of the changing political and economic climate. Divorces did occur among these families, but rarely, as Tucker also found to be the case among the elite of Nablus. Very few divorces involving members of the upper class show up in the Aleppo sources. This could simply be an indication that they kept divorces private, but other evidence suggests that marriages were quite durable. A number of factors would inhibit divorce at this level. On the practical side, a man could afford to marry a second or third wife without divorcing the first one if he wished to have a new wife. More important, since marriages were made for family reasons, ending these marriages that presumably had brought benefits to the family would not be taken lightly. Only a half dozen cases of divorce within these families appear in the sources, and only one of them gives any indication of the reason for the divorce: failure to consummate the marriage.[49]

The evidence on both polygyny and divorce, while incomplete, suggests that conditions existed that made both relatively infrequent, despite the legal sanction for them. Both were class-linked and varied with the larger social and political conditions. Because of their relative infrequency, neither was likely to devalue marriage or contribute to a sense of its impermanence, as has been suggested. However, there was a real sense in which marriage was a temporary state. The instability of the conjugal family was a fact of life, but the main culprit was not polygyny or divorce, but rather the strong possibility that one's spouse would die at a relatively young age. In this respect, Middle Eastern society was no different from other premodern societies.

There are no death records with age of death, but the inheritance records provide sufficient circumstantial evidence to show how common widowhood was in Aleppo. In 45 percent of the cases of inheritance, the deceased's spouse was already dead. While these could well be cases of older people dying after many years of marriage, much more convincing evidence comes from the number who died with young children. Thirty-six percent had minor children and were dying at an early stage in their married lives. The likelihood of losing a spouse after relatively few years of marriage was a reality confronting all classes of the population.

It is not easy to assess the psychological impact of this reality. It would seem to ensure a certain emotional distance in the relationship. Beyond that, for the lower classes, particularly for women, it must have contributed to a sense of insecurity and vulnerability, as they faced the prospect of being left with young children. It perhaps also had implications for their sense of acceptance in the family into which they married, since their link to that family was primarily through their husband.

The recognition of the demographic realities that affected the nature of marriage also raises a question about the universality of marriage and what it meant. It has been assumed that marriage was universal in Middle Eastern society; there is no religious sanction or social arrangement that would encourage celibacy. When statistical figures become available in the late nineteenth century, Duben and Behar found that only 2 percent of females in Istanbul never married.[50] McCarthy also provides evidence of universal marriage among Black Sea Turks in the nineteenth century.[51] Remarriage was common as well, as Tucker, Marcus, and Duben and Behar found in Nablus, Aleppo, and Istanbul, respectively.[52] When spouses died, remarriage followed soon after. Nevertheless, this eagerness to marry and remarry was not always the case. Linda Schilcher studied a large notable lineage of Damascus for whom she had data for several generations, spanning the period from the seventeenth century through the Second World War. She notes varying rates of celibacy among both females and males of this lineage over these centuries, with rates reaching as high as 60 percent for males in the nineteenth century in some sublineages and 56 percent for females in the earlier generations, then falling to and remaining around 40 percent in the nineteenth and twentieth centuries.[53]

In Aleppo's upper class there were many adults who had no spouse and no children. This was true for both men and women. Many of these individuals, perhaps all of them, may have been married at one time, but the marriage ended in a relatively short time due to death or divorce and did not produce surviving offspring. What this suggests is that marriage may have been universal in the technical sense that nearly everyone married at some point. However, there were also a large number of unmarried adults at any one time. Hilda Geertz refers to women in this position as the Middle Eastern version of the spinster—a woman who was married for a brief time, lost her spouse through death or divorce, and never remarried.[54] While there are no readily available figures to suggest how numerous the unmarried population was, it is clear from the information on upper-class families that relatively few divorced or widowed women remarried. We have data on the marriages for 241 upper-class women. There is evidence of only 13 women (5 percent) remarrying. Tucker's evidence on Nablus also suggests that upper-class women rarely remarried, unlike women in other classes of the city.

While in one sense marriage was the "natural" and expected state for adults, many adults at any one time were not married. Within the larger extended family, the conjugal unit was not necessarily stable, and this inevitably affected the nature of the marriage bond, leading to an emphasis on the wider kin group—though what that kin group would be might vary according to the demographics of an individual family. The explanation for this lay not in any specifically Islamic institution of marriage, but rather in the inherent demographic instability of the early modern family. The concept of marriage as political alliance, economic investment, and social insurance tended to make the end of a marriage a major point of transition. Yet not many people could count on spending decades with the same spouse.

MARRIAGE PATTERNS: MARRYING IN

The ties that bound husbands and wives were affected by structural factors—legal rights and economic obligations; societal conceptions of marriage; the possibility of divorce, polygyny, and early death—as well as by feelings of love, affection, or dependence, and the latter were shaped as much by circumstances and personality as by any conditions attached to the institution of marriage. Equally important in determining the significance of marriage were the reasons why a particular marriage partner was chosen. Spouses were chosen with familial concerns in mind, at least for the elite. Their choices provide important insights into family relationships and dynamics and shaped family and social structure in Aleppo.

Much of the scholarly discussion of marriage in the Middle East has focused on cousin marriage, which has been viewed by many as the distinctive feature of the marriage system and as something that sets the Middle East apart from other societies. Both Islamic law and customary law permit endogamy, even between very close kin, including first cousins. Cousin marriage, particularly one kind of cousin marriage—

marriage with the father's brother's daughter—has been seen as a strong cultural preference and has been linked to the particular kind of patriarchal family found in the Middle East.

In the 1950s and 1960s, many anthropologists viewed cousin marriage in general and patrilineal parallel cousin marriage (marriage to the father's brother's daughter) specifically as the defining characteristic of the Middle Eastern kinship system. There was some disagreement about whether there was a rule or simply a strong preference for patrilineal parallel cousin marriage and about the explanation of this preference. Some researchers attributed it to conscious motivations about the need to preserve property within the lineage, to secure political alliances, to ensure harmony within the family, or to protect family honor. Others, notably R. F. Murphy and Leonard Kasdan, saw this marriage pattern not as a result of calculating specific goals, but rather as a functional arrangement that promoted segmentation and therefore preserved the kinship system. Despite these disagreements, there was general agreement that cousin marriage played a critical role in the kinship system and made it unique.[55]

Since that time the uniqueness of this marriage preference and the significance of cousin marriage in general has been called into question. Richard Antoun, for example, has pointed out the problem of trying to generalize about cousin marriage in the Middle East when rates of such marriage have varied widely. He argues that even focusing on the issue of patrilineal parallel cousin marriage or lineage endogamy is an example of the tendency to look for the "unique and apparently esoteric aspects of Middle Eastern culture." Moreover, focusing on endogamy means that scholars were ignoring much important data about marriage.[56]

Antoun's critique of those who see cousin marriage as uniquely important to the Middle East is underscored by looking at marriage practices outside the region. Cousin marriage was quite common among Europeans in the medieval and early modern period as well, despite persistent and often heavy-handed efforts by the Catholic Church to prevent it. The church was obsessed with the fear of incest; any marriage between relatives closer than third cousins, as well as some in-laws, families of godparents, and sometimes others, was considered incestuous by the Catholic Church. Even with all the weight of church authority against them, cousin marriages, including marriages between first cousins, occurred regularly. The advantages of such marriages in many circumstances outweighed any fears of the church or of going to hell. In general, people preferred to marry those who were already well known to them and their families, be they kin or neighbors. The preference was for "closeness."[57] Despite the legal and ideological differences between Islamic and Christian canon law, marriage preferences in practice were remarkably similar in these two societies.

This similarity is underscored in the preferences about marriage partners expressed by Palestinians in this century, as documented by Annelies Moors. They wanted to marry someone who was *qarib* (that is, close to them), but who was included in this category changed depending on circumstances. At times this would translate into a preference for cousins, but at other times this "closeness" or "sameness" could mean "sharing space" (i.e., village or neighborhood) or "sharing class or culture" rather than "sharing blood." Moreover, the definitions of "closeness" and therefore the preferred marriage partner could vary by gender.[58]

Just as the supposed cultural preference for lineage endogamy is not as straightforward as much of the literature would suggest, the link between endogamy and patriarchy also needs to be examined critically. A number of scholars have explicitly or implicitly seen cousin marriage as a basic feature of the patriarchal family in the Middle East.[59] They assume that cousin marriage was one way of controlling females, ensuring that resources stayed within the family in the hands of the family patriarch. It also reinforced the authority of the father, husband, and uncle over the bride, given the multiple roles they played in her life, and reinforced family solidarity at the expense of individual family members, all believed to be important goals of the patriarchal Middle Eastern family. Linda Schilcher makes this linkage between endogamy and patriarchy explicit in her study of the Damascus notable lineage by using rates of cousin marriage as one of the measures of patriarchy. She associates the declining rates of male and female endogamy with the decline of patriarchy and the emergence of more egalitarian relationships within the family.[60] Assuming such a connection between endogamy and patriarchy raises a number of questions, however. If cousin marriage was important to maintaining the patriarchal system, why did the practice of cousin marriage vary so widely and remain low overall? Cousin marriage *was* common in certain situations. High rates of cousin marriage were found among pastoral groups with pronounced segmentary lineages in societies where centralized political authority was weak; among the Hamula Arabs studied by Michael Meeker (50 percent); among a holy lineage in the Turkish-Syrian border region studied by Barbara Aswad (60 percent); among an urban kin group studied by Hilda Geertz in Morocco (50 percent); and in the late nineteenth century among females of the Damascus lineage studied by Schilcher. Among most communities, however, rates of cousin marriage were low (10–15 percent).[61] Can we therefore conclude that the groups with higher rates were more patriarchal and those with lower rates, less patriarchal? Alternatively, could endogamy in fact have been a way of ensuring a better position for females within marriage by creating more equal marriages between partners who knew each other well rather than as a way of controlling women? Was it a way to level the hierarchy within the harem somewhat when a woman's mother-in-law was also her aunt, and did it therefore offset some of the potential disadvantages that a young bride faced? To raise such questions is not to deny that such a relationship between endogamy and patriarchy might exist, but rather to argue that it must be demonstrated and not taken for granted.

Rather than starting from a position that views cousin marriage as either a cultural preference or a characteristic of the patriarchal family, the approach taken here is that cousin marriage was one option among many available for families seeking spouses for their marriageable sons and daughters. It was a strategy that families could use to achieve a variety of purposes, and the reasons why cousins were chosen as spouses would be different from family to family and from one social context to another. This would also explain why the rates of cousin marriage vary as much as they do. In order to understand the role and significance of cousin marriage as a social strategy in any given historical context, it is necessary to establish the rate of cousin marriage, look for patterns in these choices that explain why it might be a preferred option, and examine its impact on the family, gender relations, and kinship ties.

To date we have very little solid evidence on cousin marriage in the past. Observations about the relative importance of cousin marriage among well-to-do urbanites in the Ottoman Empire are contradictory. On the one hand, the memoirs of Emine Foat Tugay on Ottoman-Egyptian ruling-class families detail numerous cousin marriages and a seemingly impenetrable web of relationships among family members as a result. Abdul-Rahman Hamide, writing about early-twentieth-century Aleppo and the "esprit de corps" among the upper class, says that cousin marriage was common to avoid fragmenting the family patrimony. Yet Kazem Daghestani, also writing on Syrian Muslim families in the early twentieth century, argues that cousin marriage was neither religiously sanctioned nor very common in the cities.[62] Only a few studies have attempted to provide some statistical evidence that might lend weight to one view or the other. In the study already mentioned, Schilcher found that rates of endogamy varied widely over time for both males and females. There was no male endogamy in the founding generation of the family, then endogamy among males rose and remained in the 20–40 percent range in subsequent generations. Female endogamy reached 60 percent in the late nineteenth century and then declined and remained under 20 percent in the early twentieth century. Tucker found eight cousin marriages among the wealthiest families (who made up roughly a third of her sample of 107 marriage contracts)—in other words, approximately 22 percent. Cousin marriage rates were half that for the other classes of the population. Among the landowning Shiuk tribe in late-nineteenth-century Syria, cousin marriage rates were also around 20 percent, in contrast to the holy lineage mentioned above in which they were 60 percent.[63]

The rate of cousin marriage among Aleppo's elite was comparable to what Tucker found for Nablus's upper class and Aswad found for the landowning Shiuk in the late nineteenth century. For the Aleppo group, 665 marriage choices were analyzed, and 159 of these choices were cousins (24 percent).[64] The most frequent type of cousin marriage was parallel patrilineal cousin marriage (i.e., marriage with the father's brother's daughter). Thirty men married their father's brother's daughters, which means of course that thirty women married their father's brother's sons. This represented 38 percent of all cousin marriages. Clearly, then, when cousins were chosen as spouses, there seems to have been a tendency to seek these close alliances. However, this represented only 9 percent of all marriages, a low rate that tends to confirm the conclusions of those who argue that this type of marriage had relatively little significance. It also indicates that those scholars who argue that this type of marriage pattern was characteristic but that its infrequency could be explained by changes in marriage patterns under the impact of modernization are wrong.[65] In other words, patrilineal parallel cousin marriage was no more common in the past than in the present.

Other types of cousins were also important as marriage partners. Nineteen males (23 percent) chose other close agnatic cousins to marry. Four married their father's sister's daughters. Fifteen others were married to their first cousins once removed or second cousins, five to their grandfather's brother's daughters, another five to their grandfather's brother's granddaughters, and the last five to their father's brother's granddaughters.

The cross-generational marriages were probably determined by age range. In a society in which early marriage and childbearing were the norm and polygyny and taking a much younger wife were options, a large age span could separate siblings, as much as thirty years in some cases.[66] Consequently, a large age gap would also exist among first cousins, so that a man seeking a wife among closely related kin would sometimes have found that his grandfather's brother's daughter was closer to his age than his father's brother's daughter. All these figures suggest that when cousins were chosen as marriage partners, most were chosen from among close kin; 62 percent of cousin marriages were with first or second cousins. However, marriages with more distant cousins were not insignificant. Another twenty-two males (27 percent) married more distant cousins, some of them so distant that the exact relationship between the cousins is not known, although they were members of the same lineage.

Marriages between maternal cousins also occurred. In the cases in which males married their father's sister's daughters, from the perspective of the females, these were marriages with maternal kin. Males also married maternal cousins. Eleven marriages (13 percent) with maternal relatives in eight different families took place. In two of these cases, the maternal cousins were also more distant paternal cousins, since the occurrence of cousin marriages in earlier generations had resulted in the overlapping of maternal and paternal kin. For example, Ahmad b. Isma'il Shaykhbandar married his mother's brother's daughter, who was also a paternal cousin, since his mother as well as his father were members of the Shaykhbandar family.[67] Similarly, Ahmad b. 'Abd Allah Miri married his mother's brother's daughter, who was also his grandfather's brother's granddaughter. All the others, however, were related to their spouses only through the maternal line.

As indicated, the rate of cousin marriage among Aleppo's elite was similar to rates of cousin marriage in other historical contexts. It was considerably lower than the highest rates, but probably also higher than the rate of cousin marriage for the population of Aleppo as a whole. The aggregate figures on cousin marriage, however, disguise an important point. Most families had either no cousin marriages or only one, while for a few the rate of cousin marriage was as high as 70 percent. Relatively few families account for most cousin marriages. Six families had five or more cousin marriages: the Jazmatis, Miris, Qurnas, Ubris, Tahas, and the Yakins. Four of these six families were among the largest and wealthiest merchant families in the city. These merchant families were some of the same ones that maintained undivided households throughout this period. A number of other merchant families had higher rates of cousin marriage than the average also. André Raymond found a similar pattern in Cairo, where the great merchant families were tightly knit and endogamy was common. So did Beshara Doumani in the important merchant family, the Arafats, in Nablus. This tendency of merchant families to prefer cousin marriage was directly linked to the kind of economic resources that generated the bulk of the family fortune. Given the family bases of these mercantile enterprises and the lack of corporate institutions within Middle Eastern society through which to accumulate wealth, preserving the integrity of family resources was essential. Cousin marriage was a way of ensuring that capital and property were not fragmented and did not leave the family.[68]

The other two families with the highest rates of cousin marriage were not merchant families. One, the Taha, was an ulema family (see family biography in Chapter 1); the other, the Yakin, was an 'askari family. The Yakin family were the descendants of the sister of 'Uthman Pasha, an early-eighteenth-century governor of Aleppo (governor in 1737), who was both the son and father of pashas. He was also a native of Aleppo and is probably best known as the builder of the 'Uthmaniyya Mosque. 'Uthman Pasha's direct line died out after the death of his son, and his sister's children inherited his wealth.[69] What the Taha and Yakin families had in common was their position as very prominent and long-established families. Both could trace their importance in the city back to the seventeenth century. This suggests that cousin marriage was more likely to have been chosen by older families, a suggestion that is borne out when these families are divided into groups according to the length of residence in the city. When the rate of cousin marriage is calculated among those families established in the city before the end of the seventeenth century, the rate of cousin marriage is twice as high for the group as a whole (48 percent). Both Barbara Aswad and Wolfram Eberhard, who did a study of notable families of Antakya, found similar patterns.[70] Upwardly mobile families were much more likely to marry outside the family, since they needed to establish alliances with as many different families as they could. In other words, exogamous marriages were part of a strategy of expansion. In the second or third generation, once the family was well established, its goals were directed toward consolidating its political and economic position and reinforcing its honor and status. Cousin marriage was one way to do this. In a sense, the families could now afford to have more cousin marriages.

Women also had a higher rate of cousin marriage than did men. When the aggregate figures for cousin marriage are broken down by gender, 32 percent of female marriages were made with cousins, while only 20 percent of men married cousins. Similar gender differences in rates of cousin marriage have been found elsewhere. Aswad discovered that the women of successful lineages among the Shiuk and women of holy lineages in the same area did not marry outside the kin group.[71] The notable lineage of Damascus studied by Schilcher had high rates of female endogamy in the early generations and therefore many women found their options severely limited.[72] Clearly, the limits on women's marriages were not as rigid in Aleppo. In only two families, the Jabiri and the ʿIsabi, did the women marry cousins exclusively. In both of these cases, we know very little about the marriage patterns of the women at all, so there is at least a possibility that others married outside the family. Women married outside the family twice as often as they married their cousins. Nevertheless, the higher rate among women suggests that it was more important for daughters to marry in the family than for sons. The reasons why cousin marriage was preferred for daughters might be different from one family to the next. In merchant families, as indicated above, it was connected to keeping capital within the family. In families whose wealth derived primarily from other kinds of resources less vulnerable to risks of fragmentation or in more established families, the decision to marry daughters within the family might grow out of more intangible reasons: a desire to protect females and keep them within the household or a concern with the honor and status of the family and the status of the daughters. Marrying cousins ensured that daughters did not marry their social inferiors or were not connected to families in which their honor might be compromised.

Unfortunately, there is little direct evidence that sheds any light on what these families themselves thought about the issue of cousin marriage, so that their preferences can only be judged by their behavior. Legal disputes about marriage contracts indirectly reveal some possible attitudes, however. In one case a father, on behalf of his absent son, sued his cousin's daughter and her husband, saying that he and his cousin had arranged a marriage between his son and his cousin's daughter several years ago and asking that her proposed marriage to someone else be prohibited. His suit was based on breach of contract and the unsuitability of the pending marriage (the plaintiff claimed that the other man was not a social equal of the bride). He did not base his suit on any priority that a cousin might have.[73] It is also suggestive that Alexander Russell, who writes at length about marriage and was an acute observer of Aleppo society, makes no mention of cousin marriage as a preferred or desirable option.[74]

The higher rates of cousin marriage among women, merchant families, and older families indicate that in Aleppo during this period cousin marriage was used as a strategy to protect certain kinds of wealth from fragmentation and as a strategy for consolidation of status and position. Because cousin marriage was linked to these goals, its rates were tied to gender. The effect of cousin marriage was to create a new layer of kinship ties among a relatively narrow circle of kin, and this was important in strengthening family ties and in differentiating smaller family circles within the lineage. What cousin marriage patterns suggest about family structure is that reinforcing family ties through endogamous marriages was seen as important to many. When cousins were chosen as spouses, those more closely related usually provided the pool of possible partners. Marriage with more distant cousins did occur, an acknowledgment that a sense of lineage was maintained. However, reinforcing ties among close kin was apparently more important than renewing ties with more distant ones.

MARRIAGE PATTERNS: MARRYING OUT

Cousin marriage was an important option for families when deciding on the most appropriate marriages for their children, although the reasons for that particular choice differed. However, exogamous marriages were much more common than endogamous marriages; 69 percent of all marriages took place between spouses who were not cousins. Marriage was not a means of turning families inward, reinforcing kinship and household ties at the expense of other important social connections. It was primarily a strategy for broadening kinship networks and achieving other social, economic, and political goals in the process. The point has already been made that marriage linked these notable families together in a tangled network of connections. As a result, marriage played an important role in defining the social group and marking distinctions between it and other groups. The fact that it played this role also has important implications for the nature of kinship ties.

Marriages made outside the family can be divided into two groups: marriages to individuals from other notable families and marriages to individuals from other social groups. The most frequent type of marriage was between members of two notable families. Forty percent of all marriages were alliances of this type. The general reasons are not difficult to understand. These marriages offered the best opportunity to increase family status, power, and wealth through useful connections. A closer look at who married whom and the apparent reasons for those choices provides insights into the relationship between marriage connections and other social and political ties.

The most striking characteristic of the marriage alliances among these families was their diversity. This is best illustrated by looking at a few families and the marriage choices made by individuals within them. Three families, whose marriage patterns were "typical," will be used as examples: the Ghawri family, an ʿaskari family prominent in the city since the sixteenth century; the Hamawi family, a wealthy merchant family established in Aleppo sometime in the early to mid–eighteenth century; and the Qudsi family, an ulema family from Urfa, whose scion, Muhammad ibn Hasan, arrived in Aleppo in 1785 and quickly established himself and his family as an important presence in the city.

The Ghawri family, descendants of the freed slaves of the last Mamluk sultan, Qansuh al-Ghawri, derived its wealth from rights to the large endowment created by this sultan shortly before the Ottoman conquest and from control of numerous villages in the neighborhood of Aleppo.[75] The head of the family in the middle of the eighteenth century was Hasan, who was married to Rahma bint Qasim Agha Jaliq. Not much is known about the Jaliq family, except that it was a merchant family well connected to some of the most prominent merchant families in the city. Hasan and Rahma had four children, a daughter and three sons. Nothing is known about the daughter. One son, Ahmad, married twice, once to a slave woman and once to the daughter of an agha (it is not clear from the evidence whether he was married to both these women at the same time or one after the other). The spouses of the other two sons, Husyan and Ibrahim, are not mentioned, although both married and produced children. In the next generation, three of Ahmad's four children had no descendants, nor were any spouses mentioned for them. The same is true for Ibrahim's three daughters and for Husayn's one daughter. Only Ibrahim's son, Khalil, and Ahmad's daughter, Zaynab, were married, at least long enough for there to be some mention of a spouse and to produce some surviving offspring. Zaynab married Mustafa Shaykhbandar from another old ʿaskari family (see Chapter 1 for family biography). Khalil married Zaynab Hamawi, the daughter of a distinguished and wealthy merchant, Hasan Hamawi (see below). Khalil and Zaynab had four children, two daughters, ʿAysha and Asma, and two sons, Husayn and one whose name was not given in the sources and whose wife is not mentioned, although one son, Muhammad, is. ʿAysha married Muhammad Darwish Shaykhbandar, the son of her father's first cousin Zaynab Ghawri. Her sister married a man from another ʿaskari family, the Saʿid Agha. Husayn married Fatima Jaliq, the daughter of his great-grandmother's nephew. Husayn's son ʿAbd Allah married Sufya Shaykhbandar, his father's sister's daughter. Over five generations the Ghawris intermarried with two (possibly three) other ʿaskari families and with two merchant families; with two of these families there was more than one marriage connection. Two cousin marriages and one marriage with a slave woman also occurred.

Among the marriage connections of the Ghawri was the wealthy merchant family, the Hamawi.[76] The family was presumably from Hama, although little is known about them before the middle of the eighteenth century, by which time Hasan Hamawi (d. 1773) had made a fortune in the silk trade and manufacture of soap. He lived in Frafira and had built and endowed a neighborhood mosque there. He was married three times, all to women whose social origins are unknown, although two of them appear to have been slave women. He had a very large family of five boys and seven girls. Four of the females married Hamawi cousins. Two others married sons of Aleppo merchant families, the Jurbajis and Haykals. The seventh married into the Ghawri family, as indicated above. One of the five sons married a slave woman; another married a woman whose social origins are not indicated; and another's spouse is never mentioned. The other two sons married daughters of the same merchant families into which their sisters had married. Taha Hamawi married his brother-in-law's niece, ʿAysha Haykal. Ismaʿil and Hafsa Hamawi, brother and sister, married another brother and sister, Fatima and Ahmad Jurbaji. There is a less complete record of the marriages of the following generations. One cousin marriage took place between Muhammad Hamawi and his mother's brother's daughter Zalikha bint Taha. Several females of this generation married into other prominent merchant families, the Jaliqs, Ubris, and Muwaqqits. The two daughters of Mustafa Hamawi married into an ulema family, the Ikhlas. Amana bint Mustafa married twice, once to a man whose social background is not known and then to ʿUmar Ikhlas. Her sister, Ruqayya, married ʿUmar's son by his first wife, ʿAbd al-Kafi. The other spouses for this generation could not be identified. In the following generation, another marriage took place between the Hamawi and the Ikhlas families. The granddaughter of Ruqayya Hamawi and ʿAbd al-Kafi Ikhlas married Ruqayya's father's brother's grandson. At one time or another over four generations the Hamawi family made use of every marriage option available to them: cousins, people from other upper-class families, people of obscure social background, and slave women. Certain patterns, however, are clear. One was the importance of cousin marriage, although more so in the second generation than later. Second was a strategy of allying themselves through multiple ties of marriage with several other merchant families. They were connected to six different merchant families; with three of these there was more than one marriage. They also were connected to an important and wealthy ʿaskari family (Ghawri) and an ulema family (Tibi), so they did make some effort to expand their marriage networks beyond merchant families.

The Qudsi family traced its origin to Urfa, where it was known as the Halim Zade. It only became established in Aleppo in the last decades of the eighteenth century after Muhammad settled there and became a prominent religious official and political leader.[77] Muhammad himself married three women: one in Istanbul, where he had lived for a while and where he maintained close connections with high Ottoman officials; one in Aleppo who was the granddaughter of the sister of ʿUthman Pasha; and a third whose social background is unclear. In two of his three choices he married to connect himself to influential people in these cities. His sister, ʿAysha, married into the Kucuk Ali Agha family of Aleppo, a long-established ʿaskari family; she also married an official of the governor's household, although it is not clear which of these marriages came first. Muhammad's cousin Khadija apparently also settled into his household in Aleppo, and she married the son of ʿAbd al-Qadir Jabiri. Muhammad also had a brother, Mubarak. The name of Mubarak's wife (or wives) is never mentioned, but the marriages of two of his three children are known. His daughter, Manur, married her first cousin Zaki (Muhammad's son); she also married a son of Ismaʿil Shurayyif. One brother had two wives, one whose social background is unknown, the other from the prominent merchant family, the Hariris. One of Muhammad Qudsi's grandsons married a daughter of Nuʿman Shurayyif. Two others married daughters of Ottoman officials. While one cousin marriage did take place, Muhammad Qudsi and his family were clearly pursuing a strategy of forming connections with well-established families in Aleppo and maintaining connections with the Ottoman ruling class. They married other ulema families as well as ʿaskari and merchant families. As with the Ghawris and Hamawis, multiple marriage links were often forged with another family. Two Qudsi marriages were made with the Shurayyif family. In their choice of marriage partners, the Qudsis were connecting themselves to some of the most powerful families in the city.

Taken collectively, the marriages of these three families reflected patterns that are found in other families. Most families showed considerable diversity in their choice of spouses, combining endogamous and exogamous, intraclass and interclass marriages in different ways at different points in time. Two broad tendencies are apparent in their exogamous marriages, however. They pursued simultaneous strategies of using marriage to reinforce existing social and political ties and to widen their networks. These strategies become apparent in examining the relationship between marriage ties and ties created by occupation, interfamily relationships, neighborhood, social origins, and politics.

The high-status occupations in Aleppo—commerce, religion, and control of land—helped to define membership in the elite, as discussed in Chapter 1. Professional connections and common interests were important among those who shared the same occupation, but not to the exclusion of pursuing connections across occupational lines. Marriage patterns both reflected and reinforced these relationships. Almost all families married into some families who were associated with the same occupation and some who were not. Among the three occupational categories listed above, merchant families tended to intermarry more often than others. Like the Hamawi family above, other prominent merchant families (the Amiris, Qurnas, Ghannams, Jazmatis, Ubris, etc.) made marriage alliances with other merchant families more often than with any other occupational groups. However, except in the case of the Miri family, marriage connections among these merchant families were not made to the exclusion of other kinds of alliances. As with the Hamawis, marriages with ulema and ʿaskari families were important in diversifying their economic interests and consolidating their social position in the city.

Perhaps surprisingly, ulema families were less likely to intermarry with other ulema families than merchant families were to intermarry with other merchant families. They intermarried with ʿaskari and merchant families as often as with other ulema families. Only the Kurani family, believed by Tabbakh to be the oldest family in the city and closely associated with the law courts of Aleppo in the eighteenth and nineteenth centuries, married exclusively with other ulema families.[78] This presents an interesting contrast to some other Ottoman provincial cities, in which the upper ranks of the ulema appeared to form a virtually closed caste. In Damascus, ulema married almost exclusively other ulema, except for a limited number of merchant families who were considered distinguished enough to provide marriage partners. It was not until the middle of the nineteenth century, with the formation of an upper class of landowning ulema and Ottoman bureaucrats, that their marriage choices became more diverse.[79] Batatu noted a similar sense of caste in Iraqi cities like Mosul, but not in a more cosmopolitan city like Baghdad.[80] The fact that the ulema did not appear to share this sense of caste in Aleppo may be another indication of a more open and fluid society than in Damascus. ʿAskari families also married frequently into the other occupational groups. Over the years their integration into local society had been achieved partly through marriages with prominent local merchant and ulema families, and these patterns continued after their assimilation into local society.[81]

Neighborhood ties seem to have had little effect on marriage patterns. As mentioned in Chapter 2, families were often identified with specific quarters. Some families, or branches of families, resided in the same quarter over several generations, and links with other families long-resident in the quarter were undoubtedly important, but such ties did not seem to encourage marriage alliances among quarter residents. The Ghawri family and the Shaykhbandar family were both residents of Bayyada and they intermarried, but this was the exception rather than the rule. More often families were connected across quarter lines.

Renewing links with affinal relatives also appeared to be a consideration in choosing marriage partners. All three families discussed above had multiple marriage ties with at least one other family, and there were at least fifteen other families in which this was also evident. These marriages might take various forms, from an exchange of brides (the son and daughter in one family marrying a son and daughter in another) to two cousins marrying into different branches of the same family. Sometimes the tie would be renewed once a generation, just as there was one Shaykhbandar-Ghawri marriage in each of three generations. The Kawakibi family also exchanged marriage partners once a generation with the family of the Hanafi mufti of Antakya.[82] When this occurred, the marriages in later generations were simultaneously new links between families and cousin marriages. The number of families who were connected by more than one marriage is evidence that maintaining and renewing such ties were important considerations. On the other hand, marriage ties did not separate these families into isolated kinship clusters. A few families did not intermarry regularly to the exclusion of other families, with the exception of the Trabulsi and Shukri families, who married only each other. Multiple marriage ties among families were not uncommon, but did not preclude alliances with a diversity of other families.

Marriage choices also did not create a distinction between long-established and "parvenu" families in this period of fairly rapid restructuring of the elite. For relative newcomers to Aleppo, the advantages of marrying into old and established families is obvious. Ibrahim Pasha, who acquired power and fortune through his patron Muhammad Taha, was able to marry one of his sons to a daughter of Hasan Kawakibi, head of one of the oldest and most distinguished ulema families of the city. The Qudsi family, discussed above, formed marriage connections with two families that traced their ancestors well back into the seventeenth century, the Yakins and the Kucuk Ali Aghas. For the newcomers, these marriages were part of their process of assimilation into local society. But there were advantages for the older families as well. The Ibrahim Pasha family was very wealthy, held major offices in Aleppo, and had important connections in Istanbul. The Qudsi family also owed much of its prominence to good connections in Istanbul. These factors would have benefited the local families with whom they were connected by marriage. Other marriages gave access to new sources of wealth, as Khalil Ghawri gained through his marriage to Zaynab Hamawi, a daughter of the wealthy Hamawi merchant family. A daughter of Abu Su'ud Kawakibi married 'Abd al-Rahman Muwaqqit, an up-and-coming merchant who was the wealthiest Muslim merchant in Aleppo by the 1830s, according to John

Bowring.[83] Analysis of virtually all of these marriage alliances would show a similar exchange of benefits between old and new families.

Despite the undoubted importance of these alliances, not all marriages outside the family were made within the group of notable families. A significant number of marriages (29 percent) were contracted with individuals whose social origins and background are more obscure. Since the social backgrounds of many of the non-zade marriage partners are not known, it is difficult to analyze the factors that led to these marriages in the majority of cases. Common place of origin, past family ties, economic partnerships, and patronage relationships probably influenced these choices. Where some identification of individuals is possible, it is clear that, whatever the past connections, many such marriages meant access to new sources of wealth and power for the families involved. Several of the individuals who married into these families held important offices in the city. One of the daughters of the Ubri family married the *wazzan al-harir,* an official involved in the regulation of the silk trade. He would have been not only a man of wealth but also a powerful figure in the commercial life of the city.[84] As merchants of some importance in the city, the Ubri family's economic activities would have been facilitated by this connection. Later on, ʿAbd al-Hamid Jabiri married a daughter of the holder of this office.[85] Some connections were also established with Ottoman officials assigned to the city. This connection would have provided these families with additional access to political power. The sister of Muhammad Qudsi (see above) married the seal bearer in the governor's household at the end of the eighteenth century, as did another Ubri in the 1770s.[86] In return, the individuals who married into these notable families received status and influence in local society. In other words, these marriages provided advantages for both the family and the person with whom the marriage was contracted. For the former, it allowed the assimilation of "new blood," which often brought decided advantages to the family and important new connections. For the latter, it was a means of upward mobility and integration into the local elite.

Such marriages could also extend family networks spatially. Some of these marriages were made with provincial families, either creating new ties or renewing old ones, and formed an important link between the city and the countryside. Khalil Jazmati, for example, married a daughter of a sheikh of Bab, an important town located twenty-three kilometers to the northeast of Aleppo. Her dowry included considerable land in that town, which the Jazmati family controlled throughout the period. The link to Bab was renewed in the next generation when one of Khalil's daughters, Layla, married a man from Bab.[87] The Kawakibi family had ties with Antioch, another important provincial town, through several marriages with the family of that town's mufti.[88] As is apparent from these marriages, marriage was not confined to the family or to other families in the class, and as a result, it provided the chance for new people to be assimilated into the class and for kinship ties to be widely extended.

As with cousin marriage, there was a significant difference between rates of marriage of men and women outside the group. Thirty-six percent of the men chose non-zade women, while only 16 percent of the women were married to men who were not cousins or not from another upper-class family. Equality of status was apparently important in marriage of daughters for these Aleppo families, while marriages of sons were often used to extend kinship ties beyond the social group. This was not always the case in other parts of the Ottoman Empire. Carter Findley has noted that, although members of the ruling class often sought to link themselves with families of equal status, "there are signs indicating that inequality of status rather than equality was also sometimes sought between partners to marriage."[89] He noted in particular the "son-in-law" phenomenon, found in the sultan's household and copied by other grandees. A daughter of the household would be married to an up-and-coming man of talent and usefulness whose social background was inferior. This provided a way of recruiting new talent into the household, expanding its size and connections, and tying the young man more firmly to his patron.[90] This phenomenon was not unknown in Aleppo, as discussed earlier. The founder of the Jabiri family, for example, was a man of obscure social origins who married the daughter of an Ottoman qadi. Her greater prestige was reflected in the fact that it was her father's name that became the basis of the family name.[91] Nevertheless, this pattern seems to have been less common in Aleppo relative to Istanbul.

The decisions made about marriage by each family were undoubtedly influenced by circumstances unique to that family: whether they were still climbing the social ladder or trying to avoid downward mobility in the face of adverse political or economic circumstances; whether they wanted to avoid the political entanglements of the time or were eager to forge new political links and gain greater power in hopes of taking advantage of an unsettled situation; whether they wanted to consolidate their hold over existing resources or wanted to diversify their economic

base. Collectively, these decisions about marriage reinforced existing social ties and forged new ones to integrate these families into a more or
less cohesive group. Any one family might be related by marriage to as
few as two to as many as nine other families. Through those marriages
they would in turn be connected with still other families. The Hamawis,
for example, had formed alliances with six other families. Through these
six families they were connected to eleven others, some of whom were
related to each other. Most of these families were connected directly or
indirectly with numerous others. These connections were undoubtedly
important in shaping a sense of group identity and helped to define the
boundaries of the group. This is not to deny the permeability of social
boundaries. Marriages outside the family group indicate the importance
of vertical ties and show that marriage still provided a means of social
mobility.

Nor can we deny that rivalries and feuds among these families did occur, such as existed between the Shurayyif and Ibrahim Pasha families,
with deadly consequences for both (see Chapter 1). Bodman describes
the internecine struggles over leadership of the ashraf faction between
Muhammad Taha and the Kawakibis and later between Muhammad
Qudsi and the Jabiris, struggles that could be as bitter as those between
the ashraf and the Janissaries.[92] Other rivalries, often over the appoint-
ment to important local offices, caused tensions among families like the
Khankarli and the Taha. Yet such rivalries did not preclude all social connections, including marriages. 'Abd al-Qadir Jabiri was very involved
in the political struggles of the time and was a rival of Muhammad
Qudsi. Yet his son Muhammad married Muhammad Qudsi's first cousin
Khadija.[93] Marriages also followed political alliances, but cases such as the
Jabiri-Qudsi connection suggest that marriage was also used to keep political rivalries from becoming too disruptive to the social order. Julie
Oehler argues that in Iran during the nineteenth century, in the midst of
intense competition among the Bakhtiyari khans for wealth and power,
"marriage ties became even more important for keeping peace among
families."[94] Some marriage connections in Aleppo may have worked that
way as well. In the final analysis, despite rivalries among the notables and
ties to other groups, the result of these marriage alliances was a group of
families linked together by a complicated network of family connections.

That exogamous, rather than endogamous, marriages were more frequent among Aleppo's upper-class families has important implications not
only for social structure but also for the nature of the kinship system. The

strong ideological and legal emphasis on patrilineal ties would seem to downplay the importance of ties created by marriage. However, since marriages were made for the purpose of establishing beneficial connections, it follows that these families had a strong interest in cultivating and strengthening the ties created by marriages. Sometimes this did not happen. Death, or less often divorce, would terminate the marriage before such ties between families would be cemented. In most cases, however, achieving the benefits of such alliances required maintaining them over the long run. More than one marriage between families, common economic interests through jointly owned property and as beneficiaries of endowments, and long-term political alliances among related families reflect the enduring nature of these connections among families over several generations.

Close ties among families related by marriage therefore meant that maternal kin as well as paternal kin played an important role in family life. Anthropologists and historians have noted a variety of roles that maternal kin have played in Middle Eastern societies. Ties linking the mother's brother with his nieces and nephews were often particularly strong. Ties of affection, growing out of the strong relationship between sister and brother, were often more freely expressed than those with parents. Goitein discussed the close and affectionate relationship between brother and sister in medieval Fustat.[95] The brother maintained the role of protector often long after his sister's marriage. Sisters, particularly if they happened to make good marriages, would lend a helping hand to their brothers. Protecting his sister would carry over to her children. An uncle would often help his nephew get launched in a career. The maternal uncle often became confidant as well. Peters has noted that the mother's brother was the one who could talk to his nephew about sex and marriage, topics that were taboo between father and son. The uncle could also intervene on his nephew's behalf in deciding on a marriage partner.[96]

Maternal kin played a variety of roles in Ottoman Aleppo, sometimes assuming roles that one would expect to go to paternal relatives. Maternal kin not infrequently served as guardians and executors for minor children. Mothers and paternal grandmothers often served as *wasis* (guardians) for minors; if neither of these was appointed, the mother's sister was most often chosen, and maternal grandmothers and aunts also undertook this role.[97] Maternal kin also frequently served as *wakils*, agents who would represent the interests of an individual in a variety of legal matters and who were viewed as individuals who could be trusted to do so.

Women in particular frequently chose maternal uncles or sister's sons to serve in this role. Maternal relatives also occasionally served as mentors and took over the education of children, especially in cases in which the father had died, as happened in the Kayyali family.[98] As a result of the roles that maternal kin played, of marriages among maternal cousins, and of economic ties among affines created by inheritance and endowment, these kinship ties remained active and vital. They had the effect of creating a bilateral kinship system.

CONCLUSION

The relationship between husband and wife in Aleppo was a complex one whose strength is difficult to assess, given the limited sources for the period. Certain factors undoubtedly underscored a tenuousness to these ties—the separate social worlds of men and women, real prospects of early death of a spouse, the lack of economic partnership, the threat of polygyny and divorce. Other factors, however, created a strong bond that was difficult to break. The most important of these was the key role of marriage in reinforcing connections within the family and cementing alliances between families. As a result, most upper-class marriages were relatively durable, as long as both spouses survived. Divorce was rare, and polygyny, which might threaten these alliances, was not widespread. This meant relative security for women in these marriages and had implications for their role in their husbands' households. As the link between families, a woman had some leverage to ease her way, prevent abuses, and eventually work her way into a position of some authority within the household. On the other hand, women had fewer options when marriage partners were selected, which probably meant that many more women than men never married or never remarried, once widowed or divorced. While there is less information generally on the marriage of women, it is not clear whether this simply reflects an accident of the sources or the fact that many more women never married or remained married for a very short time.

The choices of marriage partners made by these families reflected the variety of social goals that marriages helped to achieve and the diverse options open to them. The cumulative effect of their choices, however, highlight certain aspects of family and social structure and of the gender system in early modern Aleppo. Endogamous marriages showed a clear preference for choosing close kin as spouses, when kin were chosen at all. As in the formation of households, the family ties that were nurtured were those within the narrowly extended family. The kinship system was also more bilateral than often acknowledged. Patrilineal ties were important, but the very nature of marriage as social strategy and social alliance made ties among people related by marriage significant for the family. Finally, the interweaving lines of marriage among families of wealth, influence, and high status were vital in determining the sense of identity and boundaries of this social group and were part of a process of class formation that would accelerate in the late nineteenth century.

Four

INHERITANCE
AND FAMILY
STRUCTURE

Of the many decisions, large and small, that families confronted, none were as important as those surrounding the transfer of wealth from one generation to the next. These decisions affected the breakup of households, the choice of marriage partners, and the economic exchange in marriage. The breakup of the household and the division of property were closely linked, although not the same process; the point at which household fission occurred was probably determined largely by the exigencies surrounding the devolution of wealth. This was particularly true among the elite, for whom considerable resources were often involved and successful management of this transition was necessary not only to continue to enjoy a certain standard of living but also to preserve or enhance the family's status and influence. The potential for conflict between generations was great, as the younger generation wanted to obtain a share of family resources as soon as possible and the older generation resisted efforts to limit its control over the family patrimony. Similarly, potential conflict existed among those who had expectations of receiving part of this wealth and wanted to maximize their share. The strains of making such decisions were undoubtedly intensified in times of economic uncertainty and political upheaval, such as characterized late-eighteenth- and early-nineteenth-century Aleppo.

Passing on the family patrimony to the next generation could take a number of forms, including inheritance, endowments, and premortem transfers through the mahr, property sales, and gifts of cash and valuable goods. The relative importance of these different ways of transferring wealth varied historically. David Powers has argued that "[i]n pre-

modern times the application of the Islamic law of inheritance was often
the last and least important stage in the process."[1] This was not the case
in eighteenth- and nineteenth-century Aleppo, however. All these different strategies were used, but inheritance as proscribed by law was important. This chapter will focus on devolution through the mechanism of
the Islamic inheritance system.

In designating which family members had inheritance rights, the
shari'a (Islamic law) was in effect demarcating the boundaries of the family in the eyes of the law. Regardless of the existence or absence of other
economic links among family members, they were tied together through
their common legal rights as heirs or heirs apparent and their joint interests in the resources involved. The significance of these legal rights, the
ties created by them, and their impact on family structure depended,
however, on how inheritances were settled in practice, not on a legal ab-
straction. The ensuing discussion will elaborate on the Islamic inheritance system, which included not only legal texts but also the role of the
courts and judges in interpreting and applying the law; the actual practice of inheritance; and the ways in which the practice of inheritance
shaped family structure. Particular attention will be paid to two aspects of
inheritance that were critical in this regard—the partible nature of the
system and the entitlement of women—and how these affected family
boundaries and the distribution of economic resources by gender.

ISLAMIC LAW OF INHERITANCE

The way in which the Islamic legal system in
general, and the law of inheritance in particular, historically shaped family structure among Muslims was not a simple one. The shari'a is very detailed and specific on family matters, especially inheritance. Because of
the central place of family law in the Islamic legal system as a whole, there
has been a tendency on the part of Western scholars to understand the relationship between theory and practice of family law as falling at one of
two extremes. One view assumes that family structure mirrored family
law. This view—that law serves as a guide to practice—originated in
eighteenth-century notions that "laws, well ordered and well classified
statements, best describe the relations of men in society."[2] Even as views
of the relationship between law and society in the Islamic world became
more sophisticated in other respects, the view persisted that what the law

said about the family was the reality, as though one could understand family structure simply by reading legal texts. This idea was particularly prevalent in any historical discussion of the family, where the abundance of legal texts and lack of other kinds of evidence on family life made it more plausible.[3] It also reflected a view of the law as only a legal text, not as a system that included not only the texts but also the various legal institutions and practices through which the law was interpreted and applied.[4] At the other extreme was the assumption that Islamic law was ignored completely in favor of customary law. When evidence did appear that some groups did not follow the shari‘a, it was taken to mean that Islamic law was considered irrelevant by that particular group.

Neither extreme accurately reflects the complex nature of the relationship between law and practice. In regions where a hierarchy of Islamic courts and judicial and legal officials stood ready to enforce Islamic law, and the population made frequent use of them (e.g., urban areas in the Ottoman Empire), the application of the law always involved a process of interpretation. Numerous variables could intervene to make the actual settlement of an estate, for example, quite different from what the legal text might seem to suggest. On the other hand, even in areas remote from central authority, where customary law would seem to reign supreme, the shari‘a was rarely ignored completely. In many pastoral societies, women were denied the right to inheritance, but they received other rights in lieu of that, an implicit acknowledgment that they had a claim on the family patrimony.[5]

Before exploring the relationship between the theory and practice of inheritance and between inheritance and family structure in Ottoman Aleppo, some general remarks about the nature of Islamic family law and its origins, with special reference to the laws of inheritance, are in order.

In Islamic law, the family is patriarchal and patrilineal. The law awards ultimate authority to the male over the female. Descent is traced through the male line, and the close association of male agnates is reflected in the inheritance system that identified them as part of the "inner family." "The family group knitted together by the web of social rights and obligations was the extended agnatic family of males linked together through males to a common ancestor."[6] Legally, however, the patriarchal nature of the family was not absolute. The spread of Islam in the seventh century had been accompanied by a social revolution that undercut the tribal foundation of society. In place of the tribe was a community of believers. A key element in this revolution was the replacement of tribal inheritance customs by new rules outlined in the Koran.[7] Wives, daughters, mothers, and some maternal relatives were allowed to inherit, and women were given some rights in marriage, guardianship of children, and property, thus softening the impact of male dominance and raising the status of women. Under Islamic law, the power of the male was both upheld and limited—he was not free to act completely at will.[8]

Islamic inheritance law, as it emerged in the early years of the Islamic state, provided for all heirs through a carefully spelled out system of entitlement. So detailed are the codes outlining the transmission of wealth that the Islamic inheritance system is sometimes called the "science of shares" (fara'id). Islamic law recognizes two categories of legal heirs: (1) all male agnates and (2) heirs specifically designated by the Koran.[9] Heirs were ranked according to class and assigned fixed shares. All sons got the same amount, the largest share. Daughters received half of what sons received. Spouses and parents each got a smaller share. All Koranic heirs and male agnates were equally entitled to a share in the deceased's estate, and all were considered part of the "inner family." However, when the estate was actually distributed, Koranic heirs took their allotted portions first. Male agnates got the residue to divide among themselves in appropriate proportions. Even the Koranic heirs, however, did not all necessarily inherit. Only the primary heirs—spouse(s), children, and parents—were never excluded by other relatives. After these heirs came the secondary heirs: brothers and sisters and male agnates ranked according to class, the former taking precedence over the latter.[10] There was also a provision for bequests. A person was allowed to leave up to one-third of his or her estate at will. However, this third could not be left to someone already legally defined as an heir and so could not be used to give Koranic heirs more than their fair share. Islamic inheritance, then, was an apparently rigid partible system, one that left little freedom of choice to the individual over devolution of property.

The inflexibility of the Islamic inheritance laws was, however, more apparent than real. When one moves from the law as text to the law as it was interpreted by the muftis and qadis and put into practice in a given historical context, the flexibility and adaptability of the inheritance system become clear. An examination of inheritance practices among the notables of Aleppo can shed light on the nature of the inheritance system, the relationship between law and practice, and the sources of this flexibility.

PARTIBLE INHERITANCE

Inheritance systems are classified as partible and impartible, and the two systems are assumed to have different purposes and consequences. Partible inheritance may be more equitable and better for the heirs in that sense; impartible is better for the property. These assumptions have informed much of the discussion about inheritance in the Middle East. As a partible system, Islamic law was seen as a threat to economic production. If applied to agricultural and grazing lands, it would result in fragmentation of the land, and this fragmentation would only grow worse with each succeeding generation.[11] At the level of individual peasant families, this would result in the inability to make a living. From the point of view of the state, the threats to production would mean a decrease in state revenues. While partible inheritance was less ruinous when other kinds of economic resources were involved (e.g., cash, household goods, urban real estate), its implementation could still be economically damaging. For example, in families whose wealth derived from commerce, the distribution of accumulated capital among many heirs could make continued commercial undertakings impossible, especially in the absence of other institutions through which capital could be accumulated. A number of developments in Middle Eastern history are seen as responses to the need to avoid the harmful consequences of partible inheritance. The widespread emergence of state ownership of land, especially in the heyday of large bureaucratic states like the Ottoman Empire, was one such development.[12] State-appointed officials or local notables would have rights to collect revenues from the land; peasants would have tenancy rights. Tenancy rights, and sometimes revenue rights, could be inherited. The land itself, however, was not subject to Islamic inheritance laws because it was state-owned. Another way of avoiding the negative consequences of this partible system was to ignore it and use customary law. This option was used particularly in cases involving pastoral lands or in more remote agricultural regions where state control was less effective.[13]

Despite the problems that can result from partible inheritance, it does not follow that a partible system of inheritance by its very nature has negative economic consequences. Some village communities in the Middle East did practice partible inheritance without suffering economic hardship.[14] Whether or not partible inheritance had negative economic con-

sequences depended on the type and availability of resources and the relationship between population size, family size, and resources. The problem faced by many families in the past was not too many heirs, but too
few. Under these circumstances, land fragmentation was not a problem
because property was divided among at most a couple of heirs. Even if
demographic constraints did not sharply limit population, the availability
of land or other economic opportunities could offset the potentially
negative effects of fragmentation. For example, land was abundant in
parts of the Ottoman Empire in the nineteenth century. As land was divided equally among sons in each generation, each son was able to rent
or buy additional land to make his share viable. Alan Duben has argued
that the equalizing of wealth in this type of inheritance was an important
safety valve for rural society.[15]

A partible system of inheritance, then, was economically viable under
many circumstances and served other social purposes as well. Moreover,
it was a highly flexible system for settling inheritances. In discussing inheritance among peasant communities in early modern Europe, Lutz
Berkner has argued that inheritance settlements were always circumstantial, regardless of how the inheritance system was classified, and that the
actual settlement of inheritance fell somewhere on a continuum from
strict impartibility to strictly equal partibility. Where it fell on the continuum had less to do with inheritance law as such than it did with other
conditions.

> *Inheritance laws require that the family property be dis-
> tributed in certain proportions. But they rarely deter-
> mine the form of settlement, which depends on the land
> tenure, the peasant customs, or economic conditions.*[16]

As long as the law did not mandate that land be divided, partible inheritance systems allowed families to develop appropriate ways of dividing
wealth in light of economic and demographic circumstances, family
goals, and family size and resources, without breaking the law.[17] Partible
inheritance was basically a system that could accommodate changing
family circumstances and changing historical circumstances. An examination of how upper-class Aleppo families handled the transmission of
property from one generation to another demonstrates the flexibility of
the Islamic system of partible inheritance.

Elite families at all times were presented with a dilemma when faced

with decisions about the transmission of family resources from one generation to another. On the one hand, these families, concerned about
holding on to wealth, status, and political influence, were often anxious
to realize the economic benefits of an undivided patrimony. On the other
hand, they were interested in providing for all family members.[18] These
contradictory goals required a delicate balancing act, one dependent on
the careful management of family resources. For upper-class Aleppo
families in the late eighteenth and early nineteenth centuries, difficult
decisions about the transmission of property were further complicated
by major challenges and threats to the economic security of upper-class
families. As previously discussed, this was a period of intense competition
for increasingly scarce resources, as trade declined and agriculture stag-
nated. At the same time, new economic opportunities were appearing.
With the decline in central government authority, the possibility of getting tighter control of rural resources existed. So did opportunities to invest in productive land in the vicinity of Aleppo and other provincial
towns and in proto-industrial enterprises like soap factories. As trade
with Europe revived after 1830 and the first steps toward modernization
were taken by the Ottoman government, people who invested in these
areas were in a good position to take advantage of the economic
changes.[19] How families dealt with the transmission of property from one
generation to the next could have major consequences for their success
in dealing with the contradictory economic forces to which they were
exposed and for holding on to family wealth.

In their decisions about inheritance matters, these families took advantage of the partible inheritance law as well as two other aspects of the
Islamic inheritance system. First, there was no specific requirement about
when the division of inheritance had to take place. The timing of the distribution was determined by the heirs; either by all of them collectively
or by one heir who would put forward a claim to his or her share. At that
point, the entire estate might be divided up or only some resources re-
leased to honor that claim. Second, there was no requirement about the
kind of property that went to each heir. With the flexibility inherent in
the law, families were able to develop strategies that were appropriate for
their circumstances. This left families and individuals free to determine
how to handle the devolution of property without violating the law. It allowed them to balance the conflicting claims of preserving wealth and
status with the legal requirement that wealth be divided equitably and
provision made for all family members. We cannot know from existing

sources the specific motivations for any given decision about inheritance, but it is possible to see patterns in their choices that suggest connections between individual family circumstances and the way inheritance was managed.

Three different patterns were used to transmit wealth via Islamic inheritance to other family members after someone's death. The first was a straightforward division of all property—real estate, capital, and other liquid assets—among the heirs in the proscribed shares, relatively soon after the death of the legator. A variation on this pattern occurred when the original inheritance settlement was followed by a series of property sales among the heirs, in effect redistributing the property among them. The second strategy was the distribution among the legal heirs of all assets except debts owed to the deceased and real estate, again relatively soon after death. The third pattern involved leaving all or most of the estate undivided for long periods of time, from five to as many as thirty years. In some cases, liquid assets and perhaps some real estate were divided, but the bulk of the estate remained undivided. Closer examination of these patterns can suggest how often they were used, what family circumstances seemed to influence their choice, and why they would make effective inheritance strategies.

The first pattern, a straightforward division of assets following inheritance law, was common in Aleppo among all classes, including members of the notable families. Most estates were small, even those of individuals from well-to-do families. Even when the total resources of the family were very extensive, the personal fortunes of family members were often fairly meager. A man who predeceased his father, the head of the family, would have had little wealth of his own, unless he had been in a position to accumulate wealth independently of his father. The Hasabi family provides a good illustration of this point. 'Abd al-Qadir Hasabi died in 1826, leaving a fortune valued at almost 60,000 qurush. One son, Ahmad, had already accumulated a larger fortune of his own through moneylending and control of the grain trade. 'Abd al-Qadir's other son, As'ad, who had died shortly before his father, left only 172 qurush in cash to be divided among his wife, two young children, and father.[20] Similarly, many women, especially unmarried women, would have had relatively little property unless they were only daughters or there was only one son. This first pattern, then, was usually followed when estates were small. When estates were fairly modest, there was not enough wealth at stake to make their distribution other than routine.

A straightforward division of property was also not uncommon, even when larger estates were involved, if there were relatively few heirs. Family inheritance strategies were directly related to rates of reproduction and mortality. As discussed in Chapter 2, the average number of offspring among upper-class families was only 3.6.[21] Consequently, most people had relatively few heirs, despite the fact that other relatives besides children did inherit. The average number of heirs for a man from one of these families was 5.4 and for a woman, 3.2. When the estate was large and the number of heirs relatively small, the estate could be distributed among the heirs easily. The estate of Muhammad Qamari, a merchant from the quarter of Bahsita who owned considerable commercial property in and around the madina, illustrates this point. In 1786 his heirs divided his property, which included some capital as well as many shops and warehouses. Each of his heirs—his wife, two sons and two daughters—got several pieces of property and a cash sum relative to their entitlement under the inheritance system.[22] With such a large amount of real estate, each heir was able to get his or her share in whole pieces, without having to subdivide real property into shares. The large size of the total estate and the small number of heirs alleviated concerns about how to distribute property, how to avoid fragmentation, and how to ensure that each heir received an adequate inheritance.

The distribution of assets among heirs was not always the final step in the transmission of this wealth to the legatees. In some cases, the original settlement of the estate was followed by redistribution of assets among the heirs, primarily visible in extensive sales among them. This usually occurred when real estate made up an important share of the wealth and when the original division of this real estate had resulted in each heir owning partial shares in several pieces of property. As was evident in the court records, these complex arrangements often led to lawsuits and confusion over ownership rights, especially after the deaths of the original heirs. To avoid such a situation, sales among heirs redistributed shares in a way that reduced fragmentation and joint ownership. When completed, they resulted in the various heirs owning whole pieces of property or at least larger shares of fewer properties. Some heirs might even sell all their shares in exchange for cash. The assets each heir acquired were not substantially different in total value than his or her entitlement through inheritance, but the form of these assets changed.

This strategy was likely to be used if there were many heirs among whom the real estate was to be divided and if these heirs were not mem-

bers of the immediate family and not sharing a household. The settlement
of the estate of Ahmad Tabbakh offers a good illustration of this situation.
Ahmad's estate was settled in 1795 at the request of his son's widow. In
addition to the widow and her three children, the heirs were Ahmad's
other son and three daughters and his nephew (son of another brother).
His estate was extensive. It included not only the family home but also
several smaller houses and ten commercial properties. Ahmad's surviving
son received seven qirats (a qirat is one-twenty-fourth share of a property) from the family house and a four and four-fifths qirat share of the
rest of the property. The three daughters each got one and one-fifth
qirats of the family home and a one and three-fifths share of the rest. The
nephew received a three-qirat share of the family home and a one and
four-fifths share from the rest. The other son's widow and her children
received ten and one-fifth qirats of the house and a twelve and three-fifths
qirat share of the rest.[23] In the following year, a series of sales occurred in
which the widow and her children sold some shares of this property to
other heirs in exchange for other shares. It was a process of separating her
economic interests from those of her in-laws; it is likely also that she was
living in another household and was thus motivated to claim her share of
the inheritance.

Sales of real estate among heirs after settlement of an estate sometimes
followed a different pattern. One heir would "buy out" the other heirs
and in effect reconstitute the family patrimony as his own. This happened
when the person wanted to invest in real estate, often when consolidating fortune and position or in preparation for setting up a waqf. This
could only happen, of course, when one heir could afford to buy out the
others. An ambitious man on the rise could accumulate considerable
capital independently of the other members of the family, usually through
moneylending, tax farming, and investment in lucrative commercial
deals. His personal fortune allowed him to "buy out" his father's other
heirs. Hasan Kawakibi, a wealthy religious leader from one of the oldest
and most important families in the city, inherited a fourth of his father's
real estate in 1788. By 1805 he had bought up most of the rest from the
other heirs and incorporated it into two large religious endowments.[24]
When such "buy-outs" occurred, they often coincided with a sharp differentiation in wealth and even status among different branches of the lineage. Hasan's ambitions were centered largely around his own immediate
family. As he became wealthier and more powerful, the other branch of
the Kawakibi lineage remained insignificant.

In sum, many inheritance settlements took place within a relatively short time after the death of the legator, with all assets distributed among the heirs according to their entitlement under Islamic law. Such a pattern was usually followed when inheritances were small or when an inheritance was large but there were few heirs. In some cases, real estate was redistributed among heirs through sales to avoid fragmentation or joint ownership, or one heir consolidated ownership in his hands by buying out the other heirs.

Many families chose the second pattern, deciding not to divide up the real estate and/or any debts still owed to the deceased when other assets were divided. Among upper-class families, this happened more often than not when real estate and debts made up a sizable part of the estate, regardless of its total size. The sequence and timing of the distribution of Yusif Jabiri's estate provide an example of this. Yusif Jabiri died in 1819, leaving an estate valued at 28,870 qurush, the majority of which was in real estate. In 1820 a cash sum of 2,363 qurush (this was the value of the estate minus the real estate, debts owed to Yusif, and a few expenses that had to be paid out of the estate) was distributed among his heirs: his wife, mother, two grown sons, and two minor children, a son and a daughter. In the following year, his real estate, with the exception of the family residence, was also divided up. The sources do not explain why the distribution of the property took place at this time, although two factors probably explain this. Sharaf Jabiri, Yusif's mother, created a waqf out of her one-sixth share of the real estate, so she needed to claim her share of the property. Moreover, Yusif's daughter had died in the meanwhile, and the resulting need to reallocate the estate may have prompted this decision.[25] The reasons for the delay in dividing up debts and real estate were probably closely connected to advantages to the family as a whole, although the exact timing and nature of the distribution varied. The year that separated the two stages of settling Yusif Jabiri's estate was probably unusual; in most cases, real estate and debts remained undivided for a longer period. Debts could not always be collected quickly, either because the debtor could not afford to pay the debt or because the lender had made specific arrangements for payment of the debt that could not be overturned. Moreover, long-term debts were potentially a sound financial investment. Although taking interest, or at least undue interest, was prohibited by law, those who lent money often did collect interest on it. In addition, even if there was no direct financial gain, holding someone's note was a source of power. The delay in dividing real estate was more closely linked to family status and circumstances. Real estate was often the largest single asset of a family, and in symbolic and economic terms, it represented the principal share of the family patrimony. Keeping the real estate intact avoided its fragmentation among many heirs and the problems associated with managing joint property. The strains put on family relationships when many heirs owned shares in real estate were evident in the many court cases that involved disputes over jointly owned property created by inheritance.

The advantage of a pattern in which wealth was passed to heirs in stages was that it allowed the heirs to have access to some of the wealth they were due to inherit and at the same time to maintain some of the family patrimony intact. More specifically, the delay in dividing up real estate appeared to have been connected to the continuation of the joint household and the presence of minor children (see Chapter 2). When children were among the heirs to an estate, having most of the estate intact may have made taking care of the needs of the children during their minority easier. Even if no minor children were involved, as long as the household did not break up, maintaining a joint patrimony that would support the household made financial sense and may have been a financial necessity. So the final distribution of inheritance and the breakup of the joint household appear to have been closely connected. The need of one or more heirs, as in the case of Sharaf Jabiri, to claim his or her share determined when this distribution would occur.

Yet another option available for managing the devolution of wealth was to delay the distribution of property indefinitely. All the patterns of inheritance settlements discussed above assume that property was passed from one generation to the next relatively soon after the deceased's death. Some estates, however, were not divided until many years after the death of the original legator, sometimes as long as thirty years, by which time most of the original heirs were dead. In effect, this was a way to maintain an undivided patrimony. A few of the heirs may have been "paid off," especially if their shares were not large and they did not remain in the household, as might have been true for some widows. Martha Mundy found what she calls "undivided associations" to be quite common among well-to-do landowners in Yemen. "At the base of many complex and wealthy households was the refusal of a powerful man to divide the joint family patrimony." [26] Politically ambitious men consolidated control of family labor and property at some point in their careers and resisted any attempt to divide family resources. Similarly in Aleppo, a pat-

tern of joint ownership and exploitation of resources—both those inherited from their father and those they had acquired for themselves—was
found among many of those men who figured most prominently in
Aleppo politics. The heirs of Ahmad Jabiri, ʿAbd al-Rahman Shurayyif,
Ahmad Kawakibi, ʿAbd al-Qadir Hasabi, and ʿUmar Taha all maintained
these joint associations for long periods of time. In every case, the most
prominent male or males in the family—Mustafa Jabiri and his sons,
ʿAbd Allah and ʿAbd al-Qadir; the Shurayyif brothers, Ismaʿil and
Nuʿman, sons of ʿAbd al-Rahman; Ahmad Kawakibi's son Hasan; or
ʿUmar Taha's son Fayd Allah; and ʿAbd al-Qadir Hasabi's son Ahmad—
were major political figures. The advantages of such undivided association included a larger pool of readily available resources, the presence of
kinsmen to support their political causes, and the status of maintaining a
large household. However, these were not the only circumstances under
which there might be a long delay in the distribution of wealth. A number of wealthy merchant families also maintained these undivided patri-
monies. It was also the strategy used by the heirs of ʿAbd Allah Miri, a
wealthy merchant who died in 1769 but whose estate was not distributed
among his heirs until 1799, at the request of his daughter's family, who
put in a claim for their share of the estate. The reasons for the delay in
this case are less obvious. It may have been that this was a strategy adopted
by merchant families as well to preserve and ensure the accumulation of
capital for their enterprises, a connection that is also suggested by the fact
that the heirs of Salih Qurna, another wealthy merchant, also followed
this pattern. In the Miri case, it may also have been affected by the fact
that ʿAbd Allah died with a heavy burden of debt and this joint association may have been the best way of protecting the financial well-being of
the family. The Miris were also a very tight-knit family; they apparently
maintained a joint household throughout this time, and cousin marriages
were common both before and during the time that they maintained the
undivided patrimony (see Chapters 2 and 3).

　　These different strategies, all of which were fully compatible with the
law, illustrate the flexibility provided by the way in which that law was
interpreted and executed. What particular strategy a family used depended on the type of resources and amount of wealth it had, as well as
the size of the family and rates of reproduction, its position within the social hierarchy, and the ambitions of its members. It is also clear that inheritance strategies and household patterns were closely linked. Maintaining an undivided patrimony meant that family members remained

economically dependent on the household head and were not in a position to set up their own households. In these circumstances, pressure
could be applied on them not to claim their inheritance. The inheritance
strategy chosen had a long-term impact on family structure and the control of family wealth. This point will be considered further in the last section of the chapter.

WOMEN AND INHERITANCE

Much of the literature on Islamic inheritance
has focused on women as heirs. Islamic law gives rights of inheritance to
daughters, wives, mothers, and sometimes sisters; whether women realized these rights has been a point of much discussion and debate. Since
women could marry outside the family and would therefore take their
shares with them, honoring their inheritance rights ran the risk of alien-
ating the property. If they did inherit, under what conditions and what
did it mean for women?

As the extensive literature on the issue of female inheritance has
shown, there are no simple answers to these questions. Whether or not
a women inherited depended on where she lived and the social group
to which she belonged. Inheritance patterns differed significantly among
urban dwellers, peasants, and pastoralists.[27] Even within these different
groups, however, inheritance practices with regard to women could vary
in important ways. In most pastoral communities, customary law was in-
voked, Islamic law was ignored, and women were excluded from inheritance entirely. Among the Bedouin of Cyrenica, for example, property
ownership was vested in the corporate group of male agnates. Allowing
women to inherit risked fragmentation and alienation of herds and grazing lands, especially since more than half of all women married outside
the group.[28] Women of the Shiuk, a settled property-owning lineage in
southeastern Turkey, could inherit, but only in the absence of brothers.
Their shares of the property then passed to their sons.[29] In village communities, women sometimes inherited and sometimes did not. In a
Lebanese Shiʿa village, women of both upper and lower class inherited.
However, because upper-class women inherited property, their choice of
marriage partners was restricted; they had to marry within the land association.[30] In other cases, women were permitted to inherit certain kinds
of wealth, but denied access to land. In such cases, the letter of the law

was being observed, since Islamic law mandates female inheritance but
does not specify what kind of property women should receive. In the
cities, women were more likely to inherit. Ottoman historians who have
studied women's economic activities have generally concluded that
women received these rights. Since wealth was usually not in the form of
land or livestock, the economic considerations that determined inheritance practice among pastoral or agricultural groups did not have the
same imperative to limit female inheritance. Although some literature has
suggested that upper-class women may effectively have been disinherited
in the interests of the lineage or extended family, this does not seem to
have been the case in most Ottoman cities, including Aleppo. At the same
time, however, the simple fact that women inherited does not tell us
much about what this implied for women's control of property, their
power and autonomy, and their relationship to their families. Close attention to these questions in different cities and over time are needed before we can draw firm conclusions about the significance of inheritance
rights for women.

In eighteenth- and nineteenth-century Aleppo, women figured
prominently as heirs in the legal sources, through their rights as wives,
daughters, mothers, and sisters. The mukhallafat registers indicate that
women were allotted their proper shares. It is hardly surprising that these
records would show this, since court officials would see that what was
recorded would conform to the rights laid down by law. That this was
more than a legal fiction, however, comes through clearly in other evidence from these sources about women's economic activities. Like women
in other Ottoman cities, women in Aleppo, especially upper-class women,
figured prominently in the economic life of the city, buying and selling
commercial and residential property, investing in rural properties near
Aleppo and other provincial cities, controlling usufruct on state-owned
land, lending money, and setting up religious endowments.[31] Women's
access to resources that provided a basis for this level of economic activity came primarily through inheritance or through the mahr. There were
no other means for women to begin the process of accumulating the necessary resources.

The significance of this access to resources through inheritance was in
part determined by the kind of wealth they inherited. In this urban context, the kinds of resources inherited included residential and commercial
property in the city; privately owned agricultural properties like vineyards, orchards, and market gardens (usually located in the suburbs

around the city); household goods and textiles; cash; and, on rare occasions, usufruct rights on other state-owned agricultural lands. In Aleppo,
women inherited shares in all these resources, as did male heirs. In contrast to what seems to have been the case in some Ottoman cities, women
did receive their allotted share of both residential and commercial properties; in other words, they did not inherit just cash, jewelry, and household goods while the real estate went to males, nor did they inherit only
residential properties. While it is true that men controlled much more of
the commercial and productive real estate in and around the city then did
women, women did get a proportional share of this kind of property.
When women received their inheritance, it remained their own, including valuable real estate; if this had not been the case, women would not
have had the means to be economically active in so many different areas.
Thus, it does not seem that women were given their legal rights to inheritance only to be coerced into giving up the property later, in contrast
to what Faroqhi found in seventeenth-century Ankara and Kayseri.[32]
Women sometimes sold inherited property to brothers or other family
members, but not to any greater extent than men did. Moreover, women
who did sell inherited property to other family members often used this
cash to purchase other property or to invest in other ways.

The significance of this inheritance for women—how much it affected a woman's position and authority in the household and her relationship to her natal family and her husband's—depended not just on the
kinds of resources involved but also on a number of other variables. The
most important was the timing. Unlike men, women did receive some
financial provision early in life, assuming they married, since at the time
of their marriage they received a sum of money from their husbands
(mahr) as well as something from their parents, which could be in the
form of cash, jewelry, or household goods. This meant that they did not
have to wait for an inheritance to gain some access to resources, even if
these were very limited. However, their receipt of the rest of their "inheritance" from their families, the most significant part of which would
usually come from fathers, could happen early or late in life and was determined partly by chance: the age at which their fathers or other individuals from whom they inherited died. It also depended on when inherited property was divided. If a woman's parents died when she was
relatively young and the estates were divided up soon after their deaths,
she would have access to her inheritance early in life. On the other hand,
if her parents lived to old age, as some did, or the estate remained undi-

vided for many years, the woman would receive her shares late in life
or might well die before receiving anything. As indicated earlier, some
estates, especially those of wealthy and powerful males, were left undivided for long periods of time. Like other family members, women
would have a claim on the inheritance, but would not necessarily be able
to exercise it. One example was the estate of ʿUmar Taha, who left four
sons and five daughters as heirs. By the time any property was distributed
from the estate, three of his five daughters and one of his four sons were
already dead.[33]

This inheritance strategy of delaying the settlement of estates or keeping certain kinds of property undivided for longer or shorter periods of
time raises the complex question of whether women claimed the inheritance to which they were entitled. The long delay before the division of
property can be construed as—and often was—a strategy for disinheriting females, as well as most males. In this strategy, women never gained
direct control over property that was rightfully theirs, or gained it only
late in life. When property was left in this way, any of the heirs could go
to court and claim his or her share. There were many cases in which
women as well as men did this. In these situations, women had an ally in
the courts. Once such a case was brought before the qadi, he would settle
the claim. The women who did press such claims tended to be widows
seeking their share of their husbands' estates or claiming their children's
share from their in-laws. From the contexts, it appears that they were usually pressing these claims when the connections to the husband's family
were loosening or when there was a specific reason why the woman
needed ownership of the property, such as that she was preparing to set
up a waqf.[34] Rarely do these claims come from sisters or daughters. One
noteworthy exception was a suit brought by two sisters, Hanifa and
ʿAtika Fansa, against their brother ʿAbd al-Rahman. They claimed that
he had compelled them to give up their rights to their father's property.
The dispute involved real estate, the family home in the quarter of
Jallum Kubra, and olive trees and land in several provincial villages. The
women claimed that this property had been left by their father to his eight
children and his wife; four of the children had subsequently died. The sisters demanded their share of their father's estate, but their brother de-
fended himself by saying that the property was part of a waqf and that the
conditions of the waqf stipulated that women lost all rights to the revenues once they married. He claimed Hanifa and ʿAtika had agreed to
this. The sisters acknowledged this, but claimed that they had been com-

pelled to do so through violence. Nevertheless, they could produce no evidence to that effect, and the judge dismissed the suit.[35]

As has been suggested in the anthropological literature, women's failure to press inheritance claims was often deliberate and not necessarily a sign of powerlessness or ignorance of their inheritance rights. Their rights to these resources, rather then the resources themselves, may have been more important. As Peters has argued in the case of the Bedouin of Cyrenica, the critical factor in determining a woman's status and sense of security was not inheritance per se, but having a claim to inheritance. Women often chose not to exercise that claim, because it would isolate them from their natal family. Moors makes the same argument in the case of Palestinian women. As long as a woman did not claim her inheritance, she could continue to count on her family's protection and help in times of difficulty.[36] This connection to her natal family might be particularly important for a younger woman before she had had sons and had thus secured her position within her husband's family. In other words, having a claim to inheritance conferred benefits that could offset actual control of inherited wealth.

The other factor that determined the importance of inheritance for women was the amount of property involved relative to the number of heirs. For a woman who belonged to a large family, especially one in which there were many sons, her share of the inheritance would be relatively small, even if the family were quite wealthy. On the other hand, if there were only one son in a small family or only daughters, women could be significant heiresses, especially when the estate was a large one. A good example was the family of Hasan Kawakibi, who had three daughters and no surviving sons. His wealth, including the income from his large religious endowment, went to his daughters and their children. One of his daughters married a man from an Antakya family with whom the Kawakibis had exchanged marriage partners for many years. The other two daughters stayed in Aleppo. One married the son of Ibrahim Pasha, who had risen from obscurity to become governor of Aleppo at the beginning of the nineteenth century.[37] In the case of the Kawakibi family, the lineage did not come to an end with the death of Hasan. Another branch of the family still lived in the city, but it had had none of the prominence or wealth of Hasan's branch. The name survived in this branch, but Hasan's wealth went to his daughters and their children, not to more distant agnates.

Through inheritance, many women did have access to economic re-

sources in sufficient quantity to be economically active and in some cases
wealthy in their own right. Nevertheless, whether they inherited, what
they inherited, and when they inherited affected the impact that inheritance rights had on their lives. Ultimately, the protection and security
these rights implied were guaranteed only by the willingness of the men
in their family to abide by the law and by the women's willingness to assert their rights to inheritance, if these rights should be violated. The
pressure that could be brought to bear on women to give up their rights
of inheritance was undoubtedly strong, as the case of the Fansa sisters suggests. While few cases were this conspicuous, litigation over women's inheritance occurred frequently enough to suggest that this could be a con-
tentious issue. The kinds of cases that appear reveal some of the problems
that did arise for women as heirs.

One type of inheritance dispute involved property sold to women by
their fathers or husbands while the men were still alive. It can be assumed
that in most cases such premortem transfers of property took place for the
same reason they do in other societies—to avoid the "penalties" imposed
by the inheritance system. Such transfers could have been strategies to
avoid the effects of a partible system of inheritance or to guarantee that
one particular heir received certain property. Although it is usually assumed that such sales were used to prevent female inheritance, the evidence from Aleppo does not support this. If anything, it suggests that the
opposite may have been true—that property was passed on to women
through sales to guarantee them more property than they might have received through inheritance. One such case in 1823 involved litigation between a brother and sister, Mustafa and Ruqayya Shaykhbandar, both of
whom were heirs to their father's sister's son, Ahmad Shaykhbandar,
Mustafa as a first cousin and Ruqayya as Ahmad's wife. In this case,
Ruqayya sued Mustafa, claiming that he had illegally taken possession of
property sold to her by her husband several years before his death. She
presented proof that she had purchased all this property, and the judge
ruled in her favor. A case appearing just a couple of weeks after this litigation suggests at least one possible reason for these sales by a husband to
his wife. Ruqayya and Mustafa, together with a cousin, ʿAbd al-Rahman,
also an heir to Ahmad, were required to sell considerable property that
had belonged to Ahmad in order to pay debts to the provincial treasury.[38]
It is possible that Ahmad had sold some property to his wife to ensure
that she would be properly provided for if he should die encumbered by
debt. In another case, ʿAbd al-Rizzaq Jazmati sued his sister's husband,

Muhammad (who also happened to be his cousin), and his niece Ruqayya for his share of his sister's estate, which consisted of gold and jewelry and part of an orchard. However, Muhammad Jazmati, acting as guardian to his daughter, was able to prove that his wife had sold all these possessions to Ruqayya before her death.[39] Both cases suggest that the economic security of females was being assured before the death of their legators and that women had to be vigilant about protecting their rights in these situations.

Tensions over inheritance also arose among the wives and the children of different mothers in polygynous households. In some cases, the cause of the dispute is not clear; what was recorded in court was merely that the conflict had been resolved and neither party to the suit had any further claims against the other. When more details of the dispute are known, it seems that conflict arose over what had belonged to the father and should be divided among all of his children and what had belonged to one of his wives and should go only to her children. Mustafa Fallah had five children, three by one wife and two by another. The mother of the three children died in 1823, and her husband died shortly thereafter. Three years later, her children brought suit to the effect that 3,800 qurush from their father's estate was a debt owed to their mother; therefore it should come to the three of them and not be divided among five heirs along with the rest of his property.[40]

While the weight of the evidence shows that women generally inherited what they were entitled to—that is, there was no systematic effort to deprive them of their share of an inheritance—more problems seem to have arisen in the transfer of a woman's property to her heirs. The three grown children of Husayn Tutunji sued and received from the executor of their father's estate 5,000 qurush, the remainder of the money left to them by their mother and in their father's possession at the time of his death, when they were legally minors.[41] The heirs of Sufya Shaykhbandar sued her brother, who was executor of their father's estate, for Sufya's share of that estate. Her brother claimed that her share was only 2,041 qurush, which he had paid in full. The plaintiffs denied that. They stated that her share amounted to 15,000 qurush, and the judge ruled in their favor, stating that Sufya's share was based on the original estate, minus legal expenses, not on the sum remaining after their father's debts had been paid.[42] In all of these cases, the heirs of women had to fight to establish what property was properly theirs and was therefore owed to them as heirs. It suggests that women's rights as heirs were relatively well protected, but that women's rights to property and as legators of that property to their heirs were harder to protect.

The relationship of women to inheritance in practice, not just in legal theory, adds to the growing body of evidence that suggests that their legal rights gave them opportunities that they could use to their advantage under certain circumstances, if not always. This was true whether women actually took possession of the resources to which they were entitled or whether they refrained from claiming them. Moreover, premortem inheritance in the form of gifts at the time of marriage and property sales gave women some access to property at an earlier stage in their lives than if they were entirely dependent on such access through inheritance after the death of the fathers, husbands, or sons. Abuses undoubtedly occurred, pressure was brought to bear, and tensions surrounded the issue. But most women did inherit in law and in fact. Their rights to inheritance had positive consequences for upper-class women in Aleppo. They controlled some of their own resources, and for many from wealthy families, this represented considerable wealth. Having money or owning property did not automatically give women power or even much control over their lives. Many other variables affected their situations. However, this wealth provided them with a degree of economic security, as well as some influence in making economic decisions that affected the family as a whole. The ties a woman retained with her natal family through economic links also protected her in the often vulnerable position as a new wife, especially one who had not yet had children, in her husband's household. It could also affect her status in another way: those women who were bringing wealth to a marriage could not be easily discarded or ignored.

INHERITANCE AND
FAMILY STRUCTURE

The distinctive features of the Islamic inheritance system—female inheritance, partible distribution, and the mandate that certain individuals inherit—gave families considerable latitude in managing the devolution of wealth, though this freedom was not unrestricted. The interaction between the nature of the inheritance system and the choices made by these families had important consequences for family structure.

These consequences are apparent when one looks more closely at who among the wide circle of kin with theoretical rights to inheritance actually realized these rights. As discussed above, Islamic law recognizes two classes of heirs: the heirs designated by the Koran and male agnates. This wide circle of heirs was recognized because it allowed for all possible contingencies. For example, if all Koranic heirs predeceased a legator, the law would still have other heirs to fall back on. It avoided the problems of dying intestate.[43] Coulson concludes that the tension between the interests of the immediate family and the interests of the extended family (the larger group of male agnates) inherent in the development of the law was resolved in practice in favor of the latter.[44] But that conclusion was based on his reading of the law, not the study of how it was applied in actual historical situations. A close look at inheritance practices among the upper class of Aleppo can shed light on the nature of the inheritance system and the relationship between law and practice.

Who inherited depended to some extent on accidents of fertility and mortality. In a sample of 281 inheritance cases (215 males and 66 females), over half of the estates (162) were shared only by members of the elementary (children and spouses) family. In another 44 cases, parents were heirs along with spouses and children. In other words, in 75 percent of the inheritance sample, the entire estate was distributed to the spouse and the immediately ascending and descending generations. If the entire estate was not consumed by these heirs, siblings were the next most common class of heirs (36 cases). Siblings appeared most frequently as heirs when the deceased either had never married or had been preceded in death by his or her spouse and children. In effect, there were only a handful of cases in which male agnates beyond the immediate family (son, father, or brother[s]) received any part of the inheritance. In one case, a man died, survived only by his wife and one brother. In the absence of other close relatives, his first cousins (sons of his father's brother) inherited part of his estate. In another case, the only surviving Koranic heirs were daughters. Since an estate would not normally be divided solely among female heirs, male first cousins also received a share. In only one case did the estate go to a more distant relative. A woman died whose closest male relative was her grandfather's brother's grandson, and he was her sole heir.[45]

While the rights of heirship were confined largely to the elementary family for the population as a whole, some variations by class do occur. The basic model of the upper-class family as one in which economic ties across the lineage would be more important and would be reflected in in-

heritance patterns suggests that male agnates would figure more prominently as heirs. It is true that the percentage of inheritance cases in which
only members of the elementary family figure as heirs (twenty-five out of
sixty-seven) is lower and that the percentage of cases in which uncles,
nephews, and cousins inherited is slightly higher (forty-two out of sixty-
seven). That means in effect that male relatives within the first degree of
kinship were more likely to inherit and therefore that upper-class families were more likely to have economic interests in common with a wider
circle of kin than other classes. However, even among the upper class,
more distant male agnates do not appear as heirs any more frequently
than they do for the population as a whole. Close female relatives were
preferred as heirs over more distant male agnates. Only one case is recorded in which the claims of distant agnates were preferred. Two brothers, Muhammad Darwish and ʿAbd al-Qadir Shaykhbandar, claimed to
be the rightful heirs of Khalil Shaykhbandar. Their great-great-grand-
father and Khalil's grandfather were the same. They were heirs because
they were the only surviving male agnates. However, Khalil's brother,
Muhammad, who had predeceased him, had a daughter, and she had
taken possession of his estate. The judge ruled that Khalil's niece did not
inherit under these circumstances. Although daughters, wives, mothers,
and sisters had rights that took precedence over the rights of distant male
agnates, nieces did not. This was the only case in which distant agnates
were able to make such a claim against a close relative, but it does illu-
minate clearly the point at which the lineage superseded the more immediate family.[46]

Despite the entitlement of male agnates as well as close relatives in Islamic law, in practice the laws of inheritance clearly favored more immediate relatives at the expense of the lineage. Male agnates beyond the first
degree of kinship had little stake in economic resources as heirs, despite
their equal entitlement. The role of female inheritance was critical in establishing this reality.[47]

The inheritance system as practiced in Aleppo among the upper class
had the effect of strengthening the elementary family at the expense of
the lineage. Male agnates more distant than first cousins only came into
the picture if the surviving Koranic heirs were all women. Even in those
cases the bulk of the property remained in the hands of the women. Because women inherited, women and their children had an interest in the
family patrimony, and this undoubtedly had an impact on decisions made

about marriage. Anthropologists and others usually cite this as one explanation for cousin marriage, since such marriages provided a way for keeping wealth within the family, even when women did inherit. While cousin marriages did occur, more women by far married outside the lineage than within it.[48] Yet their position as heirs reinforced the links to their natal families, and it gave their children, members of a different patriline, some ties to their maternal relations. In effect, it promoted family-to-family connections. Although variations occurred from one family to the next, affinal ties were important. Agnatic relationships were not all-encompassing in economic terms, any more than they were in emotional or psychological terms, a point that is usually not sufficiently recognized in the literature on the Middle Eastern family.

The fact that upper-class women were able to exercise their rights of inheritance guaranteed by the law and that some were significant property owners reflected a number of considerations. One was that the status of a family was dependent on the status of daughters as well as sons, a point that Jack Goody argues convincingly in his study of family structure outside of Europe.[49] Moreover, neither the economic base of this urban upper class nor the system of land tenure in the Ottoman Empire presented insurmountable barriers to female inheritance. Since the economic base of this class was not grounded in rights to pastoral lands or ownership of agricultural properties, the effects of female inheritance on property was not disruptive to the same degree that it might have been under other circumstances. Because of the organization of the economy, the lack of compelling reason to limit female inheritance, and the family's own concern with the status of all their children, upper-class women had the means to acquire property through inheritance. Inheritance practice affirmed the access to property that the legal system gave them.

While female inheritance was decisive in determining who among eligible heirs actually inherited, the strategies chosen by different families for transferring their wealth from one generation to another determined the strength and durability of economic ties among heirs. Three different patterns of economic association emerge from these choices. For many families the economic ties created by common rights as heirs were severed completely soon after the death of the legator. The property was divided up and each heir accepted his or her share, without having any further claims on or common interest with the other heirs. At the other extreme were the "undivided associations" mentioned earlier in which inherited wealth remained undivided for long periods of time and was in effect held as corporate property, although not recognized as such by the law, usually under the control of the most powerful male in the family. Family members were linked economically to each other by their rights to inherit, sometimes over the life span of more than one generation. In the final pattern, which fell somewhere in between these two, each heir would receive all or some of the wealth to which he or she was entitled as individual property, but would continue to have common economic interests through shares in jointly owned property or rights to uncollected debts for a period of time.

CONCLUSION

Inheritance created one economic network among kin—a network that encompassed a fairly narrow circle (primarily spouses, children, and parents), that changed over time, and that was usually not maintained too long after the death of the individual from whom they inherited. The partibility of inheritance and the fact that women inherited helped determine the way in which devolution of property occurred and had an impact on family structure as well as the position of women and men within the family.

The devolution of property also occurred in another form, outside the workings of the inheritance system, through the family religious endowment. The following chapter will take up this issue and consider whether this alternative to the inheritance system established a significantly different economic relationship among family members and altered the relative position of males and females within it.

Five

ENDOWMENT
AND FAMILY
STRUCTURE

Common right to inheritance was the most basic economic tie between family members and one that existed regardless of any decision on the part of the people involved, but it was by no means the only one. Nor was the inheritance system the only way of transmitting property from one generation to another. In addition to premortem transfers through sale, gift, and dowry, there was the family religious endowment (*waqf dhurri*), probably the most important alternative to devolution through inheritance. The religious endowment (waqf) has a long history in Islamic societies. It was first established in the early centuries of Islam for purposes of supporting religious activities and institutions and of establishing a system of social welfare. Over time the original institution came to be known as *waqf khayri* (public or charitable endowment). Another kind of waqf—waqf dhurri—also developed, in which the recipients of the income from the endowment were members of the endower's family; the waqf only reverted to religious or charitable purposes if the line of designated beneficiaries died out. In effect, it became a means of transmitting property from one generation to another outside the inheritance system.

The attractiveness of the family endowment as a means of transmitting property from one generation to the next has often been noted. It was the only corporate form of property control recognized in Islamic law, and it therefore avoided the complex and cumbersome legal arrangements that could be involved in de facto joint ownership created through inheritance and other processes. Moreover, in theory, waqf property was tax exempt and could not be confiscated by rapacious government officials. In other words, it provided both a tax shelter and long-term security of property for the family.

Since it was a means of devolution running parallel to the inheritance system, the use of the waqf clearly would have an impact on family structure. The waqf resembled the entail in Europe and similar institutions elsewhere that kept property inalienable and undivided from generation to generation while the income from the endowment was distributed among its beneficiaries as set up in the original deed of endowment. At issue is whether it was also used as a way of establishing primogeniture or unigeniture or as a way of disinheriting women. In other words, was it used as a way of circumventing certain requirements—perceived as problems—of the Islamic inheritance system? If so, its impact on family structure could be radically different than that of the inheritance system. Given its nature and purpose, it could have operated as a way of establishing a more permanent and encompassing economic relationship among members of the extended kin group and of assuring tighter control over family resources and family members by the head of the family—a very different kind of family economic network than that created by the inheritance system.

The family waqf is a particularly interesting source for the historian interested in the family because it is one of the few sources that offers some insights into prevailing attitudes toward the family.[1] Since the Islamic system of inheritance allowed relatively little free choice in how property was to be divided among heirs, the setting up of a family waqf was one of the few occasions when the personal preference of the property owner determined how his or her property was to be passed to succeeding generations. The deeds of endowment (waqfiyyas), like wills studied by European historians, are valuable indicators of how individuals perceived the ideal family and of relationships within particular families. Moreover, these ideal images of the family can be compared to the realities of family life as revealed in other evidence from the archives. The waqf shaped family structure and relationships by creating long-standing economic ties among family members and reflected their ideal and actual forms. Through the deeds of endowment and numerous other documents related to waqf, a picture of this connection emerges.[2]

To address the question of the relationship between the institution of religious endowment and family structure, this chapter will examine the political, economic, and religious significance of the waqf in Ottoman Aleppo and the role of Aleppine notables in establishing these endowments. It will then focus on waqf as a form of devolution and on its impact on family structure and relationships through the way in which it set the boundaries of the family.

THE WAQF IN
OTTOMAN ALEPPO

By the Ottoman period the central role of the religious endowment in Islamic society generally, and Syrian society specifically, was already well established. Large expanses of agricultural land as well as many commercial and residential properties in all major towns and cities formed part of one or another religious endowment. While the full extent of waqf property in Syria at the time of the Ottoman conquest awaits a definitive study, it is clear that the Mamluk rulers of Syria had encouraged the establishment of endowments and had themselves been active as religious endowers. The last Mamluk sultan, Qansuh al-Ghawri, had established extensive waqfs in both Syria and Egypt, and the beneficiaries of these were scattered throughout the region and continued to benefit from these endowments until the nineteenth century. (For more discussion of the Ghawri family in Aleppo and the extensive litigation that surrounded the Ghawri endowment, see below.)

The establishment of waqfs continued at a brisk pace under the Ottomans. Although the Ottoman government attempted periodically to reform the whole system of endowments—in an effort to reclaim revenues lost when land was transformed to tax-exempt status through the process of endowment—these efforts had little effect on the proliferation of endowments throughout the empire.[3] In Syria the largest endowments, and the ones most likely to include substantial amounts of *miri* (state-owned) land, were created by Ottoman governors. The largest and richest waqfs in Damascus, for example, apart from those of the Ummayyad Mosque, were the sixteenth-century endowments of Murad Pasha and Sinan Pasha.[4] In Aleppo, at least fourteen governors or members of their families set up endowments in the sixteenth and seventeenth centuries, including the very extensive endowments of Khrusru Pasha (1544), Muhammad Pasha Dukakin (1555), Bahram Pasha (1583), and Ibshir Pasha (1653). Agricultural land, most in the province of Aleppo but some as far away as Gaza and Cairo, generated a significant percentage of the income from these endowments.[5]

Ottoman inability to control endowments and curb the transfer of revenue-producing miri lands into waqf lands was closely connected to the relationship between these endowments and Ottoman religious and economic policies in the provinces. As a state whose legitimacy depended on its religious identity, the symbolic importance of encouraging the construction of new religious buildings was enormous. The construction of the great religious complexes, first in Edirne and then in Istanbul, under the patronage of members of the imperial family, was imitated in the provinces, under the patronage of Ottoman governors and officials. The minarets of distinctly Ottoman mosques still dot the skyline of Aleppo, Damascus, Cairo, and the other major and less-important provincial cities and towns. The support of such large institutions—both for the construction and maintenance of the buildings themselves and for the salaries of the many officials to staff them—required extensive endowments.

Moreover, these religious endowments were directly linked to the economic development of the Arab provinces. The Ottoman conquest brought a period of economic revival and growth to the Arab provinces, particularly to Aleppo. With its incorporation into the empire, Aleppo became a center of both international trade and intra-empire trade, with enormous benefits to the local economy. The most visible reflection of these benefits was the physical growth of the city and particularly the expansion of its central commercial districts. Overall, Aleppo grew from 238.5 hectares to 349 hectares, an increase of 50 percent, between the Ottoman conquest and 1800. The madina, the area of Aleppo's extensive markets, grew from four to nine hectares.[6] The building of these new commercial areas went hand in hand with the building of the new religious complexes. Each of the latter was supported by the construction of *khan*s (buildings that combined the functions of residence, exchange center, and warehouse for traveling merchants), *qasariyya*s (buildings that served either as workshops for craftsmen or residences/warehouses for merchants), and shops to provide income for the endowment. For example, the ʿAdliyya Mosque, built and endowed by Muhammad Pasha Dukakin, was supported by three khans, three qasariyyas, and 157 shops in four different *suq*s (markets), covering an area of three hectares.[7] Virtually all the new commercial development inside the city walls was taking place south of the line from Bab Antaki to the Citadel, and most of this development was connected with the endowment of one or another of these great religious complexes.

The expansion and redevelopment of the city continued after the sixteenth century. In the seventeenth century, there was major development outside the city walls, most notably in the quarter of Judayda in conjunction with the waqf of Ibshir Pasha.[8] In the first half of the eighteenth century, the building and endowment of mosques by ʿUthman Pasha and Hajj Musa Amiri, and a madrasa and library by Ahmad Taha, were accompanied by redevelopment in the quarters of Dakhil Bab al-Nasr, Suwayqa ʿAli, and Jallum. The connection between religious endowment activity and the economic life of the city was important in other ways as well. The large rural endowments of the sixteenth century and earlier provided a way of transferring the rural surplus to the city. Instead of this income going to Istanbul in the form of taxes, it stayed in the province for local needs. Much of it was used for the upkeep of buildings in Aleppo and for the employment of religious officials.[9] The existence and management of endowment property was also closely tied to the urban economy, since most of the khans, many of the qasariyyas and other kinds of workshops, and a significant number of shops—all essential to the health of this mercantile economy—were tied to endowments.

The most conspicuous development in the history of Aleppine endowments during the Ottoman period was an important shift in the number, scale, and patronage of religious endowments after the beginning of the eighteenth century. The number of endowments increased significantly, and smaller endowments became the norm. In the eighteenth century, 561 endowments were founded, compared to 61 in the sixteenth and 80 in the seventeenth century. This upward trend continues in the nineteenth century; in the first half of the century, 483 new endowments were set up.[10] Between 1770 and 1840, the period under consideration in this study, 468 new waqfs were established in Aleppo.[11] Even when the better preservation of records from the later centuries is taken into account, the number of new endowments in the eighteenth and nineteenth centuries represented a significant increase in the rate at which endowments were founded. Most of this increase came from the proliferation of small endowments. Sixty-two percent and 75 percent of endowments founded in the eighteenth and early nineteenth centuries respectively were classified as size "seven" (the smallest size—basically endowments including only one or two pieces of property) by al-Ghazzi. In earlier centuries, small endowments were less common (19 percent of endowments in the sixteenth century and 53 percent of endowments in the seventeenth).

Along with changes in the number and scale of endowments came a

significant change in patronage of the larger endowments. In effect, imperial patronage was replaced by local patronage. As mentioned above,
three very large endowments, similar in scale to earlier endowments by
Ottoman governors, were founded in the first half of the eighteenth century. Each of these was connected with the building of new religious
monuments—the ʿUthmaniyya Mosque under the patronage of ʿUthman Pasha, the Ahmadiyya Madrasa under the patronage of Ahmad Taha,
and the mosque of Hajj Musa Amiri named for its endower. All three endowers were members of the local elite. ʿUthman Pasha was an Ottoman
official, as his father had been before him, and he had served as governor
of Aleppo, among other appointments. However, he was from a prominent local family and made his home in Aleppo between appointments
and after his retirement, and his family lived in the city.[12] The changing
economic base of these large endowments also reflected changing patronage. Instead of revenue-producing grain lands, urban real estate and
rural properties such as orchards, vineyards, gardens, ciftliks, and various
kinds of processing facilities formed the basis of all three of these endowments as well as all other endowments founded during this period. For
example, Hajj Musa Amiri's endowment included ten houses, sixty-seven
shops, seven qasariyyas, four khans, two storerooms (*makhzan*), several
dying plants and baths, three bakeries, and one *adasa,* one *madar,* and one
tabuna—all in Aleppo—as well as eight orchards, three gardens, and unspecified land outside the city.[13] The change in patronage was closely tied
to broader political and economic changes discussed in the introduction.
Local notables were in a position to establish endowments of this kind in
the early eighteenth century because of the wealth being generated by the
local economy and because of their newly acquired access to local resources that formerly had been sent to Istanbul. As part of these changes,
the notables were taking on civic roles previously performed by Ottoman
officials.

The large increase in the number of new endowments and the larger
percentage of small endowments reflected other significant changes in
endowment activity. A wide spectrum of property owners were now involved in setting up these endowments. Sixty-two percent of them were
set up by individuals who were not from upper-class families, most of
whom were probably smaller property owners. Endowment activity
therefore was not confined to one class, nor was it gender specific. Women
were quite active as founders of endowments. Two hundred fifteen endowments were founded by men, 241 by women, and 11 jointly.[14] The

type of endowments indicates that a variety of motivations and purposes influenced decisions to set up endowments. Roughly half of the endowments set up during the Ottoman period were established for charitable purposes; the rest were family waqfs.[15]

The fact that people from different social classes were engaged in founding religious endowments, however, should not obscure the critical role of the upper class as founders and beneficiaries of endowments. Waqf property was dominated, if not monopolized, by this class. The notables of Aleppo were very active as endowers. One hundred sixty-five endowments (35 percent of the total) were established by these families, 86 by men, 77 by women, and 2 jointly. Forty of the 104 notable families (38 percent) included in this study were involved in setting up new endowments. Their control of waqf property was even greater than these overall figures suggest, however. A much larger percentage of the total *property* that became waqf belonged to this group, since they were the ones who set up the very large endowments. Although ownership of real estate was widespread, a disproportionate amount of urban real estate, both residential and commercial, was concentrated in the hands of relatively few families. The notables, therefore, were the ones able to establish large endowments, if they so chose. In addition to the new endowments they set up, many were also beneficiaries of older endowments, some dating back to the sixteenth century and some of which were very large. Others had control of waqfs as administrators, even when they had not established these endowments or were not named as beneficiaries of them.

Like individuals from other social groups, the upper class established both family and charitable endowments. Sixty-two percent (102) of their endowments were waqf dhurri, while 38 percent (63) were waqf khayri. Their charitable endowments were generally quite small. In contrast to the first half of the eighteenth century and to the sixteenth century, the wealthiest element of Aleppo society was not endowing large new religious institutions, nor were they devoting extensive resources to other kinds of charitable activities.[16] This group, like others in the city, took its religious obligations seriously and was concerned about providing for relief for the poor, the upkeep of religious monuments, and the salaries of religious officials. Nevertheless, they were not devoting the same scale of resources to this as in the past. The large endowments they established were family endowments. In contrast, among the population as a whole, endowments were split evenly between family and charitable ones in the eighteenth century, and charitable ones became more common (increasing to 62 percent) in the nineteenth century.

While the notables were involved in charitable and religious activities, the use of the waqf for family purposes clearly took priority for many. The reasons why some families chose the family endowment as a way of managing and transmitting resources between generations is discussed below. It is through these endowment activities that we can begin to get a sense of how the institution of waqf was connected to the family economy and how it reflected family relationships and shaped family structure.

FAMILY ENDOWMENTS AND FAMILY RELATIONSHIPS

The distinction between a waqf khayri and a waqf dhurri has long been recognized. However, the distinctions between different types of waqf within each category have been largely ignored. Once one begins to look closely at family endowments, it becomes clear that they cannot all be lumped together. The purposes of these endowments and their terms varied considerably. A waqf dhurri that included extensive real estate, movable goods, and cash and was used as a way of transferring much of the family patrimony from one generation to another was quite different from a waqf dhurri that consisted of a single piece of property. The social and economic significance of the act of endowment and the consequences for family structure and relationships would obviously be quite different as well. For analytical purposes, then, family endowments need to be divided into at least two different categories based on size: (1) small endowments limited to one or two pieces of property and (2) very large endowments consisting of twenty-five to one hundred pieces of property. (A handful fell somewhere between these two extremes, but they more closely resembled the smaller endowments in their conditions and impact.) The variation in size was more than a quantitative difference; it reflected very different purposes for the establishment of these endowments. Although both kinds of family endowment offer insights into family, they also provide evidence about different kinds of family relationships. This section will consider the small endowments.

Deeds of endowment have survived for fifty-eight of the one hundred two family waqfs set up by members of these notable families between 1770 and 1840. Thirty-five of the fifty-eight (60 percent) consisted of only one or two pieces of property. Among the elite, as in other social groups, the waqf was used during this period to transfer selected pieces of property to other family members, not just as a strategy for passing down the family patrimony. What is interesting about this group of upper-class endowers is that twenty-six of the thirty-five were women, a much higher percentage than the total number of women represented among all endowers (74 percent as opposed to around 50 percent). Given the gender context of these endowments, an analysis of the type of property involved, the conditions of these endowments, and the beneficiaries named offers insights into family ties and obligations and women's roles in the family.

The decision to establish one of these small family endowments was not primarily an economic one. The economic benefits were limited, either for the individual endower and beneficiary or for the family as a whole, since there was so little property involved. Setting up such a waqf had little impact on the distribution and control of wealth within families. In most cases, this endowed property represented only a small part of the property owned by the endower. Instead it seems that they were used to respond to special needs of individuals or special circumstances within the family. The relative frequency with which people, especially women, founded small family endowments during this period suggests that they were believed to serve an important purpose.

The most frequent use of these endowments was to provide a residence for designated family members. In twenty-four of these thirty-five endowments, only a single house was involved, eighteen of these the residences of the endowers and were designated to be the residence of the beneficiary or beneficiaries of the endowment. (In one case, the deed of endowment specifically stated that the house was to be rented out and the proceeds divided among the beneficiaries. In the other five cases, there is no indication one way or another of the disposition of the house. It may well have been a residence as well.) Most of the endowments of this type were established by women.

A number of factors may have affected a decision to turn a residence into waqf property rather than simply letting it be passed to the next generation through the inheritance system. It was a way of ensuring that the family residence was not divided into shares. This avoided difficulties down the road that might result from joint ownership, including disputes among heirs over the management of and rights to the property. A family waqf could avoid at least some of these problems, for example, by removing questions about selling the house. Setting up this kind of waqf might also have been extra insurance in the somewhat uncertain times of the late eighteenth and early nineteenth centuries by providing security of tenure and preventing one's house from being taken in case of bad debts or political misfortunes.

It is not surprising that converting a residence from *mulk* (private property) into waqf tenure seemed to be a good strategy for avoiding problems with this most basic of family resources. More important for understanding family relationships, however, is how these endowments were set up and who was included within the households created by them. As indicated in Chapter 2, the usual arrangement of the family waqfs was a trust for the benefit of the endower's descendants, with a life interest guaranteed for the endower and sometimes his or her spouse. These small endowments involving a residence followed this model for the most part, with the benefits accruing in the form of rights to reside in the house. In the majority of cases, no distinction was made between male and female descendants. Residential rights were shared equally, with no mention that females would forfeit their rights if they married, although it was probably assumed that most women would move into their husband's house at this point. The exceptions to this arrangement, however, were numerous enough to show that people did have a choice in these arrangements and that they exercised that choice. These choices provide some important insights into family dynamics, including the position of women in the family, and into the sense of what constituted the family through underscoring certain relationships and obligations.

One important exception to naming all children and descendants as beneficiaries was the situation in which certain children would be designated by name as beneficiaries ahead of their siblings. It was usually females endowers rather than males who made this distinction. For example, one woman deliberately excluded her husband from a life interest in her endowment. Her daughters and any other children born subsequently were named as primary beneficiaries; only if they died and had no surviving heirs did her spouse become a beneficiary of the endowment, along with his sons from a previous marriage.[17] One wonders if she made this arrangement to avoid any claim that her stepsons might make to the endowment when her husband died and her own children were still alive. Another interesting arrangement involved what were in effect joint endowments by mothers and daughters. Zalikha Hamawi and her daughter, Layla Hamawi (Zalikha had married her cousin Muhammad), each owned shares in a house in Frafira called Dar Hamawi Zade. Zalikha owned sixteen shares of the harem part of the house; Layla owned eight shares of the harem as well as all of the dar al-uta, inherited from her father and brothers. They each set up an endowment, naming each other as primary beneficiaries. After their deaths, the house went to Layla's husband and their children and descendants.[18] In another example, the wife and four daughters of Hashim Muqayyid had inherited nineteen shares of their residence in Frafira from him. With this property they set up an endowment to benefit themselves, stating very clearly that no one else would share in it or dispute their arrangements.[19] What is interesting about both of these cases is that most or all of the family home was inherited by women and through these women would pass out of the family. It is possible that the endowments were being used to protect their rights against claims to the traditional family home made by brothers or cousins. In the Hamawi case, Layla was the only surviving child of Muhammad and Zalikha Hamawi, but there were male cousins who might feel entitled to live in the house. In the Muqayyid case, there was a brother involved who presumably owned the other five shares of the house.

These examples, as well as the number of women who established endowments of this sort, raise some interesting questions about the kind of property owned by women and the composition of households. In order to be used to establish a waqf, property had to belong to the endower as mulk. In effect, then, in all cases in which women were establishing endowments consisting of their residence for the purpose of providing a future residence for their designated beneficiaries, women were the owners of their residences. Moreover, in many of these cases, other evidence indicates that the endowers were widows. These two factors taken together would seem to suggest that at least some of these were female-headed households. In the Hamawi case, for example, there was a man, Layla's husband, Muhammad Hariri, who would have been considered the head of the household; yet he was living in a house owned by his wife and his mother-in-law. Many scholars have commented on the increased authority of women as they grew older and took on the running of the household, but none have suggested that they might be heading their own households. Among the lower classes, female-headed households were probably not uncommon, as the greater instability of the family caused by economic pressures and the absence of males from home would often leave women on their own. It has been assumed, however, that upper-class women would have been protected from such a position by greater availability of economic resources and concerns about status and position. Nevertheless, some of these assumptions about household composition and the position of women in the household need to be reexamined.

Joint endowments by mothers and daughters are part of a pattern among these small endowments—both those involving residences and others—that suggests another purpose common to many of these endowments: women taking care of other women. Many of these endowments were set up specifically to provide for and protect the rights of women. Judith Tucker indicates that some endowments in nineteenth-century Egypt seem to have been set up as a "limited form of matrilineal inheritance" or "to provide specifically for females heirs whose claims on inheritance would normally be weaker than those of men."[20] The waqf dhurri often served a similar purpose in Aleppo. In addition to examples already mentioned, Fatima Ubri set up an endowment with a coffeehouse and two shops she owned to benefit herself and her three unmarried daughters, as long as they remained unmarried. Once they married, they as well as her other children (she had four sons and one married daughter) and descendants shared in the benefits of the endowment.[21] The wife of Hashim Muqayyad, mentioned above, also set up another endowment consisting of some shops and storerooms she owned in Judayda, the income from which would be used to support herself, her daughters, and the daughter of her deceased son. Not all women were interested in preserving the interests of other females, however. Sharafkhan Amiri, the daughter of Hajj Musa Amiri, stipulated that the income from two shops that she had endowed would go first to her two minor sons and their descendants and then to her grown sons and their descendants, only if and when the line of the first two brothers died out. Her daughter, 'Aysha, was not even a residuary beneficiary in this case; instead the endowment went to the support of her father's mosque if the line of her sons died out.[22] However, it was highly unusual to exclude women in this fashion. Only two of the thirty-six endowments of this kind excluded women. Women were not being deprived of property rights or access to resources through these endowments. More often the situation was just the opposite.

Most endowments were set up with the immediate family in mind: spouses, children, and descendants. However, they were not the only beneficiaries of these small family endowments. Another purpose for this kind of endowment was to provide for relatives other than one's children or descendants. Who among other family members were named as beneficiaries—and who were not—reveals important family ties beyond the immediate family. Nine of these thirty-five endowments named beneficiaries other than a spouse or direct offspring, a sufficiently large number to suggest that these arrangements were not uncommon. Most of these beneficiaries were either siblings or nieces and nephews or both. In 1807, 'Aysha b. 'Abd al-Rahman Ghuzuli set up an endowment for her deceased brother's daughter, the daughter of another brother (probably also dead), and three other brothers. This endowment involved about half of a house in Suwayqa Hatim that was located next to the endower's house. It was the residence of the designated beneficiaries. 'Aysha had inherited this share of the house, presumably from her father and deceased siblings. Rather than selling her share to her brothers and nieces, she established an endowment with her share of the house. The strength of the brother-sister relationship has often been noted, and this type of endowment provides further evidence of its importance.[23] Strong bonds between sisters seem to have been equally important. Mirim Zanabili set up an endowment in 1813 for her sister Zaynab. The property, a house in Shari'tli, was left to Zaynab first and then to her two daughters; only after their deaths did the income go to Zaynab's three sons and their descendants.[24] The close ties to siblings were continued in the close connections with nieces and nephews.

The quasi-familial relationship of many household slaves to the families of their masters and among slaves of the same master was also reflected in some endowments. Several were set up to provide a life interest for manumitted female slaves, probably former concubines. One was set up by Hanifa, a freed slave of the Amiri family, for another freed slave, Mirim, who had been slave to 'Uthman Amiri. After her death, the income from the endowment went to a daughter of 'Isa Amiri and her descendants and then to a son of 'Isa Amiri and his descendants. In light of these arrangements, it seems likely that Hanifa had been a slave of 'Isa, who had died before this endowment was set up.[25] 'Abd al-Qadir

Hamawi also left a life interest in an endowment he established for his wife and seven children to a freed slave of his father. The endowment was a house in Bayyada that 'Abd al-Qadir had inherited from his father and that served as residence for himself and his family.[26]

Small family endowments were important for accomplishing certain goals, such as providing a secure residence and some income for family members, particularly those who might not have equal or undisputed rights to other family resources. Women, especially widows dependent on the good will of their husbands' or their own families or of their step-sons, and orphans and younger children were frequent beneficiaries. While family arrangements allowed for inclusion of these relatives within existing households, their position would often be on sufferance. By giv-ing them legal rights to live in the house or to some additional income, their position within the family was strengthened.

The importance of certain kinds of family relationships was also reflected in these endowments. Close relationships with siblings and the children of siblings are suggested by the number of endowments specifi-cally naming these relatives as either primary or secondary beneficiaries. On the other hand, more distant relatives were not named as even resid-uary beneficiaries. If the direct line of the endower or the original bene-ficiaries died out, the property went to some charitable purpose rather than to more distant relatives. How these arrangements actually worked out over time—whether those who had rights did live in the family home, how often the lines died out—is rarely known with any certainty and not enough to provide a sense of the frequency with which these provisions were actually put into practice.

The involvement of most individuals from these upper-class families in endowment activities was limited to either charitable endowments or to small family endowments used for specific purposes. For these indi-viduals, relatively few of their economic resources were tied up in waqfs. So while these waqfs did create economic ties among family members, the ties were not very binding, given the limited resources involved.

In contrast, for some individuals and families, the waqf was used as a primary means of transmitting family resources from one generation to the next, and income from endowments formed the basis for the wealth and economic power of the family, as a significant portion of the family patrimony was tied up in waqf property. The next section will look at these large endowments.

ENDOWMENTS, THE
DEVOLUTION OF PROPERTY,
AND FAMILY STRUCTURE

While the sheer number of small endowments is impressive, large endowments, though fewer in number relative to the smaller ones, had a much greater impact on the urban fabric and economy and on the families for whose benefit they were set up. A significant percentage of the most valuable commercial and residential property in the city and agricultural properties in the surrounding suburbs were part of one of these large endowments. Most of the large endowments were at least in part family endowments, and most were controlled by notable families. Some families were connected to long-standing endowments as beneficiaries and/or administrators. Others established new endowments in the eighteenth and nineteenth centuries. Because of the different ways in which these families were connected to endowments, we are able to look at the relationship between endowment, the devolution of property, and the family from two different perspectives: the circumstances under which endowment was used as an inheritance strategy and the impact of this form of devolution on family and property over time.[27]

Thirteen large endowments were set up in Aleppo in the sixteenth and seventeenth centuries.[28] Another ten large endowments were established in Aleppo in the eighteenth century and first half of the nineteenth. Most of the sixteenth- and seventeenth-century endowments were established by Ottoman governors, as mentioned earlier, and many were connected to urban development projects and the building of major Ottoman monuments. Some of these governors, such as Bahram Pasha and Khrusru Pasha, lived only briefly in the city. While that part of the income from these endowments designated for charitable purposes still benefited the city, the rest went into the pockets of the endower's descendants who lived in Istanbul or other places.[29] Other Ottoman officials, however, left descendants in the city who continued to be beneficiaries of these endowments and mutawallis for them. The 'Adili family were descendants of Durakin Muhammad Pasha, governor of Aleppo in 1557 and patron of the 'Adliyya Mosque. The Shaykhbandar family had rights to the waqf of Buyuni Agri Muhammad Pasha (governor in 1656) through a maternal ancestor. The Qabbad Bey family were administrators for and beneficiaries of the waqfs of Mawtyab Ahmad Pasha and his wife, Humayun Khanim, founded in 1595 and 1584 respectively. The Nasir al-Din Bey family controlled the waqf of Ahmad Pasha Mar'ashli, established in 1666. Like the Shaykhbandar family, these two families were connected to the founders of these endowments through maternal lines. In addition to large waqfs created by Ottoman governors, there were the extensive endowments set up by the last Mamluk sultan, Qansuh al-Ghawri, shortly before the Ottoman conquest. This waqf included extensive tracts of land in Syria and Egypt to be shared by his freed slaves, who settled in various parts of Ottoman Syria and Egypt after the conquest. The Ghawri family, descendants of one of these freed slaves, was still prominent in Aleppo during this period. Two other large waqfs, that of Muhammad 'Ulabi (1590) and that of Ahmad Zuhrawi (1654), were not established by Ottoman officials, but rather by wealthy merchants. By the eighteenth century, both of these endowments were controlled by the Kawakibi family. One Kawakibi ancestor, Ahmad (d. 1614), had married a daughter of 'Uthman 'Ulabi; his great-grandson, another Ahmad (d. 1712), had married 'Afifa Zuhrawi.[30] With the end of the male line in each case, the descendants of the female line became the beneficiaries of the waqf. In four of these six families, in other words, the families benefiting from the long-established endowments had acquired rights to the endowment through females. The importance of women in transmitting critical economic resources, as represented by these endowments, needs to be underscored.

The largest and most visible of the eighteenth-century endowments were those of 'Uthman Pasha (1724), Ahmad Taha (1752), and Hajj Musa Amiri (1764), mentioned above. Like the large endowments of Ottoman officials of an earlier period, all three endowments were established in conjunction with the building of new monuments, and part of the income from each was used to endow these buildings. The rest went to the families of the endowers.[31] The other large waqfs were only family endowments. They included two waqfs set up by 'Abd al-Wahhab 'Imadi in 1731; one by 'Abd al-Rahman Pasha in 1751; one each by Mustafa Jabiri (1784) and his two sons, 'Abd al-Qadir and 'Abd Allah (1787); two by Hasan Kawakibi (1801, 1804); two by Qasim Fansa (1811, 1816); seven by Isma'il Shurayyif (1824–1826); and two by Ibrahim Siyyaf (1834).[32] In looking at these large endowments, almost all of which were used as a form of property devolution in addition to other purposes they might serve, two points stand out. One is that all of these endowments were controlled by local notable families, even those originally founded by Ottoman officials. The second is that using the waqf as a means of managing the family patrimony was a strategy chosen by relatively few families or individuals. In all, thirteen families (roughly 13 percent of the total) were associated with the large endowments during the period under investigation, either through older endowments for which they were the beneficiaries or through new endowments. This was not a large number of families. However, the amount of property under their control as waqf makes their activities in this regard an important topic to pursue.

The large endowments established in the early years of Ottoman rule provide a unique opportunity to see what happens to these endowments over time and to track the economic and symbolic importance and effectiveness of this kind of inheritance strategy. The Ghawri endowment will be used as a case study to examine the impact of this way of managing the family patrimony. This waqf was unusual because it was so large and because there was extensive litigation surrounding it in this period, making it highly visible in the sources. At the same time, the issues surrounding it were similar to those for other long-standing endowments, if not to the same degree, and makes it a valid case study.

The mutawallis who administered the Ghawri endowment, all members of this family, faced three major problems during this period. One was a series of lawsuits brought by individuals claiming that they had been denied their share of the income from the endowment. Some of these individuals asserted that they were from collateral branches of the family. Efforts to prove or disprove these claims ran into serious obstacles. The claimants declared that they were descendants of the same freed slave as the acknowledged Ghawri family, but the connections between the family lines often went back almost two hundred years, and few records existed that could resolve the dispute unequivocally. Other lawsuits were cases in which descendants in female lines argued that they had beneficiary rights, but had been denied these rights because they were descended from women. A total of fourteen suits were filed in the courts between 1772 and 1841. In some cases the judges ruled on behalf of the plaintiffs, feeling that proof was sufficient. In other cases they ruled against them. Whether these claims were legitimate or not, the prominence and size of the Ghawri endowment, as well as the difficulties of documenting all family members through many generations, made the waqf a likely target for such claims. It is also possible that the suits resulted from actions of the mutawallis themselves, who may have been attempting to exclude people from receiving benefits to prevent further fragmentation of the income.

This fragmentation of income was the second problem faced by long-established endowments and explains to some extent the resistance the mutawallis put up against new claims on the endowment. The income that any individual received from the endowment, even such extensive and prosperous endowments as the Ghawri, diminished over time if the number of people with rights to the endowment increased. One lawsuit makes this very clear. A member of the family brought suit against the mutawalli, arguing that he should have received an income equivalent to his deceased father's share of the endowment rather than the sum other members of his generation received. He based his claim on his father's early death and his having inherited his father's share. The motivation behind his claim was the sizable difference in income received by the two generations. His father had received an annual income from the endowment of 500 qurush; he would receive only 140 qurush. The judge ruled against him.[33]

Other pressure on the endowment came from the Ottoman government. How serious this pressure had been over the two hundred years or so of the endowment's existence is hard to judge without some extensive research in the Ottoman archives. Nevertheless, it seems likely that at various times the state tried to tax or confiscate all or part of the endowment. Endowments consisting of grain-producing land, as was true for the Ghawri case, cut into Ottoman revenues, and periodic efforts were made by the state to reclaim these lands.[34] At least twice during this period the government tried to tax land that was part of the Ghawri waqf, as evidenced by cases in which the mutawallis were called on to defend the endowment against such encroachments.

Despite these problems, it seems that the connection between founding endowments and the long-term wealth, power, and status of the family was a significant one. By the time that several generations had passed, the direct economic benefits to those who were entitled to income from the endowment had diminished considerably. Even when an endowment was very large, the income received annually from the endowment by each individual was reduced in most cases. Even if the number of beneficiaries did not increase with each generation, the effects of inflation and economic fluctuations could erode the income. In other words, a beneficiary from the income of a large family endowment could not depend on that alone if he (or she, in some cases) wished to be rich and powerful and be able to protect position and status.

Indirect economic benefits, however, could be very important. Much of the wealth of the Ghawri family by the middle of the eighteenth century was generated by moneylending. They frequently lent money to villages on land that formed part of the endowment for purposes of paying taxes, buying seed and animals, and other needs associated with agriculture. Moreover, they would extend long-term loans if the villagers were unable to meet their payments to the endowment. This long-term indebtedness relationship was a very lucrative one for the Ghawri. Additionally, since payments to the waqf were often made in kind, they acquired access to some of the grain supply of the province.[35] Moneylending and involvement in the grain trade meant not only wealth but also, at least potentially, power.

The administrators of these large endowments also reaped important benefits from their positions. While they received some direct economic benefits through their salaries, the more significant benefits were the economic power and influence derived from the management of extensive properties in Aleppo and elsewhere and the opportunities to serve as administrators of other endowments. These benefits were evident in the case of the ʿAdili family. Unlike the Ghawri family, the ʿAdili family was not much in evidence in the court registers of this period. The family, or branch of the family living in Aleppo, seems to have been fairly small. They resided in a large house in Bayyada and were not economically active in ways visible in the sources: buying and selling property, lending money to villages, or engaging in disputes over the waqf. Their principal economic base was the land and other kinds of property that they controlled through their waqf. Some were members of the ulema, including ʿAbd al-Latif ʿAdili, who served as mudarris as well as mutawalli in the Madrasa ʿUsruniyya and also served briefly as naqib al-ashraf in 1780.[36] What is interesting about the ʿAdili situation is that members of this family served as mutawallis for several other religious institutions, including the Khusruwiyya.[37] It is probably not a coincidence that members of the family who controlled the ʿAdliyya endowment were also appointed to serve as mutawallis for another large Ottoman endowment and were therefore in a position to benefit from their access to the extensive lands that formed part of this endowment.

Less tangible and harder to document is the connection between the waqf and the status and long-term survival of a family. As discussed in Chapter 1, there were few "old" families among the upper class of Aleppo in the second half of the eighteenth century. Most of these families could only trace their ancestry to the end of the seventeenth or beginning of the eighteenth century. It is suggestive that most of the surviving "old" families, who could trace their origins to the first century of Ottoman rule, were associated with a large waqf. Whether this was coincidental or whether it was connected to tangible and intangible benefits of these endowments cannot be answered with any certainty. A study of these families over the centuries, one that looked at a variety of factors that affected their economic, political, and social position, would be needed to answer this question. Nevertheless, the direct and indirect economic benefits mentioned above, as well as the status and perhaps a sense of family identity and solidarity fostered by sharing interests in these endowments, were most likely important.

The long-term benefits from these endowments undoubtedly played a role in the decision by other individuals to use this form of property devolution for the family patrimony in the eighteenth and nineteenth centuries. Relatively few families or individuals chose this way of passing on the bulk of the family patrimony, but the great wealth involved and prominent position of the endowers in Aleppo give these endowments special significance. Who these endowers were and the way in which these endowments were set up can suggest why some chose this option for passing on family resources to the next generation, as well as what its consequences for family boundaries and relationships were.

The thirteen endowers of these large family waqfs were all wealthy men, of course, since they would not otherwise have been in a position to establish large endowments. Furthermore, with the exception of Hasan Kawakibi, they were from families that had been established in Aleppo for only a couple of generations at the time when they set up their endowments.[38] In other words, the establishment of a large endowment was connected to the process of consolidating one's position in the elite.[39] These endowers had made fortunes or inherited wealth that could have come from a variety of sources, including commerce, moneylending, tax farming, landowning, or government service, and they then converted a sizable part of this wealth into real estate. The Jabiri family endowments are a good example of this. Two different endowments were involved, that of Mustafa and a joint waqf created by his sons, 'Abd al-Qadir and 'Abdallah, three years later. However, they should effectively be treated as a single endowment, since their provisions were exactly the same. The original basis of the Jabiri family fortune is unclear. By the middle of the century, however, the family was a well-established ulema family, and Mustafa's father, Ahmad, had established a family waqf, although not on

the scale of the endowments created by his son and grandsons. By the
latter part of the eighteenth century, Mustafa and his sons had made an
additional fortune, probably largely through tax farming and moneylending. In the five years immediately preceding the creation of the first
endowment, a significant part of this fortune was used to purchase real estate. Some of the purchases were made from other family members, but
most were of new properties. These newly purchased properties were
added to those that Mustafa had inherited from his father and formed the
basis of the endowments. Similar patterns of extensive purchases of property are evident in other cases. Isma'il Shurayyif's seven endowments
were set up over a period of three years, beginning in 1824. Between 1819
and 1826 he purchased considerable property and acquired other properties through waqf exchanges. Isma'il also inherited property from his
brother and close associate, Nu'man (d. 1822), who had himself been
purchasing large amounts of property since 1817. In 1824, Isma'il set up
the first of his seven endowments, and his last was established just before
his death in 1826.[40]

Using other forms of wealth to purchase property was a common
practice among these Aleppo notable families during this period. It was
presumably a strategy for ensuring the long-term stability of the family
by investing in a less lucrative but more secure and stable form of wealth.
Nevertheless, relatively few upwardly mobile families—even close relatives of some of these endowers, such as Yusif Jabiri (Mustafa's brother)
or 'Abd al-Qadir Shurayyif (Isma'il's uncle)—took the next step of using
this property to establish an endowment. So the decision to tie up property in an endowment was influenced by more than just wealth, property
ownership, and the desire to consolidate one's status. The other apparently decisive factor was active involvement in the political fray of this
turbulent period in Aleppo's history. With the exception of Musa Amiri
and Qasim Fansa, who were both wealthy merchants and did not get involved in local politics, all of these endowers held political or semipolitical
offices in Aleppo at some point in their lives. These ranged from 'Uthman Pasha, an Ottoman official who was governor of his native city for
a year, and Isma'il Shurayyif, who was mutasallim of the city from 1824
to 1826, to 'Abd Allah Jabiri, Hanafi mufti from 1786 to 1790 and again
from 1794 to 1798 and 1800 to 1805, a position that was not "political"
in the strict sense of the term but could be used as a platform from which
to exercise political power and one that entitled its holder to sit on the
local divan. In addition to holding offices, several of these endowers were

in the thick of the factional struggles in the city. The political activity of the endowers suggests that those people who chose to set up large endowments and to use that as a way of transmitting a significant percentage of their resources to the next generation were probably motivated by more than just a desire to show that they had "arrived." The timing of these endowments is also illustrative, since a number of them were set up soon after a political crisis in which the vulnerability of those involved was apparent. It seems as though the desire for some security for their families was critical. These endowers had planned carefully to establish their endowments, and they were undoubtedly aware of the risks involved in their political activities. The waqf provided a much better chance of saving their families from disaster in the event that they were defeated politically or died, leaving their estates heavily encumbered with debts.

While the decision to transfer significant economic resources into endowments was part of a process of consolidating status and influence and was linked to political ambitions and circumstances, it was also connected to internal family dynamics. The ways in which these endowments were set up provide insights into conceptions of authority, gender relations, and family boundaries within these families. When endowments were used as a primary means of transferring wealth from one generation to the next, as was the case with these large ones, there were clear efforts to ensure greater patriarchal control. The nature of the waqf itself, as a corporate form of property tenure that gives great power, at least in theory, to the administrator of the endowment, limited the rights of other beneficiaries to receiving income rather than controlling the property itself. The impact of this limitation on individuals' access to economic resources was obviously much greater when endowments included the bulk of the family patrimony rather than part of it. In these large endowments, the endowers went further to secure patriarchal authority by stipulating male priority in terms of benefits and male authority in the management of the endowments and by limiting women's rights vis-à-vis the property. All the large endowments except one allowed women only half the share of men. The exception was one of the waqfs of Ibrahim Siyyaf, and the exception may be more apparent than real, since his other waqfs limited the rights of females descendants.[41] Moreover, specific conditions limiting the rights of females or the rights of their descendants were frequently included in the larger endowments. One such condition limited the rights of women to endowment income once they married;

another prevented married daughters from living in the family home. Other conditions either denied beneficiary rights entirely to all descendants of females or allowed only certain descendants, such as the male descendants of females, to have these rights. For example, ʿAbd Allah and ʿAbd al-Qadir Jabiri stated in their waqfiyyat that women would be excluded from rights to the endowment when they married and that their male descendants had some rights to the endowment, but only half of those of the male descendants of males.[42] Hasan Kawakibi restricted the right to reside in the family house in Bandara to unmarried females of his children and descendants.[43] In other words, these endowments made provision for women who were left single or widowed, but cut off others once they were married. Not all of these endowments imposed such restrictions, but many did. The contrast to smaller endowments in which women were given equal rights to men as beneficiaries in many cases and were even privileged beneficiaries in some underscores the differences between these endowments.

Women were also largely excluded from the management of these large endowments, in marked contrast to other public and family endowments in which women were usually named as possible mutawallis and not infrequently were able to turn this theoretical right into actual control of the endowment. In most of these large endowments, however, women were not allowed to be mutawallis. Only Mustafa Jabiri did not exclude female descendants from this post. Hasan Kawakibi did allow the sons of females to serve as mutawallis, a condition that turned out to be important, since his only surviving descendants were daughters.[44] Management of his endowment passed into the hands of his son-in-law Mustafa Ibrahim Pasha Zade and his descendants. Ibrahim Siyyaf allowed female descendants to serve as mutawallis, but only after all male descendants had died out.[45]

The significance of the stipulations of these large endowments is made clear not only by comparing them to smaller endowments but also by comparing them to those of a few relatively large waqfs set up by women of these families. None of the endowments set up by these women were as large as the largest male-initiated endowments. Nevertheless, there were three waqfs established by women—Sharaf Jabiri, Saliha Taybi, and Afifa Ghannam—that were considerably larger than other female endowments and also larger than many male endowments. Sharaf Jabiri was the sister of ʿAbd Allah and ʿAbd al-Qadir Jabiri and the widow of Muhammad b. Yusif Jabiri, her first cousin. When she established her endowment in 1820, her husband had been dead for almost thirty years, and her son, Muhammad, her only surviving child, had recently died. The endowment she set up was designated for her grandchildren and their descendants equally. The mutawalli of the endowment after her death would be the most worthy of these descendants, without regard to gender. Saliha Taybi, the wife of 'Isa Amiri, a son of Hajj Musa Amiri, established an endowment in 1785 consisting of a dozen pieces of mostly commercial properties for the sake of her children and their descendants. The children were to share the proceeds equally; in subsequent generations, males would receive twice the share of females. In this case, no mutawallis were mentioned.[46] Finally, 'Afifa Ghannam established an endowment in 1794 from property she had inherited from her husband, Isma'il Za'im, as well as some she had purchased. Of the dozen pieces of property, two were half shares in her residence, apparently her share of her husband's house. The others were all commercial properties. The endowment was established for her daughter and only child, Sharaf; after her death it would be shared equally by her male and female descendants, all of whom would have rights to reside in the house.[47]

Although the number of endowments of this kind is small, they share some interesting patterns. All three involve substantial property, enough to provide some economic security to the beneficiaries, even if it did not represent all or the major part of their patrimony. All these endowments were created right around the death of the significant males involved: Sharaf Jabiri's soon after the death of her son, with whom she had resided during the long period of her widowhood, and the other two after the deaths of their husbands. Furthermore, when women set up endowments, they were more likely to provide equal treatment to males and females. That is, they seemed less concerned about preserving the property and income intact for, and under the management of, male members of the family than did the men. The gender differences in this respect are significant.

Compared to the more inclusive conditions concerning women in many smaller endowments and in the larger endowments set up by women, the restrictions on female beneficiaries in the larger male-initiated endowments are clearly important. Nevertheless, it is also significant that females were not completely excluded from the benefits of the endowment. The family waqf was generally not used by these Aleppo notables to deny women *any* share in inheritance or to establish male primogeniture, though one waqf did seem to move in this direction.

Qasim Fansa set up an endowment in which his son, 'Abd Allah, was given clear preference over the other children. Half of the proceeds of the endowment were set aside for 'Abd Allah; the other half was to be shared by 'Abd Allah, his five sisters, and Qasim Fansa's wife, Amat Allah Khanji, as well as by any other children born to the endower, with males receiving twice as much as females. In a second family endowment, set up five years later, Qasim Fansa did not set 'Abd Allah apart; the latter was a beneficiary along with his four sisters, with the two-to-one ratio applying. (The other sister and Qasim's wife had died in the intervening five years.)[48] The terms of the first Fansa endowment are significant for their uniqueness. There were no other examples of males receiving unusually large shares of the proceeds. In all other cases, daughters received half the share of sons, as they would have under the Islamic inheritance system.

The effort by male endowers to ensure that the family patrimony remained intact and firmly under the control of the male head of the family was not always successful, however. Even when their rights were restricted, women did end up assuming control of endowments. In two of these families, women had assumed control of the endowments within a generation. In 1832, about two years after Qasim Fansa's death, a dispute arose among his surviving children and grandchildren over who had rights to the endowment. At this time, the mutawalli of Qasim's waqf was his daughter Zaynab, since his son, 'Abd Allah, as well as one daughter, Layla, had died before Qasim. Zaynab and her two surviving sisters, 'Aysha and Fatima, had claimed all the proceeds of the waqf as theirs exclusively. In this case, they were being sued by their two minor nieces, 'Afifa, Layla's daughter, and Khadija, 'Abd Allah's daughter. The plaintiffs claimed that as children of original beneficiaries to the endowment, they should have been receiving their share of the endowment income for the previous two years. Zaynab denied this, saying that since her brother and sister had died before their father and had therefore never come into the rights that would have been theirs on his death, their descendants had no right to the proceeds of their endowment. In other words, whatever rights they had anticipated, died with them. The case was referred to the mufti, who ruled on behalf of the plaintiffs.[49] This case raises some of the complicated questions about rights to endowments inherent in the way they are set up and offers one of the few clear rulings on the legal issues surrounding these rights. Simultaneously it points out how different the reality can be from what the endower intended. It seemed that Qasim

wanted to set aside at least part of this patrimony for exclusive use of his
only son and his son's descendants. However, given the unpredictability
of succession, his son not only predeceased him, but died leaving only
a young daughter. The bulk of the property, as well as the management
of the endowment, came into the hands of Qasim's three surviving
daughters.

The case of Hasan Kawakibi was similar. At his death, his only surviving children were three daughters, one of whom was no longer mentally
competent. One of his daughters assumed the position of mutawalli of his
endowments, as well as of two other family endowments, her grandfather
Ahmad's and their ancestor Ahmad ʿUlabi's, for a short time. She was followed in this position by her son and then her cousin Khadija's son. The
family home in Bandara became the residence of her children and grandchildren from the Ibrahim Pasha family. The older Kawakibi endowments, including those attached to the family mosque in Jallum, passed to
her cousin, but he had no claim on these newer family endowments. In
the absence of male children, the latter were transferred to the Ibrahim
Pasha and Muwaqqit families.[50]

Through the conditions set out in the waqfiyyat, these endowers not
only came down on the side of patriarchal authority but also were explicit
about who did or did not belong to the family. In most endowments, the
endower, and sometimes his wife or wives, and his direct descendants
were designated as the original beneficiaries. Among these endowments,
there was only one exception to that pattern: the endowments established
by Ismaʿil Shurayyif. The original beneficiaries of his collective waqfs, after his death, were his two sisters, Nafisa and Amana. By the time of
these endowments, his brother, Nuʿman, was already dead, as was another sister, Zabida. Both surviving sisters were apparently widowed,
since there is no indication of a husband in either case. After his sisters,
the beneficiaries were his deceased brother's eight children, as well as
Ismaʿil's grandchildren (both of his sons, his only children, were dead by
this time).[51] In choosing to include his brother's children as beneficiaries
of this endowment, Ismaʿil was reflecting the close relationship between
himself and his brother. During Nuʿman's lifetime, the two brothers had
been joined not just by family ties, but had also formed a political and
economic partnership. In effect, this was a joint endowment, although
Nuʿman had been assassinated before it could be set up. Ismaʿil clearly felt
a sense of obligation to his brother's children, as well as to his widowed

sisters. Apart from this exception, the original beneficiaries of all other endowments were direct descendants of the endowers; siblings or children of siblings were not included.

To understand more clearly the boundaries of the family as they were defined in these endowment documents, it is necessary to look at what happened to the endowment if the direct line of the endower became extinct. By law, the ultimate beneficiary of the endowment had to be a charitable trust to benefit the poor of the endower's city or neighborhood, the poor of the Holy Cities, or a specific religious institution with which the endower or his family had some connection. In this way, the charitable intentions of the waqf institution were preserved. However, the endower had some flexibility about the disposition of the endowment in the event that his direct line of descendants died out. He or she could determine if some other relatives or associates would have access to the endowment before it passed to its ultimate beneficiary. But these endowers rarely took advantage of this opportunity to name secondary beneficiaries to pass the endowment on to collateral branches of the family. Only ʿAbd Allah and ʿAbd al-Qadir Jabiri specified that the endowment would pass to relatives (unnamed) in the event that their line died out. In all other cases, collateral lines of the family existed, but they were never designated as beneficiaries. Instead, clients or freed slaves of the endower and their descendants were named as secondary beneficiaries, while cousins were ignored. This pattern clearly suggests that economic resources were not considered to be the property of the lineage, defined as people with a common surname and descendants of a single ancestor, but rather as rightfully belonging to a fairly narrow circle of kin.

The failure to designate relatives from other branches of the family as residuary beneficiaries of the endowment brings us back to the connection between the history of the family and the use of the endowment as an inheritance strategy. It suggests that the establishment of these endowments was closely connected to the process of change within the family—specifically the separation of the family into distinctive family branches. It has been argued that many notable families established family endowments at some point in the process of consolidating their status in society.[52] In a general way, this was true, but at the same time it disguises a more complex process. A closer look at these endowments indicates that they were designed to consolidate the position of one particular branch of the family, not the lineage as a whole. The creation of the endowment signaled the definitive breakup of the larger family group into distinct branches, and the division of economic resources. It was also usually associated with growing disparities of wealth and status among different branches of the family. This is most clearly seen in families who were the beneficiaries of older endowments and who established new ones during this period. The Shurayyif family, for example, was a relatively new family in Aleppo, one that became prominent in the middle of the eighteenth century. The six children of ʿAbd al-Wahhab by his second wife, Fatima ʿImadi, had acquired rights to the income of the large ʿImadi waqf through their mother, and they and their descendants continued to profit from this. However, Ismaʿil Shurayyif, ʿAbd al-Wahhab's grandson, subsequently set up his own endowment, from which all but his descendants and those of his siblings were excluded. This endowment set his branch of the family apart from the others. In fact, his and his brother's descendants remained prominent in the city well in to the twentieth century, while his cousins' descendants slipped into obscurity. The waqf served to prevent other relatives from pressing a claim to the resources of this particular branch.

CONCLUSION

The waqf was a multifaceted institution that served a variety of social, religious, and economic needs in Aleppo, as it did elsewhere in the Islamic world. Among other roles, it provided one means of transmitting resources from one generation to another within the family context. It was used in conjunction with the Islamic inheritance system, but never replaced it as the primary form of inheritance. In some cases, it provided a way of transmitting specific and limited kinds of resources, like the family residence, to serve a very specific purpose. In other cases, a significant part of the patrimony of an individual was transferred to his or her heirs in this fashion. The decision to transmit resources in this way was in only a limited sense an economic one; other factors made the establishment of an endowment the preferred way of handling this process.

The impact on the family of using this form of devolution, whether to supplement or replace the transmission of the bulk of family resources, was not significantly different from the impact of inheritance. In other words, this form of devolution was not used to circumvent the supposedly "undesirable" features of the inheritance system. It was not used to create unigeniture or primogeniture among offspring and descendants; with a very few exceptions, all were treated equally or received benefits in the same shares as they would have under the system of inheritance. The resources devolved on a relatively small circle of kin, usually children and spouses, occasionally other close kin such as brothers or sisters and their children. In particular, the waqf was not used as a way of disinheriting women. Not only did women create their own waqfs, serve as administrators for their own and other endowments, and receive benefits from the endowments of their fathers, husbands, brothers, and uncles, but they also played an important role in the transmission of these endowments over time. In more than a few cases, demographic realities meant that women remained the surviving beneficiaries of these endowments, and therefore assumed primary responsibility for them and passed them on to their offspring. Even in the case of the large endowments, in which women's benefits and rights to manage the endowment were more restricted by terms of the endowment, women often found themselves in charge of the endowment because they outlived their male relatives.

The waqf in theory created a more permanent economic network among those family members who benefited from it than did the inheritance system. The sources provide examples of interaction among people, all with rights to an endowment, several generations after the original endowment was created. It is possible that the common benefits helped keep a sense of family identity alive. Just how strong these ties were, however, is unclear. Over time the economic significance of the endowment lessened in many cases; as the number of people with rights to the endowment grew, the value of each share decreased. This did not always happen, however, since families did not necessarily grow in size over time, as discussed in Chapter 2. Nevertheless, the income from the endowment was rarely the only or the most important source of support for most of the people who benefited from it. They still had to create their own economic base independent of the waqf. Moreover, in some cases the waqf became part of the process of fission within the family, when resources of one branch are being separated from resources of another. So the waqf, like the inheritance system, served to define an economic network among family members that encompassed a fairly small circle of kin — the narrowly extended family at most — and that changed over the life cycle of the family members.

CONCLUSION

The first part of the title of this book is taken from an Arab proverb that says (loosely paraphrased): "The kin who count are the kin who show up on the day of the battle." As this proverb suggests, the strongest ties and most meaningful relationships within the family exist among those relatives who "show up," who are there for you when the going gets tough, drawn by a sense of responsibility or mutual obligation and/or feelings of affection that can exist independently of the formal structure of family ties—patrilineage, household, inheritance rights, marriage bonds. When all is said and done, after the effort to identify kinship structures and determine the boundaries of the family and to analyze institutions of household and marriage, the essence of family—understanding just who are the "kin who count" and why—remains elusive. Our sources do not answer many of the questions we wish to ask. This is a constant source of frustration for the family historians trying to understand family dynamics from a distance of (in this case) two hundred years.

Nevertheless, what we glean from the religious court archives is a dynamic picture of families, and even, on occasion, glimpses of the drama of family life, as people went about the routine matters of daily life: marrying, buying and selling property, negotiating inheritance rights, arranging for the guardianship of children, forming and dissolving households, settling disputes. What stands out most clearly from this is the diversity of ways in which these notables organized their families, the constantly changing shape of these families, and the multiplicity of factors that affected the actual arrangements of household and family life,

despite the fact that they were all part of the same class, subscribed to a
widely shared set of social norms and cultural values, and acted under the
same system of family law.

From this complex and fluid picture of family life, however, certain
conclusions can be drawn. One is that most members of this elite "belonged" to three family groups: the lineage, the narrowly extended family (husband, wife or wives, children, parents and siblings and their children), and the elementary family (husband, wife or wives, and children).
How significant the ties to each of these were depended on the context.
The lineage provided a sense of identity and connection to past and future generations of the patrilineage and conferred status and a sense of
one's place in the social order. Beyond that, there did not appear to be
close interaction, reflecting strong ties of kinship, among members of
the lineage who were not closely related. Patrilineages were not formally
structured groups, and individuals did not have common economic interests just by virtue of being lineage members. Despite the law that
defined all male agnates as members of the "inner family" for inheritance
purposes, male agnates who were not brothers, uncles, or first cousins
rarely inherited. When endowments were established, the beneficiaries
were almost always direct descendants of the endower, both male and female; collateral branches of the patrilineage were not even designated as
residual beneficiaries. Over time the benefits of an endowment might be
shared by distant cousins, as the lineage grew over the generations. By
that point, however, the shares of each beneficiary would have become
so small that they did not provide the basis for common economic interests. Moreover, more distant cousins did not share households. They
were rarely chosen as marriage partners in endogamous marriages; it was
more common to see marriage partners chosen from other families connected by marriage than from more distant cousins within the patrilineage. Larger kinship groups were inherently unstable. Over time they
would expand and then often contract, as the difficulties of reproducing
the lineage each generation intervened. If they continued to grow and
expand, they divided up into distinct branches that shared a sense of common family identity through having the same family name, but did not
appear to have much contact in other ways.

The strongest ties of kin were forged with one's close relatives, by
birth and by marriage: parents, spouses, children, siblings, nieces and
nephews, and first cousins. It was from among this group that one found
marriage partners and sought guardians for children; with them one

shared a household and inheritance and other economic interests. Over the course of individual life cycles, the strength of these ties often changed as the boundaries of these families shifted. An individual moved in and out of these family groups, and the group of significant kin changed. At certain points or under certain circumstances the strongest and most active ties were between members of the conjugal family. When the death of parents in a joint family household was followed by the breakup of the household and the prompt settlement of inheritance, the severing of economic ties and reversion to simple households would reinforce the conjugal family. At other times, the extended family—parents, siblings, aunts and uncles, and/or cousins—would constitute the family. Joint family households would incorporate a wider circle of kin, although which ones would depend on whether these were joint family households of fathers and sons, or of brothers, or of uncles, nephews, and cousins. New marriages among cousins, both paternal and maternal, produced new layers of kinship ties that affected relationships among kin inside and outside the household. Individuals whose economic activities and control of resources had been completely independent would find themselves connected by common economic interests that resulted from inheritance or the establishment of family endowments. A variety of factors determined whether an individual spent most of her or his life in simple or joint households and how much contact they had with which family members: the extent and kind of resources, levels of fertility and rates of mortality, personal relationships among family members, the way in which a particular family was affected by the vagaries of political life and economic change.

The fact that kinship ties were strongest among close relatives had another important implication for the nature of the kinship system. Despite the strong patrilineal emphasis in the law and in the ideology of kinship, close maternal relatives were also very important. Marriages with maternal kin, as well as common economic ties created by inheritance and endowment, reinforced these links outside the patriline. This was, in effect, a bilateral kinship system.

Two important points about the elite families in Aleppo during this period follow from the emphases on kinship ties among close relatives, on the fluidity of family boundaries, and on the multiplicity of factors that influenced household structures, marriage choices, and economic arrangements. One is that the ideal of the large patriarchal, patrilineal family—reproducing itself generation after generation and characterized

by the immense power of the patriarch, joint ownership or management
of economic resources, joint family households, and restrictions on the
economic and social autonomy of family members, especially women—
was rarely achieved. Some families came close to achieving it in Aleppo
during this period: a few wealthy merchants and a few of the politically
ambitious and powerful. But even among these families it rarely lasted beyond the death of the powerful patriarchs around whom the family had
centered. Subsequent generations were not able to reproduce it. While
the ideal may have been shared by many families, the reality was too hard
to achieve for more than short periods of time; too many factors intervened to prevent it from happening.

The second point is that different family arrangements had important
implications for the gender system. The difficulties of reconstructing the
lives of women in the past remain formidable, despite the progress that
has been made in recent years. The biggest difficulty is our inability to see
the lives of women through their own eyes; the absence of women's
voices before the nineteenth century is an overwhelming obstacle. The
few exceptions to this bleak picture only highlight what we are missing
without these voices. Leslie Peirce's work on the Ottoman royal harem is
a brilliant study of the structure and dynamics of this complex institution
and the nature of the authority and power of royal women. It also gives
"voice" to these women in a way that not only humanizes them but also
forces us to reevaluate our perceptions of these women of the harem and
of their role as political actors. They cease to be the manipulative, power-
hungry, and self-serving schemers of the "reign of women"; instead they
emerge as legitimate political actors whose role was shaped by the very
nature of the Ottoman system, who exercised power and sovereignty in
ways that were expected of them, and who were concerned about the interests of the Ottoman state.[1] Without women's voices, discussions of
gender and patriarchy that attempt to take a long historical view too easily fall into the trap of changelessness, even among scholars who are sen-
sitive to the complexities, ambiguities, and nuances of gender relations in
the present and more recent past.

The late eighteenth and early nineteenth centuries in Syria do not offer us much more in the way of texts through which women can speak.
Yet as a source in which women appear as frequent actors, the religious
court archives provide a record of the daily experiences of women's lives
that offer the best substitute for actual voices. The high visibility of
women in these sources indicates that many used the means available to

them through the law and the courts to negotiate their position within
the family and in some cases to play an active role in the outside world as
well. What the court records reveal about the nature of the household,
the importance of marriage as a social strategy and mechanism for the integration of this social group, and the role of women as transmitters of
wealth and property suggests that there were opportunities for women in
the way in which the processes of family life unfolded. Household
arrangements were flexible and dynamic. Within the household, age hierarchies were as important, if not more important, than gender hierarchies. Older women exercised great influence in these households over
both males and females. Young men were often as vulnerable and powerless as young women. With maturity, women, as well as men, acquired
positions of greater authority and responsibility. Moreover, short life
spans and male mortality sometimes made women de facto heads of
households. Marriages were key to the successful reproduction of a family, both in a literal and a figurative way. Marriages produced offspring
to continue the family line, but were also instrumental in maintaining
wealth, power, and status over time. Women, key actors in the system as
marriage partners and as marriage brokers, were essential to its successful
functioning. A concern for the status of daughters and the connections
that females maintained with their natal families, particularly close ties
between brothers and sisters, provided them with protection, especially
in the early years of marriage in a new household where they had little
clout as yet. Their access to and control over property, as well as their role
as transmitters of property, also gave them some leverage. These situations
influenced the realities of women's lives and redressed the imbalance between the genders.

This is not to deny the many ways in which women's freedom of action was restricted and their ability to resist the dictates of males with authority over them limited by law and social norms. The gender system in
Ottoman Aleppo remained a patriarchal one in which men by law, custom, and practice were in a dominant position. The power that men had
over women, and the ways in which women could be abused, mistreated,
and deprived of their rights, were very real. Nevertheless, in most cases
the importance of women to the family had an impact on how they were
treated and provided them with opportunities that are often overlooked.
The family could be a structure through which women's subordination
was reinforced and reproduced under certain conditions. However, the
family could also be a structure that empowered them. The way in which

many families were organized and the patterns of family life over time gave women important roles to play and the authority and status associated with these roles.

The larger significance of these conclusions about the family and about gender relations in Ottoman Aleppo remains unclear in the absence of more studies of the family in the early modern period, in other parts of the Middle East, and in other classes. Were these family arrangements and gender relations fairly typical, at least among elite families, before the social transformations of the nineteenth century, or did the early modern period witness important changes in the family and kinship, as has been suggested? Did the use of family names among the elite reflect a new sense of "dynasty" that was symptomatic of a new emphasis on family and kinship ties? Were larger kinship structures becoming more or less important than before? Did a more decentralized Ottoman state mean an enhancement of the power of the family patriarch or more opportunities for women to have access to resources, take advantage of the political climate, and therefore have greater autonomy? Were these families more or less patriarchal? There are no answers to any of these questions in this study, since we still know too little about the family in the early modern Ottoman Empire to be able to make generalizations about family patterns. We know even less about the family before this period, so cannot begin to determine the direction and significance of whatever changes might be occurring. However, I hope that this study helps to identify some of the critical questions we need to pursue and underscores the need for more case studies to help us find those answers.

Appendix One THE NOTABLE
FAMILIES OF
ALEPPO

The following table is a list of the 104 families included in this study. In addition to the family name, there is information about each family that provides supporting evidence for the discussion in Chapter 1 of the social bases of elite status and of social mobility among these notables. "Occupation" refers to the professional category with which family members were associated when the family rose to prominence in the city: ulema, merchant, or 'askari. Two of the families, the Ghawri and Munqar, are not included in any of these categories, but rather are referred to as Mamluk families, since they both claim to trace their roots back to freed slaves of Mamluk officials. They are included with the 'askari families, that is, among those who were called "secular notables" by Hourani, when calculating the relative numbers of families in each occupational category. The "Sharif" column indicates whether or not the family belonged to the ashraf, those who claimed descent from the Prophet Muhammad. The "Resident in Aleppo" columns indicate the approximate times when these families were prominent in Aleppo, before, during, or after the period under study. The "1770" column shows which families were notable families at the beginning of the period under study. The "1830" column indicates those families who had notable status by the last decade of this period and therefore shows how much upward mobility there was, as well as which families had disappeared from the sources by the end of this period. The "1570," "1670," and "1930" columns show long-term patterns of social mobility.

Family Name	Occupation	Sharif	Resident in Aleppo				
			1570	1670	1770	1830	1930
ʿAbd al-Baqi	ʿaskari	Y			x	x	x
ʿAbd al-Rahman Pasha	ʿaskari	N			x	x	x
ʿAbdi Agha	ʿaskari	N			x		
ʿAddas	merchant	Y				x	x
ʿAdili	ʿaskari	Y	x	x	x	x	x
Ahmad Pasha	ʿaskari	N			x	x	
ʿAjami	merchant	Y			x		
Alwand Pasha	ʿaskari	Y		x	x	x	
Amiri	merchant	Y			x	x	x
ʿAqqad	ulema	Y			x	x	x
Arihawi	merchant	Y		x	x		
Asadi	ulema	Y			x		
Babi	ʿaskari	Y			x	x	
Bakhsha	ulema	Y		x	x		
Batruni	ulema	Y	x	x	x	x	
Bayazid	merchant	N			x	x	x
Bayyan	ʿaskari/merchant	N			x		
Biri	ulema/merchant	Y			x	x	
Dadikhi	ulema	Y			x	x	x
Dahana	merchant	?				x	x
Dhahir	merchant	?				x	x
Fakhri	unknown	Y			x	x	
Fansa	ulema/merchant	Y			x	x	x
Ghannam	ulema/merchant	Y			x	x	x
Ghawri	Mamluk	Y	x	x	x	x	x
Ghazu	merchant	Y			x		
Ghuzuli	merchant	Y			x	x	
Halawi	ulema	Y			x	x	x
Hamawi	merchant	Y			x	x	x
Hamid	ulema	Y			x	x	
Hamza Bey	ʿaskari	Y			x	x	x
Hanbali	ulema	Y	x	x	x	x	
Hariri	merchant	Y			x	x	x
Hasabi	ulema	Y			x	x	x
Hatab	merchant	Y			x	x	
Haykal	merchant	Y			x	x	
Hijazi	ulema	Y			x		

Family Name	Occupation	Sharif	Resident in Aleppo				
			1570	1670	1770	1830	1930
Ibrahim Pasha	ʿaskari	Y				x	x
Ikhlas	ulema	Y			x	x	
ʿImadi	ulema	Y	x		x		
ʿIsabi	unknown	Y			x		
Jabiri	ulema	Y			x	x	x
Jaliq	merchant	Y			x	x	x
Jamili	merchant	Y			x	x	x
Jawbi	unknown	N			x	x	x
Jazmati	merchant	Y			x	x	x
Jurbaji	merchant	N			x	x	
Kabisi	ulema	Y			x	x	
Kahya	unknown	N				x	
Kanj ʿAli	ʿaskari	N		x	x	x	x
Katkhuda	unknown	Y			x	x	x
Kawakibi	ulema	Y	x	x	x	x	x
Kayyali	ulema	Y		x	x	x	x
Khanji	merchant	N				x	x
Khankarli	ʿaskari	Y			x	x	
Kucuk ʿAli Agha	ʿaskari	Y		x	x	x	x
Kurani	ulema	Y	x	x	x	x	x
Labaq	ulema/merchant	Y		x	x	x	x
Madhir	unknown	N			x		
Miri	ulema/merchant	Y			x	x	x
Misri	ulema	Y			x		
Mudarris	ulema	Y				x	x
Muharram	ulema	Y			x		
Munqar	Mamluk	Y	x	x	x	x	
Muqayyid	ulema	Y			x	x	x
Muwahibi	ulema	Y			x	x	
Muwaqqiʿ	ulema	Y			x	x	x
Muwaqqit	ulema/merchant	Y			x	x	x
Naqib	ulema	Y		x	x		
Nasimi	ulema	Y			x		
Nasir al-Din Bey	ʿaskari	Y		x	x	x	
Nawaʿi	unknown	Y			x	x	
Qabbad Bey	ʿaskari	Y		x	x	x	
Qabbani	ulema	Y			x	x	x
Qamari	merchant	Y			x	x	

Family Name	Occupation	Sharif	1570	1670	1770	1830	1930
				Resident in Aleppo			
Qana'a	merchant	N				x	x
Qudsi	ulema	Y				x	x
Qulaqsuz	ulema	Y		x	x	x	
Qurna	merchant	Y			x	x	x
Rajab Pasha	'askari	N				x	x
Rifa'i	ulema	Y			x	x	x
Sabba'i	merchant	N				x	x
Sadiq	unknown	Y		x			
Safari	unknown	Y		x	x		
Sa'id Agha	'askari	N			x		
Sharabati	ulema	Y		x	x		
Shaykhbandar	'askari	Y		x	x	x	
Shukri	ulema	Y		x	x		
Shurayyif	merchant	Y			x	x	x
Siyyaf	merchant	Y			x	x	x
Tabbakh	ulema/merchant	Y			x	x	x
Tabla	merchant	Y			x	x	
Taha	ulema	Y		x	x	x	x
Taybi	unknown	Y			x	x	
Trabulsi	ulema	Y		x	x	x	x
Ubri	merchant	Y			x	x	
'Ulabi	merchant	Y	x	x	x	x	
'Uqayli	ulema	Y				x	x
'Uthmani	merchant	Y			x	x	
Yahya Bey	'askari	Y			x		
Yakin	'askari	N			x	x	x
Za'im	unknown	Y			x	x	
Zanabili	merchant	Y			x	x	x
Zayyat	merchant	Y			x	x	

Appendix Two S E L E C T E D
G E N E A L O G I E S

        To keep this appendix to a manageable length, I
have included genealogies for only ten of the families in this study. These
ten were chosen for a number of reasons. All of them are mentioned on
several occasions in the text. The Taha, Shaykhbandar, and Shurayyif
families are used as examples of "typical" notable families in Chapter 1.
The Jabiri family is used to illustrate household patterns in Chapter 2, and
the Ghawri, Hamawi, and Qudsi families to illustrate marriage patterns
in Chapter 3. The latter three are also mentioned at other times. The
choice of the other three families—the Amiri, the Kawakibi, and the
Ibrahim Pasha—was more arbitrary; there were many other families that
could have been chosen as well. However, each of these families was
prominent in Aleppo during the period of study, albeit for different reasons, and each illustrates some important features of elite families during
this time. As a group, these ten families represent different occupational
categories and political positions; some of them were old families and
some new. In other words, in terms of social characteristics, they represent the diverse elements in Aleppo's social elite.

    The genealogies are arranged alphabetically. In some of them, names
have been shortened or omitted because of space limitations. In the few
cases where names are omitted, sex is indicated (i.e., "2 daughters" or "3
sons" might be used instead of giving the name of each). Names are usually omitted only for individuals who were not known to be married and
did not have any known offspring. Women or, in a couple of cases, men
who were originally slaves are indicated, as they were in the sources, by
the patronymic "bint (daughter of) ʿAbd Allah" or "ibn (son of) ʿAbd
Allah." The abbreviation "M." stands for Muhammad.

AMIRI

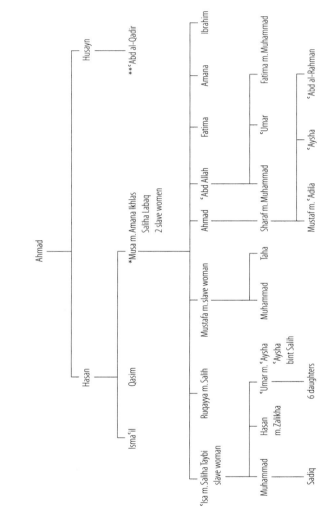

(* Because Musa had so many children, they would not all fit on one page. The rest of his offspring and their descendants appear on the next page.)
(** ʿAbd al-Qadir's line can be found on the page after next.)

AMIRI (2)

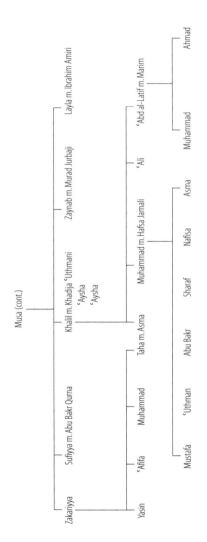

Musa (cont.)

Zakariyya — Sufiyya m. Abu Bakr Qurna — Taha m. Asma — Khalil m. Khadija ʿUthmani — Zaynab m. Murad Jurbaji — Layla m. Ibrahim Amiri

ʿAfifa — Muhammad — Abu Bakr — ʿAysha / ʿAysha — Muhammad m. Hafsa Jamali — ʿAli — ʿAbd al-Latif m. Marim

Yasin — ʿUthman — Sharaf — Nafisa — Asma — Muhammad — Ahmad

Mustafa

AMIRI (3)

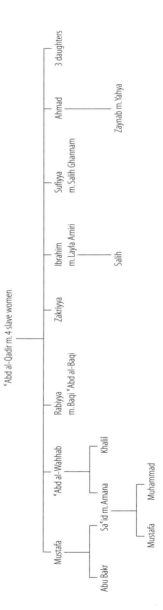

'Abd al-Qadir m. 4 slave women

Mustafa — 'Abd al-Wahhab — Rabiyya m. Baqi 'Abd al-Baqi — Zakriyya — Ibrahim m. Layla Amiri — Sufiyya m. Salih Ghannam — Ahmad — 3 daughters

'Abd al-Wahhab: Khalil

Mustafa: Abu Bakr, Sa'id m. Amana

Sa'id m. Amana: Mustafa, Muhammad

Ibrahim m. Layla Amiri: Salih

Ahmad: Zaynab m. Yahya

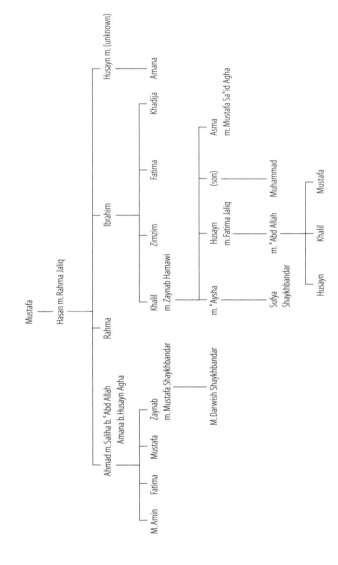

GHAWRI

Mustafa
Hasan m. Rahma Jaliq

Husayn m. (unknown)
Amana

Ibrahim
Khadija
Fatima
Zimzim
Khalil m. Zaynab Hamawi

Asma m. Mustafa Saʿid Agha
(son)
Husayn m. Fatima Jaliq
m. ʿAbd Allah
Muhammad

m. ʿAysha

Sufya Shaykhbandar
Husayn
Khalil
Mustafa

Rahma

Ahmad m. Saliha b. ʿAbd Allah
Amana b. Husayn Agha
Zaynab m. Mustafa Shaykhbandar
M. Darwish Shaykhbandar
Mustafa
Fatima
M. Amin

HAMAWI

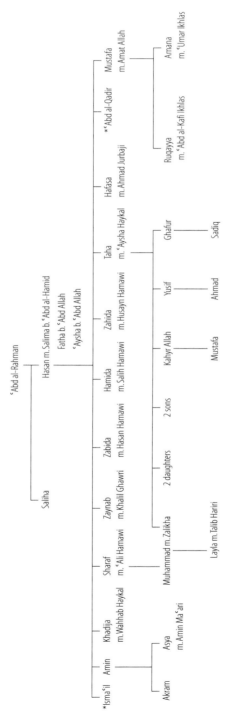

'Abd al-Rahman

Saliha

Hasan m. Salima b. 'Abd al-Hamid
Fatha b. 'Abd Allah
'Aysha b. 'Abd Allah

*Isma'il

Amin
— Akram
— Asya m. Amin Ma'ari

Khadija m. Wahhab Haykal

Sharaf m. 'Ali Hamawi
— Muhammad m. Zalikha
— Layla m. Talib Hariri

Zaynab m. Khalil Ghawri
— 2 daughters

Zabida m. Hasan Hamawi
— 2 sons

Hamida m. Salih Hamawi
— Kahyr Allah
— Mustafa

Zahida m. Husayn Hamawi
— Yusif
— Ahmad

Taha m. 'Aysha Haykal
— Ghafur
— Sadiq

Hafasa m. Ahmad Jurbaji
— Ruqayya m. 'Abd al-Kafi Ikhlas
— *'Abd al-Qadir

Mustafa m. Amat Allah
— Amana m. 'Umar Ikhlas

(* see following page)

HAMAWI (2)

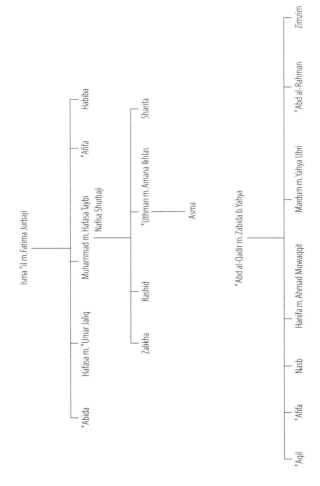

Isma'il m. Fatima Jurbaji

'Abida

Hafasa m. 'Umar Jaliq

Zalikha

Rashid

Muhammad m. Hafasa Taybi
Nafisa Shurbaji

'Afifa

Habiba

'Uthman m. Amana Ikhlas

Asma

Sharifa

'Abd al-Qadir m. Zabida b. Yahya

'Aqil

'Afifa

Nasb

Hanifa m. Ahmad Muwaqqit

Mardum m. Yahya Ubri

'Abd al-Rahman

Zimzim

IBRAHIM PASHA

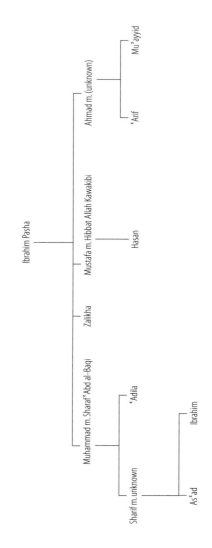

JABIRI

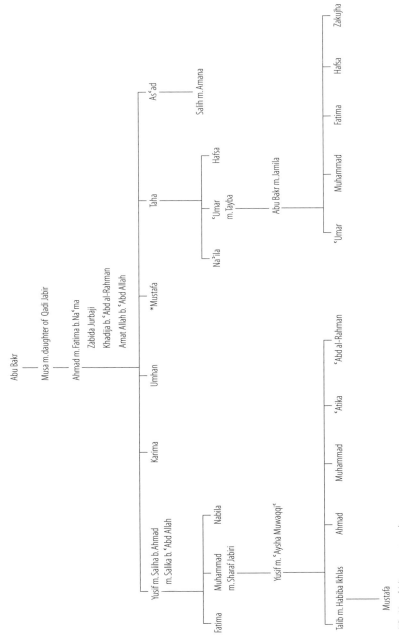

Abu Bakr
Musa m. daughter of Qadi Jabir
Ahmad m. Fatima b. Naʿma
Zabida Jurbaji
Khadija b. ʿAbd al-Rahman
Amat Allah b. ʿAbd Allah

Karima   Umhan   *Mustafa   Taha   Asʿad

Salih m. Amana

Naʾila   ʿUmar m. Tayba   Hafsa

Abu Bakr m. Jamila

ʿUmar   Muhammad   Fatima   Hafsa   Zakujha

Yusif m. Saliha b. Ahmad
m. Salika b. ʿAbd Allah

Fatima   Muhammad m. Sharaf Jabiri   Nabila

Yusif m. ʿAysha Muwaqqiʿ

Talib m. Habiba Ikhlas   Ahmad   Muhammad   ʿAtika   ʿAbd al-Rahman

Mustafa

(*For Mustafa's line, see next page.)

JABIRI (2)

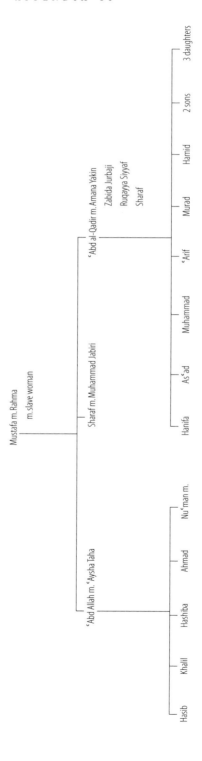

Mustafa m. Rahma
m. slave woman

'Abd Allah m. 'Aysha Taha

Sharaf m. Muhammad Jabiri

Hasib

Khalil

Hashiba

Ahmad

Nu'man m.

Hanifa

As'ad

Muhammad

'Arif

'Abd al-Qadir m. Amana Yakin
Zabida Jurbaji
Ruqayya Siyyaf
Sharaf

Murad

Hamid

2 sons

3 daughters

KAWAKIBI

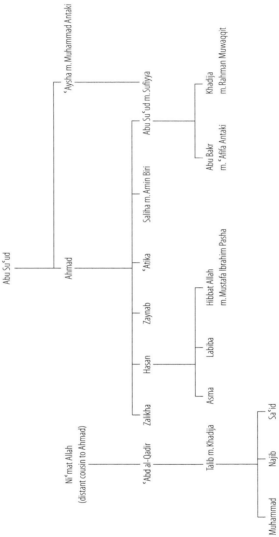

Abu Suʿud

Ahmad

ʿAysha m. Muhammad Antaki

Abu Suʿud m. Sufiyya

Saliha m. Amin Biri

ʿAtika

Hibbat Allah
m. Mustafa Ibrahim Pasha

Zaynab

Labiba

Hasan

Asma

Zalikha

Abu Bakr
m. ʿAfifa Antaki

Khadija
m. Rahman Muwaqqit

Niʿmat Allah
(distant cousin to Ahmad)

ʿAbd al-Qadir

Talib m. Khadija

Saʿid

Najib

Muhammad

QUDSI

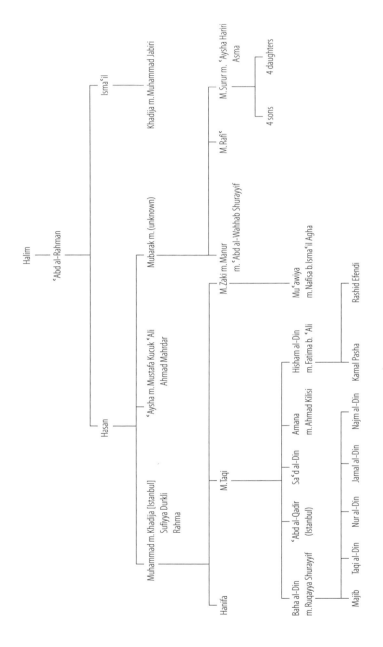

Halim

ʿAbd al-Rahman

Ismaʿil

Hasan

ʿAysha m. Mustafa Kucuk ʿAli / Ahmad Mahrdar

Khadija m. Muhammad Jabiri

Mubarak m. (unknown)

Hanifa

Muhammad m. Khadija [Istanbul] / Sufiyya Durkli / Rahma

M. Taqi

M. Zaki m. Manur / m. ʿAbd al-Wahhab Shurayyif

M. Rafiʿ

M. Surur m. ʿAysha Hariri / Asma

4 sons   4 daughters

ʿAbd al-Qadir (Istanbul)

Saʿd al-Din

Amana m. Ahmad Kilisi

Hisham al-Din m. Fatima b. ʿAli

Muʿawiya m. Nafisa b. Ismaʿil Agha

Baha al-Din m. Ruqayya Shurayyif

Majib   Taqi al-Din   Nur al-Din   Jamal al-Din   Najm al-Din   Kamal Pasha   Rashid Efendi

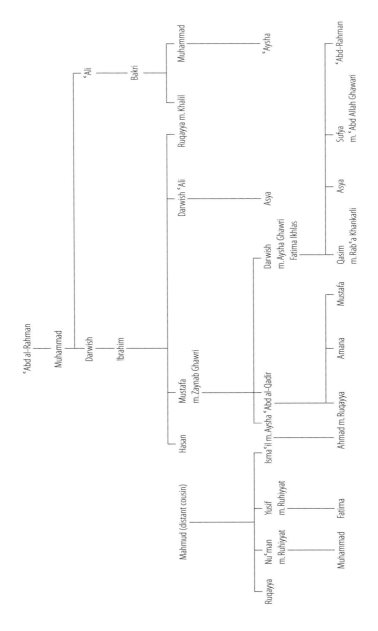

SHAYKHBANDAR

SHURAYYIF

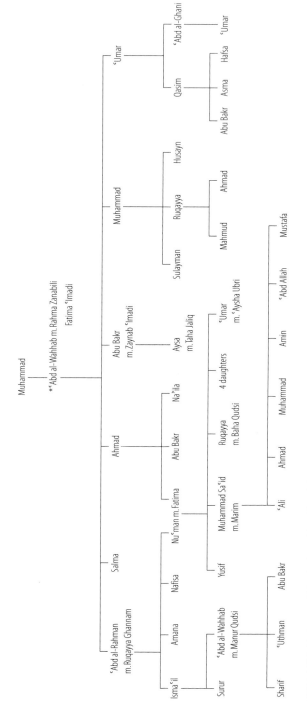

(*ʿAbd al-Wahhab had so many children that they could not all be included on this page. See following page for the rest of his children and their descendants.)

SHURAYYIF (cont.)

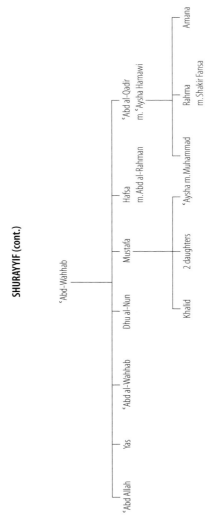

'Abd-Wahhab

'Abd Allah — Yās — 'Abd al-Wahhab — Dhu al-Nun — Mustafa — Hafsa m. Abd al-Rahman — 'Abd al-Qadir m. 'Aysha Hamawi

Khalid — 2 daughters — 'Aysha m. Muhammad — Rahma m. Shakir Fansa — Amana

TAHA

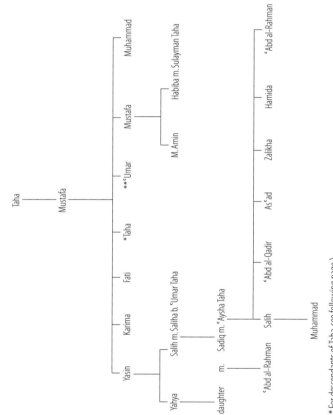

(* For descendants of Taha, see following page.)
(** For descendants of ʿUmar, see page after the next.)

TAHA (2)

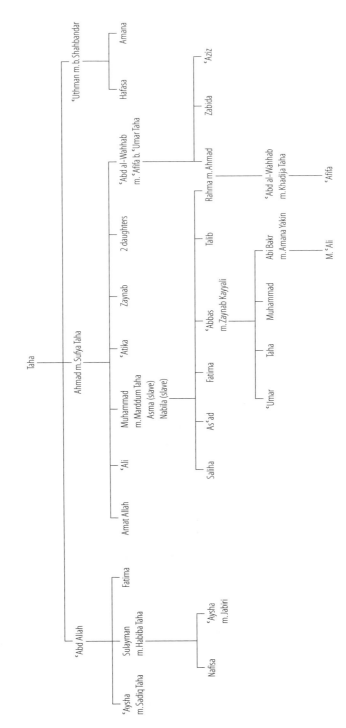

TAHA (3)

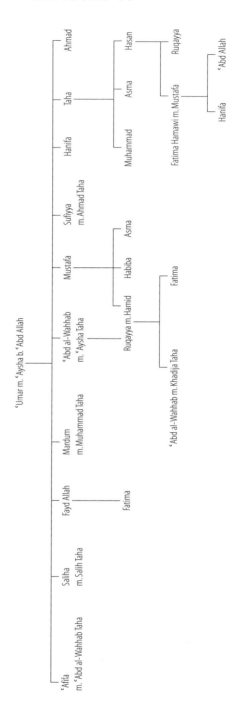

'Umar m. 'Aysha b. 'Abd Allah

'Afifa m. 'Abd al-Wahhab Taha

Saliha m. Salih Taha

Fayd Allah — Fatima

Mardum m. Muhammad Taha

'Abd al-Wahhab m. 'Aysha Taha

'Abd al-Wahhab m. Khadija Taha

Ruqayya m. Hamid — Fatima

Mustafa — Habiba — Asma

Sufiyya m. Ahmad Taha

Hanifa

Taha

Ahmad

Muhammad — Hasan — Asma

Fatima Hamawi m. Mustafa

Hanifa — 'Abd Allah

Ruqayya

Notes

INTRODUCTION

1. Lawrence Stone, "Family History in the 1980's," *Journal of Interdisciplinary History* 12 (1981), p. 82.

2. Ibid., p 87.

3. The only book-length historical study of the family to date is by Alan Duben and Cem Behar, *Istanbul Households: Marriage, Family, and Fertility, 1880–1940.* Duben has also written two articles on related topics, "Turkish Families and Households in Historical Perspective," *Journal of Family History* 10 (1985): 75–97, and "Understanding Muslim Households in the Late Ottoman Period," *Journal of Family History* 15 (1990): 71–86; Kenneth Cuno has written two articles on Egyptian households, "Joint Family Households and Rural Notables in Nineteenth-Century Egypt," *International Journal of Middle East Studies* 27 (1995), and "A Tale of Two Villages: Family, Property, and Economic Activity in Rural Egypt in the 1840's." Judith Tucker has published two articles on the family in Nablus (Palestine), "Marriage and Family in Nablus, 1720–1856: Towards a History of Arab Marriage," *Journal of Family History* 13 (1988): 165–179, and "Ties That Bound: Women and Family in Eighteenth- and Nineteenth-Century Nablus," 233–253, and she has also written "The Arab Family in History," in *Arab Women: Old Boundaries, New Frontiers,* which she edited. The volume edited by Nikki Keddie and Beth Baron has a chapter on marriage in Egypt by Beth Baron: "The Making and Breaking of Marital Bonds in Modern Egypt." Other articles on the family include Beshara Doumani's "Endowing Family: *Waqf,* Devolution, and Gender in Greater Syria, 1800–1860," *Comparative Studies in Society and History* 40 (1998): 3–41; Linda S. Schilcher's "The Lore and Reality of Middle Eastern Patriarchy," *Die Welt des Islams* 28 (1988): 496–512; Haim Gerber's "Anthropology and Family History: The Ottoman and Turkish Families," *Journal of Family History* 14

(1989): 409–421; and chapters by Peter Gran, Abdal-Rehim Abdal-Rahman Abdal-Rehim, Nelly Hanna, and Mary Ann Fay in the volume edited by Amira E. Sonbol, *Women, the Family, and Divorce Laws in Islamic History.*

4. Duben and Behar, *Istanbul Households,* pp. 48–86; Duben, "Turkish Families," pp. 81–82. There is a more complete discussion of Duben's work on households in Chapter 2.

5. Gerber, "Anthropology and Family History," p. 419.

6. Chapter 2 deals with households, and a full discussion of the present state of our knowledge of Ottoman households is included there.

7. For example, see the recent book by Judith Tucker, *In the House of the Law: Gender and Islamic Law in Ottoman Syria and Palestine.*

8. Tucker, "Marriage and Family in Nablus," pp. 177–178.

9. Tucker, "Ties That Bound," p. 250.

10. Duben and Behar, *Istanbul Households,* chs. 3–4; Beth Baron, "Marital Bonds in Modern Egypt," pp. 275–291.

11. Deniz Kandiyoti, "Islam and Patriarchy: A Comparative Perspective," in *Women in Middle Eastern History: Shifting Boundaries in Sex and Gender,* ed. Nikki Keddie and Beth Baron, pp. 23–42; Mervat Hatem, "Class and Patriarchy as Competing Paradigms for the Study of Middle Eastern Women," *Comparative Studies in Society and History* 29 (1987): 811–818.

12. Raphael Patai sums up these characteristics in *Society, Culture, and Change in the Middle East,* p. 84.

13. Gerber, "Anthropology and Family History," p. 411.

14. See questions raised by Tucker in "Ties That Bound," p. 234.

15. Hatem, "Class and Patriarchy," pp. 816–818.

16. Mervat Hatem, "Politics of Sexuality and Gender in Segregated Patriarchal Systems: The Case of Egypt in the Eighteenth and Nineteenth Centuries," *Feminist Studies* 12 (1986), p. 255.

17. Schilcher, "Lore and Reality," pp. 497–498.

18. Nelly Hanna, "Marriage among Merchant Families in Seventeenth-Century Cairo," in *Women, the Family, and Divorce Laws in Islamic History,* ed. Amira E. Sonbol, pp. 143–144; Afaf Marsot, *Women and Men in Late Eighteenth-Century Egypt,* pp. 14–15, 153–154.

19. See "Sources and Methodology" in the Introduction for a discussion of terminology.

20. Tucker, *In the House of the Law;* Annelies Moors has done an excellent review of this literature in a chapter, "Debating Islamic Family Law: Legal Texts and Social Practices," in *Social History of Women and Gender in the Middle East,* ed. Margaret L. Meriwether and Judith Tucker.

21. Hatem, "Politics of Sexuality," p. 256.

22. Leon B. Alberti, *The Family in Renaissance Florence.*

23. Tucker's article "Marriage and Family in Nablus" is based on marriage contracts found in the religious court archives of that town, and chapters by Hanna and Abdal-Rehim in Sonbol are based on these contracts for Cairo, which has a particularly large collection.

24. Galal al-Nahal, *Judicial Administration in Ottoman Egypt in the Seventeenth Century,* p. 13.

25. Haim Gerber, *State, Society, and Law in Islam,* p. 56.

26. Abraham Marcus, *The Middle East on the Eve of Modernity,* p. 10; Judith Tucker, *Women in Nineteenth-Century Egypt,* p. 13.

27. Compare Tucker, *Women in Egypt,* p. 14.

28. Julius Kirshner, "Some Problems in the Interpretation of Legal Texts *re* the Italian City-States," *Archiv für Begriffgeschichte* 19 (1975): 16−27.

29. The form of family names in the sources follows the common usage in the Ottoman Empire at the time: a proper name (usually that of the first prominent member of the family), or an adjective denoting occupation, place of origin, or some other distinguishing characteristic, is followed by the Persian suffix -*zade,* which means "son of." The use of -*zade* distinguished family names from such adjectives used in a descriptive way. Confirmation of this connection of families with family names and notable families comes from the honorific titles often given to members of these families and from biographical dictionaries and other literary sources. See comments by Hanna Batatu in *Old Social Classes and the Revolutionary Movements of Iraq,* p. 319, for use of similar family names among the upper class in other parts of the Ottoman Empire.

30. For a discussion of family reconstitution, see Andrejs Plakans, *Kinship in the Past: An Anthropology of European Family Life, 1500−1900,* pp. 25−50; Richard T. Vann, "The New Demographic History," in *International Handbook of Historical Studies: Contemporary Research and Theory,* ed. George E. Izzus and Harold T. Parker; and E. Anthony Wrigley, "Reflections on the History of the Family." *Daedalus: The Family* 106 (1977): 71−85.

31. Diane Owen Hughes, "Toward a Historical Ethnography: Notarial Records and Family History in the Middle Ages," *Historical Methods Newsletter* 7 (1974): 63, 61−71 passim.

32. Plakans, *Kinship in the Past,* p. 39.

33. Kazem Daghestani, *Étude sociologique sur la famille musulmane contemporaine en Syrie,* pp. 147−149, 189−190.

34. I have deliberately chosen to avoid the use of "nuclear" family, since its close association with a particular kind of family found in Western industrialized societies has given it connotations that are not appropriate to the early modern Middle Eastern context.

35. Marcus, *Eve of Modernity,* pp. 330−331.

36. Karl Barbir, *Ottoman Rule in Damascus, 1708−1758,* pp. 8−10.

37. André Raymond, *The Great Arab Cities from the Sixteenth to the Eighteenth Centuries: An Introduction*, p. 3.

38. The most thorough discussion of this political history is still Herbert Bodman, *Political Factions in Aleppo, 1760-1826*. See also Marcus, *Eve of Modernity*, pp. 73–101.

39. For further discussion of these events, see below.

40. Charles Issawi, "Economic Change and Urbanization in the Middle East," in *Middle Eastern Cities*, ed. L. Carl Brown; Jean Sauvaget, *Alep: Essai sur la développement d'une grande ville syrienne, des origines au milieau du XIXe siècle*; Niels Steensgaard, *The Asian Trade Revolution of the Seventeenth Century: The East India Company and the Decline of the Caravan Trade*.

41. Bruce Masters, *The Origins of Western Economic Dominance in the Middle East: Mercantilism and the Islamic Economy in Aleppo, 1600-1750*, pp. 3, 29.

42. Antoine Abdel-Nour, *Introduction a l'histoire urbaine de la Syrie ottomane*, p. 271.

43. Ibid., pp. 66–69. Other historians accept Abdel-Nour's conclusion about population trends in the city—that is, a population of 60,000 in the early decades of the sixteenth century, then a population decline before it begins to grow significantly after 1570; rapid population growth in the seventeenth century, followed by a slower rate of growth in the early part of the eighteenth century. However, there is disagreement about the size of the population at the end of the seventeenth century, as well as about population trends in the second half of the eighteenth century. Masters uses a figure of 115,000 in 1683, in contrast to Abdel-Nour's 83,000. Masters also believes that there was a sharp decline in the population between 1750 and 1800, so that the population in 1800 was about 80,000 (p. 41). Abdel-Nour estimates the population in 1800 at 120,000, a result of extensive rural migration in the wake of worsening conditions in the countryside in the latter decades of the eighteenth century (pp. 67–70); this figure is also accepted by Raymond.

44. For a full discussion of migration to Aleppo, see Bruce Masters, "Patterns of Migration to Ottoman Aleppo in the Seventeenth and Eighteenth Centuries," *International Journal of Turkish Studies* 4 (1987): 75–89.

45. For more on these families and their origins, see Chapter 1.

46. Suraiya Faroqhi used the phrase "men of modest substance" to describe property owners in two Anatolian cities (see *Men of Modest Substance: House Owners and House Property in Seventeenth-Century Ankara and Kayseri*. This group of small property owners seems comparable to what was found in Aleppo.

47. Ralph Davis, *Aleppo and Devonshire Square*, p. 27.

48. Abdel-Nour, *Introduction*, p. 279.

49. Masters, *Economic Dominance*, pp. 217–218.

50. Ibid., p. 218.

51. Christina Phelps Harris, *The Syrian Desert: Caravan, Travel, and Exploration*, p. 76.

52. William G. Browne, *Travels in Africa, Egypt, and Syria*, p. 386.

53. Batatu, *Old Social Classes*, pp. 226–234.

54. Compare Batatu's comments on the "migratory" nature of the caravan trade and its ability to flourish, despite difficult circumstances, by shifting routes. See *Old Social Classes*, p. 233.

55. Paul Masson, *Histoire du commerce français dans le Levant au XVIIIe siècle*, p. 325.

56. Abdel-Nour, *Introduction*, pp. 118–124. Some of Abdel-Nour's discussion of changes in the real estate market and housing conditions from the seventeenth to the eighteenth century and therefore his interpretation and conclusions are problematic, but his basic point about a housing shortage in the late eighteenth century seems valid.

57. Edward B. B. Barker, *Syria and Egypt under the Last Five Sultans of Turkey: Being the Experiences during Fifty Years of Mr. Consul-General Barker*, 1: 24–25.

58. Muhammad Raghib al-Tabbakh, *Iʿlam al-nubala bi taʾrikh halab al-shahba*, 3: 376.

59. The clearest evidence of this are the many cases over the next ten years in the court records about religious endowment property. In these cases, the administrators state that the property was destroyed by the earthquake and that there was no money in the endowment to pay for rebuilding it and no income coming into the endowment from rental of the property.

60. Bruce Masters, "The 1850 Events in Aleppo: An Aftershock of Syria's Incorporation into the World Capitalist System," *International Journal of Middle East Studies* 22 (1990): 3–20.

61. John Bowring, *Report on the Commercial Statistics of Syria*, pp. 77, 88.

62. Masters, "The 1850 Events in Aleppo," p. 5.

63. Ibid., pp. 3–20.

CHAPTER 1

1. Ira Lapidus, "The Evolution of Muslim Urban Society," *Comparative Studies in Society and History* 15 (1973): 21–50.

2. Richard Bulliet, *The Patricians of Nishapur*, pp. 20–21 and 26–27; Ira Lapidus, *Muslim Cities in the Later Middle Ages*, pp. 188–190.

3. Richard Bulliet, *Conversion to Islam in the Medieval Period*, pp. 137–138.

4. Albert Hourani, "Ottoman Reform and the Politics of Notables," in *Beginnings of Modernization in the Middle East*, ed. William Polk and Richard Chambers. This article has provided the framework for much of the discussion of notable politics, especially for the Syrian provinces.

5. Hourani, "Politics of Notables," p. 48.

6. Halil Inalcik, "Centralization and Decentralization in Ottoman Administration," in *Studies in Eighteenth-Century Islamic History*, ed. Thomas Naff and Roger Owen, pp. 37–38.

7. Bodman, *Political Factions*, p. 35.

8. Karl Barbir, *Ottoman Rule in Damascus, 1708–1758*, pp. 72–73.

9. Philip Khoury, *Urban Notables and Arab Nationalism: The Politics of Damascus, 1860–1920*, pp. 11–12.

10. Kemal Karpat, "The Transformation of the Ottoman State, 1789–1908," *International Journal of Middle East Studies* 3 (1972): 243–281.

11. Khoury, *Urban Notables*, pp. 12–13.

12. Batatu, *Old Social Classes*, p. 11.

13. I frequently use the term *upper class* in this study, but I use it as a descriptive phrase interchangeably with *social elite* or *notables*. I am not suggesting that these notables were a class in an analytical sense.

14. Masters, *Economic Dominance*, pp. 48–53.

15. Marcus, *Eve of Modernity*, p. 48.

16. Batatu, *Old Social Classes*, p. 319.

17. Ninety-one families appeared in the registers in the first decade of the period under study; ninety-nine families were present in the middle decade of this period; and only eighty-two in the final decade. Appendix 1 provides a full list of these families.

18. Alexander Russell, *A Natural History of Aleppo*, 1: 337.

19. Sources for this biography of the Taha family include Bodman, *Political Factions*, pp. 100–101; al-Tabbakh, *I'lam al-nubala*, 6: 469–474, 484–486 and 7: 59–60, 67–78, 522–523; Laurent d'Arvieux, *Memoires de Chevalier d'Arvieux*, 5: 536–537, 563–565, 581; as well as numerous entries in the religious court archives.

20. John Lewis Burckhardt, *Travels in Syria and the Holy Land*, p. 649.

21. Sources for this biography of the Shaykhbandar family include al-Tabbakh, *I'lam al-nubala*, 3: 354–355, and numerous entries in the religious court archives.

22. *'Askari*, literally meaning "military," and used to differentiate the ruling class of the Ottoman Empire from the subject class, will be used as a shorthand to designate those families who were descendants of Ottoman soldiers or officials (Hourani's "secular notables"), whether or not they were still actually "'askari." Included in this category will be the two families who were descendants of freed slaves of Mamluk officials, the Ghawris and the Munqars.

23. The biography of the Shurayyif family is based on al-Tabbakh, *I'lam al-nubala*, 7: 14, 239; Bodman, *Political Factions*, pp. 117–126; and numerous entries in the religious court archives.

24. See Appendix 1 for a breakdown of these families by occupations.

25. Khoury, *Urban Notables*, p. 13.

26. Masters, *Economic Dominance*, p.167.

27. Archives of the mahkama shar'iyya of Aleppo (hereafter cited as MSA), 223: 127 (28 Sha'ban 1248).

28. Al-Tabbakh, *I'lam al-nubala*, 5: 310.

29. This figure is a very rough estimate based on the fact that Muhammad was owed outstanding debts by eighty-six villages; these debts ranged from a few thousand qurush to 65,000 qurush. The larger debts were paid over time—usually twenty-

five or thirty years. This yearly income figure is probably low. ʿAbd al-Rahman Ubri's estate can be found in MSA 230: 264 (24 Muharram 1252).

30. Hourani, "Politics of Notables," p.54.

31. Batatu, *Old Social Classes,* p. 153.

32. See Appendix 1. This was also the case in Iraq. Compare Batatu, *Old Social Classes,* p. 153.

33. Hourani, "Politics of Notables," p.46.

34. Al-Tabbakh, *Iʿlam al-nubala,* 3: 373−374, 7: 172−174.

35. Muhammad Khalil al-Muradi, *Silk al-durar fi aʿyan al-qarn al-thani ʿashar,* 4: 248.

36. Khoury, *Urban Notables,* p. 12.

37. For a fuller discussion of marriage patterns and their role in cementing family alliances, see Chapter 3.

38. For Damascus, see Linda S. Schilcher, *Families in Politics: Damascene Factions and Estates in the Eighteenth and Nineteenth Centuries,* pp. 8−10.

39. Russell, *Natural History,* 1: 11−12.

40. Marcus, *Eve of Modernity,* p. 63.

41. Suraiya Faroqhi et al., *An Economic and Social History of the Ottoman Empire,* 2: 550, 590−592; Gerber, *State, Society, and Law,* p. 147.

42. Gerber, *State, Society, and Law,* pp. 149−151.

43. Carter Findley, *Bureaucratic Reform in the Ottoman Empire,* pp. 31−32; Madeline Zilfi, "Elite Circulation in the Ottoman Empire: The Great Mollas in the Eighteenth Century," *Journal of the Economic and Social History of the Orient* 26 (1983): 320; Batatu, *Old Social Classes,* p. 319.

44. Zilfi, "Elite Circulation," p. 320.

45. Schilcher, "Lore and Reality," pp. 497−498.

46. Al-Tabbakh, *Iʿlam al-nubala,* 7: 163−165; al-Muradi, *Silk al-durar,* 3: 176−177.

47. MSA 108: 23 (22 Jumada al-ula 1188); 117: 112 (4 Dhu al-Hijja 1192); 117: 146 (15 Safar 1193).

48. A partial exception to this statement would be the waqf that will be discussed in detail in Chapter 5.

49. The extent of patriarchal authority and power will be discussed more thoroughly in later chapters, especially Chapter 2.

50. Not all of these individuals would necessarily have been alive at the same time. At least some members of the earlier generation might have been dead by the time all the youngest generation had been born.

51. Kamil al-Ghazzi, *Nahr al-dhahab fi taʾrikh halab,* 2: 85.

52. The 104 figure refers to all the families of notables who were included in this study between 1770 and 1840, although there were never that many at any one time, given the processes of social and geographical mobility as well as demographic reality. See comments on page 36 and Appendix 1.

53. Al-Tabbakh, *Iʿlam al-nubala,* 7: 15.

54. For Damascus, see Schilcher, *Families in Politics,* pp. 234–236; for Aleppo, see Meriwether, *The Notable Families of Aleppo, 1770–1830: Networks and Social Structure,* p. 240.

55. Al-Tabbakh, *I'lam al-nubala,* 3: 349, 356–357; 4: 14.

56. For more discussion of these legal battles and their implications, see Chapter 5.

57. Marcus, *Eve of Modernity,* p. 68.

58. Bulliet, *Patricians of Nishapur,* p. 57.

59. Al-Tabbakh, *I'lam al-nubala,* 7: 337–338.

60. Bodman, *Political Factions,* pp. 56–57; Burckhardt, *Travels in Syria and the Holy Land,* p. 649; al-Ghazzi, *Nahr al-dhahab,* 2: 156, 203 and 3: 316–317, 334; al-Tabbakh, *I'lam al-nubala,* 3: 373–374, 413–414.

61. Masters, *Economic Dominance,* p. 64.

62. Ibid., p. 64.

63. MSA 140: 267 (23 Jumada al-akhira 1208).

64. Masters, *Economic Dominance,* p. 64.

65. Al-Tabbakh, *I'lam al-nubala,* 7: 136.

66. Al-Tabbakh, *I'lam al-nubala,* 6: 510–512; 7: 160, 178.

67. MSA 137: 194 (22 Rabi' al-awwal 1205); 116: 348 (19 Rabi' al-awwal 1193); 108: 106 (7 Jumada al-akhira 1188).

68. Ruth Roded, "Social Patterns among the Urban Elite of Syria during the Late Ottoman Period (1876–1918)," in *Palestine in the Late Ottoman Period,* ed. D. Kushner, p. 152.

69. Muhammad Amin al-Muhibbi, *Khulasat al-athar fi tarajim ahal al-qarn al-hadi 'ashar,* 2:84–87.

70. Al-Tabbakh, *I'lam al-nubala,* 7: 169–171.

71. Al-Ghazzi, *Nahr al-dhahab,* 2: 177–324.

72. Al-Tabbakh, *I'lam al-nubala,* 3: 373–374, 413–414; 7: 305–308.

73. Al-Tabbakh, *I'lam al-nubala,* 6: 469–474, 484–486; 7: 59–60, 67–78, 522–523.

74. Roded, "Social Patterns," p. 161.

CHAPTER 2

1. William Goode, *World Revolutions and Family Patterns,* p. 124.

2. Given the ambiguity surrounding the term *household,* a few preliminary comments are in order. In the context of Ottoman society of the seventeenth and eighteenth centuries, *household* is often used to describe the network of connections between a powerful political figure and his clients, retainers, and dependents of various categories. Used in this way, the household is a political structure at the heart of the political system found at both the center of the Ottoman Empire in these cen-

turies of decentralization and in some areas on the periphery, most notably Egypt under the Mamluk beys. These households may or may not have been residential groups, depending on the circumstances. The role of kinship ties in cementing relationships within the household also varied significantly; in many cases actual ties of "blood" were nonexistent. See Fay, "Ties That Bound," p. 161, and Jane Hathaway, *The Politics of Households in Ottoman Egypt,* pp. 17–31. When I use the term *household,* however, I am specifically referring to a residential unit at the center of which was a group of kin who lived and ate together in the same house or compound. The life cycles of these family members, the relationships among them, and their perceptions of what served the interests of the family determined the dynamics of household formation and fission.

3. Gerber suggests that the language about future generations was formulaic and that endowers were basically interested only in their own children. However, I think he misses the significance of these endowment deeds for what they can tell us about people's view of the family, if not necessarily about what happened in practice. See his "Anthropology and Family History," p. 417. A recent article by Beshara Doumani, "Endowing Family," offers the best refutation of Gerber's argument. Doumani shows significant differences in designated beneficiaries between Nablus and Tripoli, a clear indication that these were not just formulas.

4. Abdel-Nour, *Introduction,* p. 98. Damascus houses were more likely to have a second story, according to Abdel-Nour (p. 129). Houses in Cairo and other places could have several stories.

5. On the relationship between domestic architecture and family size and structure, see Jean-Louis Flandrin, *Families in Former Times,* pp. 92–93. For the Middle East, see Duben, "Turkish Families," pp. 79–80, and Faroqhi, *Men of Modest Substance,* for a lengthy discussion of urban architecture and the arrangement and uses of domestic space.

6. Peter Laslett, *Household and Family in Past Time,* pp. 1–16.

7. John Hajnal, "European Marriage Patterns in Perspective," in *Population and History,* ed. D. V. Glass and D. E. C. Eversley, pp. 23–69.

8. Duben, "Turkish Families," pp. 84–86.

9. Ibid., p. 92.

10. Justin McCarthy, "Age, Family, and Migration in Nineteenth-Century Black Sea Provinces of the Ottoman Empire," *International Journal of Middle East Studies* 10 (1979), p. 314.

11. Cuno, "Joint Family Households," p. 486.

12. Cuno, "A Tale of Two Villages," pp. 23–24.

13. Kenneth Cuno, "Egyptian Rural Notable Families: The Village of Sandub, 1847–68," paper presented to the Third Carleton Conference on the History of the Family, Ottawa, May 1997, pp. 5–6.

14. Cuno, "Joint Family Households," p. 491. Cuno takes this model from an article by James Lee and Jon Gjerde, "Comparative Household Morphology of Stem,

Joint, and Nuclear Household Systems: Norway, China, and the United States," *Continuity and Change* 1 (1986): 90.

15. Duben, "Turkish Families," pp. 83–84.

16. Cuno, "Joint Family Households," pp. 495–496.

17. Duben and Behar, *Istanbul Households,* p. 75.

18. Ibid., Chapter 3.

19. Ibid., pp. 4–5.

20. Gerber, *State, Society, and Law,* p. 149; idem, "Anthropology and Family History," p. 419.

21. Gerber, "Anthropology and Family History," pp. 413–419; idem, *State, Society, and Law,* p. 149.

22. This indirect way of getting at family size through inheritance records is inconvenient and not without risks. Nevertheless, calculating family size in this way provides a rough estimate that is useful. Moreover, if the question we are concerned with is the impact of family size on household structure and formation, rather than absolute rates of fertility, the total number of children born to a couple is less important than the number who survive to adulthood, marry, and have children of their own. For upper-class families in this study, information on family size is not dependent on inheritance records. The process of family reconstitution makes it possible to see these families at other moments than the death of family members. While not all of the genealogies are complete, many are, and others are more complete than inheritance records alone would indicate.

23. The phrase *conjugal family* is used here instead of the simpler and clearer term *couple* to take into account the effects of polygyny and concubinage. A conjugal family consists of a husband, wife or wives and (on rare occasions) concubines, and children. Most conjugal families were couples, since polygyny and concubinage were not particularly common among this elite. However, using this frame of reference allows for greater consistency when it is not possible always to know which children belonged to which mother. The average number of children per conjugal family for the population as a whole was determined by using a sample of 427 mukhallafat documents and calculating the average number of surviving children. For the upper class, additional information of family size was obtained through the reconstruction of families.

24. Haim Gerber, "Social and Economic Position of Women in an Ottoman City, Bursa, 1600–1700," *International Journal of Middle East Studies* 12 (1980), p. 244, footnote 79; Tucker, "Ties That Bound," p. 243; Omer Barkan, "Essai sur les données statistiques des registres de recensement dans l'Empire ottomane au XVe et XVIe siècles," *Journal of the Economic and Social History of the Orient* 1 (1958), p. 12; McCarthy, "Age, Family, and Migration," p. 313; Duben, "Turkish Families," p. 88.

25. Henri Guys, *Essai sur la statistique politique et religieuse du Pachalik d'Alep, en 1845,* p. 61.

26. Tucker, "Ties That Bound," p. 241.

27. Evidence suggests that age of marriage was low for both men and women.

This topic, as well as the question of the percentage of people who married, will be discussed in Chapter 3.

28. Basim Musallam, *Sex and Society in Islam*, pp. 118−119.

29. MSA 139: 12−17 (12 Jumada al-akhira 1205).

30. Bodman, *Political Factions*, pp. 48, 116−117; al-Ghazzi, *Nahr al-dhahab*, 2: 197; al-Tabbakh, *I'lam al-nubala*, 7: 154−160, 214.

31. MSA 181/1: 110 (12 Jumada al-ula 1229); 196: 20 (16 Muharram 1237); 219: 99 (16 Shawwal 1245).

32. MSA 141/1: 48−51 (7 Jumada al-ula 1207); 191: 140 (9 Rabi' al-awwal 1236); 197: 79−80 (6 Sha'ban 1237).

33. Most of the evidence on the break-up of households comes from documentation about the distribution of inheritance, since these two processes went hand in hand. However, other evidence does appear in passing; for example, reference will be made to an individual living in a different quarter or on a different street than before, mostly likely as a result of the process of household fission. It is in acquiring information like this that the methodology of "historical ethnography"—being able to trace the activities of individuals over time—is particularly useful to this study.

34. Gerber has shown in the case of Bursa that grown sons who predeceased their fathers often had productive property of their own, and he believes that it may indicate that grown sons left their fathers' households and established their own ("Anthropology and History," p. 414).

35. Russell, *Natural History*, 1: 281.

36. Daghestani, *Famille musulmane*, p. 186.

37. MSA 117: 172 (22 Jumada al-ula 1192).

38. MSA 204: 7−11 (6 Sha'ban 1240); Bodman, *Political Factions*, pp. 117−126.

39. Al-Tabbakh, *I'lam al-nubala*, 3: 373−374, 413−414; Bodman, *Political Factions*, pp. 117−126.

40. André Raymond, *Artisans et commerçants au Caire au XVIIIe siècle*, 2: 245.

41. MSA 113: 287−288 (27 Shawwal 1190).

42. Daghestani, *Famille musulmane*, p. 154.

43. MSA 139: 229 (8 Rabi' al-thani 1206); 141/1: 17 (13 Jumada al-ula 1207); 185/2: 132 (15 Rabi' al-awwal 1232).

44. MSA 185: 200−201 (16 Jumada al-akhira 1231).

45. MSA 117: 172 (22 Jumada al-ula 1192); 144/1: 13 (12 Rabi' al-thani 1210); 185/1: 171 (13 Dhu al-hijja 1231); 203: 80−81 (8 Dhu al Qa'da 1241).

46. Abdel-Nour discusses the contrast between the seventeenth and eighteenth centuries. In the former there was still considerable vacant land in the center of the city; by the middle of the eighteenth century, this land had been built on. A serious housing shortage had occurred as the result of demographic pressures. See *Introduction*, pp. 68−70.

47. MSA 107: 411−415 (5 Muharram 1188); 145: 124 (1 Safar 1214); al-Ghazzi, *Nahr al-dhahab*, 2: 106.

48. MSA 139: 12–17 (17 Jumada al-ula 1205); 149: 149–150 (20 Shaʿban 1216); al-Tabbakh, *Iʿlam al-nubala,* 6: 90.

49. For a discussion of these questions, see Abraham Marcus, "Privacy in Eighteenth-Century Aleppo: The Limits of a Cultural Ideal," *International Journal of Middle East Studies* 18 (1986): 165–183.

50. Duben and Behar, *Istanbul Households,* p. 61.

51. Findley, *Bureaucratic Reform,* p. 35.

52. Hathaway, *Politics of Households,* pp. 19–20.

53. Abdel-Nour, *Introduction,* p. 130.

54. Bodman, *Political Factions,* p. 39.

55. Duben, "Turkish Families," pp. 78–79.

56. Tucker, *Women in Egypt,* p. 179.

57. Findley, *Bureaucratic Reform,* p. 35.

58. Tucker, *Women in Egypt,* pp. 165–166.

59. Bowring, *Commercial Statistics,* pp. 39–40.

60. Tucker, *Women in Egypt,* p. 167.

61. This is not to suggest that all female slaves had a sexual relationship with their masters. In fact it is probable that relatively few females slaves did, but these few are the most visible in the sources.

62. S. E. Marmon, "Concubinage, Islamic," in *Dictionary of the Middle Ages,* ed. Joseph R. Strayer et al., 3: 527–529.

63. MSA 108: 547 (12 Shawwal 1191).

64. MSA 237: 188 (8 Muharram 1257).

65. Russell, *Natural History,* 1: 271.

66. MSA 231: 143 (1 Safar 1252).

67. MSA 108: 37–38 (28 Rabiʿ al-awwal 1189).

68. Marsot, *Women and Men in Late Eighteenth-Century Egypt,* p. 85.

69. Tucker, "Ties That Bound," p. 250.

70. Hanna, "Marriage among Merchant Families," p. 149.

71. Kandiyoti, "Islam and Patriarchy," p. 32.

72. Tucker, "The Arab Family in History," p. 199.

73. Martha Mundy, "Women's Inheritance of Land in Highland Yemen," *Arabian Studies* 5 (1979), p. 165.

74. MSA 223: 127 (28 Shaʿban 1248).

75. Cuno, "Joint Family Households," p. 494.

76. Duben, "Turkish Families," p. 87.

77. Leslie Peirce, *The Imperial Harem: Women and Sovereignty in the Ottoman Empire,* pp. 48–49.

78. Mundy, "Women's Inheritance," p. 165.

79. Cuno, "Joint Family Households," p. 491.

80. MSA 223: 127 (28 Shaʿban 1248).

81. Peirce, *Imperial Harem,* passim.

82. Afaf Marsot, "The Revolutionary Gentlewoman," in *Women in the Muslim Middle East,* ed. Lois Beck and Nikki Keddie, p. 265.

83. MSA 194: 50–52 (no date).

84. MSA 110: 92 (3 Shawwal 1187).

85. MSA 143: 34 (5 Rabiʿ al-awwal 1209); 196: 248 (1 Jumada al-akhira 1237); 229: 283–284 (12 Rabiʿ al-awwal).

86. Kandiyoti, "Islam and Patriarchy," p. 32.

87. Peirce, *Imperial Harem,* p. ix.

88. For a full discussion of this issue, see Margaret L. Meriwether, "The Rights of Children and the Responsibilities of Women: Women as Wasis in Ottoman Aleppo, 1770–1840," in Sonbol, pp. 219–235.

89. Duben and Behar, *Istanbul Households,* pp. 9–10.

CHAPTER 3

1. Musallam, *Sex and Society in Islam,* p. 11.

2. Russell, *Natural History,* 1: 283.

3. Ibid., 1: 282. Compare Dale Eickelman's comments about marriage negotiations today: "If questioned, men aver that marriage arrangements are their concern alone, since they claim to have an understanding of the social obligations superior to that of women. Women take a different view of the process and in fact take quite an active role in suggesting marriage partners and in preliminary negotiations" (*The Middle East and Central Asia: An Anthropological Approach,* pp. 165–166).

4. Annelies Moors, *Women, Property, and Islam: Palestinian Experiences, 1920–1990,* p. 85; N. J. Coulson, *Succession in Islamic Family Law,* p. 11.

5. MSA 143/1: 81 (1 Dhu al-Qaʿda 1209).

6. MSA 222: 60 (28 Jumada al-awwal 1247).

7. Russell, *Natural History,* 1: 281.

8. Tucker, "Marriage and Family in Nablus," p. 173.

9. MSA 222: 160 (28 Jumada al-awwal 1247).

10. MSA 141/1: 61 (27 Rajab 1207).

11. Russell, *Natural History,* 1: 283.

12. Most notably Phillipe Aries, *Centuries of Childhood.*

13. A recent chapter by Leslie Peirce in the volume *Women in the Ottoman Empire: Middle Eastern Women in the Early Modern Era,* edited by Madeline C. Zilfi, presents some exciting new research on individual life cycles and ways in which gender identity changed over time. See "Seniority, Sexuality, and Social Order: The Vocabulary of Gender in Early Modern Ottoman Society," pp. 169–196.

14. Duben and Behar, *Istanbul Households,* p. 141.

15. Hanna, "Marriage among Merchant Families," pp. 150–153; Abdal-Rehim Abdal-Rahman Abdal-Rehim, "The Family and Gender Laws in Egypt during the Ottoman Period," in Sonbol, pp. 98–101, 110.

16. Moors, *Women, Property, and Islam*, pp. 149–150.

17. Russell, *Natural History*, 1: 285; Daghestani, *Famille musulmane*, p. 27.

18. Moors, *Women, Property, and Islam*, p. 127.

19. Since the delayed mahr was usually required to be paid to the wife, if divorced, this sum was included in the divorce record. It was also listed as a liability against the estate of the deceased husband or an asset still owing to the women in female inheritances.

20. Tucker found a similar range in delayed payments in Nablus in the eighteenth and nineteenth centuries. See "Marriage and Family in Nablus," p. 169.

21. MSA 238: 120–121 (13 Dhu al-Hijja 1250); 226: 120 (13 Dhu al-Hijja 1250). Moors also found that class did not correlate with the size of dower payments. See *Women, Property, and Islam*, p. 94.

22. J. Lewis Farley, *Two Years in Syria*, pp. 38–39.

23. MSA 105: 59 (11 Muharram 1186).

24. Baron, "Marital Bonds in Modern Egypt," pp. 292–309.

25. Duben and Behar, *Istanbul Households*, p. 96.

26. Daghestani, *Famille musulmane*, p. 13.

27. S. D. Goitein, *A Mediterranean Society*, vol. 3, *The Family*, p.165.

28. Peirce, *Imperial Harem*, pp. 63, 87.

29. Russell, *Natural History*, 1: 291–293.

30. Duben, "Turkish Families," p. 90.

31. Bowring, *Commercial Statistics*, p. 4; Russell, *Natural History*, 1: 277–278.

32. Gerber, "Social and Economic Position of Women," p. 232.

33. Tucker, "Marriage and Family in Nablus," p. 176.

34. Cuno, "A Tale of Two Villages," p. 23.

35. Duben and Behar, *Istanbul Households*, pp. 148–152.

36. Ibid., p. 122.

37. McCarthy, "Age, Family, and Migration," pp. 320–323.

38. Cuno, "A Tale of Two Villages," p. 23.

39. Barbara Aswad, *Property Control and Social Strategies in Settlers on a Middle Eastern Plain*, pp. 72–75.

40. Duben and Behar, *Istanbul Households*, p. 156.

41. Hanna, "Marriage among Merchant Families," p. 147.

42. Abdal-Rehim, "Family and Gender Laws," pp. 99–100, 109.

43. Russell, *Natural History*, 1: 271.

44. Ibid., 1: 280.

45. Tucker, "Ties That Bound," pp. 240–241.

46. Moors, "Debating Islamic Family Law," p. 5; Abdal-Rehim, "Family and

Gender Laws," pp. 102−103; Svetlana Ivanona, "The Divorce between Zubaida Hatun and Esseid Osman Aga," in Sonbol, p. 123.

47. Madeline Zilfi has written an interesting and insightful discussion of khul⁶ divorce in eighteenth-century Istanbul entitled "'We Don't Get Along': Women and *Hul* Divorce in the Eighteenth Century," in *Women in the Ottoman Empire,* pp. 264−296.

48. Russell, *Natural History,* 1: 280.

49. MSA 144: 175 (23 Dhi al-Hijja 1212).

50. Duben and Behar, *Istanbul Households,* p. 125.

51. McCarthy, "Age, Family, and Migration," p. 323.

52. Marcus, *Eve of Modernity,* pp. 196−198; Tucker, "Marriage and Family in Nablus," p. 176−177; Duben and Behar, *Istanbul Households,* p. 129.

53. Schilcher, "Lore and Reality," p. 502.

54. Hilda Geertz, "The Meaning of Family Ties," in *Meaning and Order in Moroccan Society,* ed. Clifford Geertz, Hilda Geertz, and Lawrence Rosen, p. 327.

55. Some examples of this debate include articles by James M. B. Keyser, "The Middle Eastern Case: Is There a Marriage Rule?" *Ethnology* 13 (1974): 293−309; Fuad Khuri, "Parallel Cousin Marriage Reconsidered: A Middle East Practice That Nullifies the Effects of Marriage on the Intensity of Family Relations," *Man* 5 (1970): 597−618; R. F. Murphy and Leonard Kasdan, "Agnation and Endogamy: Some Further Considerations," *Southwestern Journal of Anthropology* 23 (1959): 1−14.

56. Richard Antoun, "Anthropology," in *The Study of the Middle East,* ed. Leonard Binder, pp. 166−168.

57. Beatrice Gottlieb, *The Family in the Western World from the Black Death to the Industrial Age,* p. 57.

58. Moors, *Women, Property, and Islam,* pp. 87−90.

59. Patai, *Society, Culture, and Change,* p. 84.

60. Schilcher, "Lore and Reality," p. 509.

61. Antoun, "Anthropology," p. 168; Geertz, "Family Ties," p. 325; Barbara Aswad, "Key and Peripheral Roles of Noble Women in a Middle Eastern Plains Village," *Anthropological Quarterly* 40 (1967), p. 141; Michael Meeker, "Meaning and Society in the Near East: Examples from the Black Sea Turks and Levantine Arabs," *International Journal of Middle East Studies* 7 (1976), p. 394.

62. Emine Foat Tugay, *Three Centuries: Family Chronicles of Egypt and Turkey;* Abdul Rahman Hamide, *La Ville d'Alep: Étude de geographie urbaine,* pp. 32−33; Daghestani, *Famille musulmane,* p. 21.

63. Schilcher, "Lore and Reality," p. 508; Tucker, "Marriage and Family in Nablus," p. 174; Aswad, "Key and Peripheral Roles," p. 139.

64. To establish marital patterns, the number of marriages was calculated by counting the number of marriage choices made by each individual rather than the absolute number of marriages. A marriage between a man and his father's brother's

daughter is one marriage. However, it is "double-counted" because each marriage must be viewed from the perspective of both bride and groom, since we are interested in determining the kinds of marriage choices that were made.

65. Raphael Patai, "Structure of Endogamous Unilineal Descent Groups," *Southwestern Journal of Anthropology* 21 (1965): 325–350.

66. MSA 107: 118 (6 Dhu al-Qaʿda 1185); al-Tabbakh, *Iʿlam al-nubala,* 7: 329.

67. See Shaykhbandar genealogy in Appendix 2.

68. Raymond, *Artisans et commerçants,* 2: 425; Beshara Doumani, *Rediscovering Palestine: Merchants and Peasants in Jabal Nablus,* pp. 66–67.

69. Al-Ghazzi, *Nahr al-dhahab,* 2: 177 and 3: 299; al-Muradi, *Silk al-durar,* 3: 151–159; MSA 137: 194 (22 Rabiʿ al-awwal 1205); MSA 214: 194 (1 Rabiʿ al-awwal 1243).

70. Wolfram Eberhard, "Change in Leading Families in Southern Turkey," in *Peoples and Cultures of the Middle East;* Vol. 2, *Life in the Cities, Towns, and Countryside,* ed. Louise E. Sweet, pp. 251–254; Aswad, *Property Control,* p. 92.

71. Aswad, *Property Control,* p.64; Aswad, "Key and Peripheral Roles," p. 141.

72. Schilcher, "Lore and Reality," p. 502.

73. MSA 108: 37–38 (28 Rabiʿ al-awwal 1189).

74. Russell, *Natural History,* vol. 1, passim.

75. Information on the Ghawri family marriages comes from numerous cases in the court records. For further discussion of the economic interests of this family, see Chapter 5.

76. Information on the Hamawi family and their marriages comes from numerous cases in the mahkama sharʿiyya archives.

77. For information on the Qudsi family in general, see al-Ghazzi, *Nahr al-dhahab,* 2: 156 and 3: 315; al-Tabbakh, *Iʿlam al-nubala,* 3: 373–374 and 7: 172–174. Information on Qudsi marriages come from various entries in the archives.

78. Al-Tabbakh, *Iʿlam al-nubala,* 6: 251–269 and 7: 114–116, 236–237.

79. Khoury, *Urban Notables,* p. 12. At least this was the situation as stated by these ulema families. However, as Antoun has pointed out in discussing the discrepancy between a stated preference for father's brother's daughter's cousin marriage and its low rate of occurrence, what people say they do in choosing marriage partners and what they finally do are not necessarily the same (see Antoun, "Anthropology," p. 166). Whether the ulema of Damascus were in fact as exclusive in their choice of marriage partners as they stated can only be determined by an analysis of marriage patterns that has not yet been done.

80. Batatu, *Old Social Classes,* p. 160.

81. See Karl Barbir, "From Pasha to Effendi: The Assimilation of Ottomans in Damascene Society," *International Journal of Turkish Studies* 1 (1980): 68–83, for discussion of this process in Damascus.

82. See genealogies of the Kawakibi, Ghawri, and Shaykhbandar families in Appendix 2.

83. Bowring, *Commercial Statistics,* p. 80.

84. MSA 116: 63 (23 Dhu al-Qa'da, 1190).

85. MSA 210: 127 (4 Rabi' al-awwal 1242).

86. MSA 148: 48 (15 Shawwal 1214); MSA 212: 14 (11 Ramadan 1242).

87. MSA 219: 190 (28 Dhu al-Qa'da 1245).

88. MSA 110: 34 (? Jumada al-thani 1187).

89. Findley, *Bureaucratic Reform,* p. 32–33.

90. Ibid., p. 33.

91. Al-Tabbakh, *I'lam al-nubala,* 7: 154.

92. Bodman, *Political Factions,* p. 142.

93. See genealogies of Jabiri and Qudsi families in Appendix 2.

94. Julie Oehler, "Bibi Maryam: A Bakhtiyari Tribal Woman," in *Struggle and Survival in the Modern Middle East,* ed. Edmund Burke, p. 136.

95. Goitein, *Family,* pp. 21–26.

96. Emrys L. Peters, "Status of Women in Four Middle Eastern Communities," in *Women in the Muslim World,* ed. Lois Beck and Nikki Keddie, p. 318.

97. See Meriwether, "Rights of Children," in Sonbol, p. 230.

98. Al-Tabbakh, *I'lam al-nubala,* 7: 317.

CHAPTER 4

1. David S. Powers, "The Islamic Inheritance System: A Sociohistorical Approach," in *Islamic Family Law,* ed. Chibli Mallet and Jane Connors, p. 29.

2. Martha Mundy, "The Family, Inheritance, and Islam: A Re-examination of the Sociology of Fara'id Law," in *Islamic Law: Social and Historical Context,* ed. Aziz al-Azmeh, p. 4.

3. Joseph Anderson, "The Eclipse of the Patriarchal Family in Contemporary Islamic Law," in *Family Law in Asia and Africa,* ed. J. N. D. Anderson, pp. 221–222.

4. Mundy, "Family, Inheritance, and Islam," p. 8.

5. Peters, "Status of Women," p. 324.

6. Coulson, *Succession,* p. 22.

7. Just how revolutionary the change in inheritance laws was has been the subject of some debate. Until recently, the generally accepted view was the "superimposition" theory, according to which Islamic laws of inheritance did not amount to a new system but rather to a modification of the existing tribal system. This was the view of the Islamic legal scholar Joseph Schacht, which is accepted by Coulson (*Succession,* p. 33). Recently, David S. Powers has challenged this view, arguing convincingly that Koranic rules on inheritance totally replaced rather than modified tribal law (*Studies in Qur'an and Hadith: The Formation of the Islamic Law of Inheritance,* p. 87). Powers also argues that the rules of inheritance set out in the Koran are not what was codified into Islamic law. The Koran was reinterpreted to bring the law into harmony with contemporary social, political, and theological realities (see especially pages 101–102 and 188).

8. For a good general discussion of the changes that occurred, see W. Montgomery Watt, *Muhammad: Prophet and Statesman,* passim.

9. Coulson, *Succession,* p. 30.

10. Ibid., pp. 30–40.

11. Ibid., p. 2; for a concise statement of this point of view, see Marshall Hodgson, *Venture of Islam: Conscience and History in a World Civilization,* 2: 123–124.

12. Hodgson, *Venture,* 2: 124.

13. Peters, "Status of Women," pp. 329–330.

14. Mundy, "Family, Inheritance, and Islam," pp. 60–61; Mundy bases her remarks on a study by A. Latron, *La vie rurale en Syrie et au Liban.*

15. Duben, "Turkish Families," p. 86.

16. Lutz K. Berkner, "Inheritance, Land Tenure, and Peasant Family Structure: A German Regional Comparison," in *Family and Inheritance: Rural Society in Western Europe, 1200–1800,* ed. Jack Goody, Joan Thirsk, and E. P. Thompson, pp. 71–72.

17. Berkner, "Inheritance," pp. 71–74; Lutz K. Berkner and Franklin F. Mendels, "Inheritance Systems, Family Structure, and Demographic Patterns in Western Europe, 1700–1900," in *Historical Studies in Changing Fertility,* ed. Charles Tilly, p. 213.

18. For a discussion of similar issues in a different historical context, see Jack Goody, "Inheritance, Property, and Women," in *Family and Society,* ed. Robert Forster and Orest Ranum, p. 36.

19. For a more detailed discussion of these economic changes, see Margaret L. Meriwether, "Urban Notables and Rural Resources in Ottoman Aleppo, 1770–1830," *International Journal of Turkish Studies* 4 (1987): 55–73; and the introduction to this book.

20. MSA 209: 68 (1 Dhu al-Hijja 1242); 238: 107–108 (25 Rabiʿa al-awwal 1250); 238: 151–154 (5 Rabiʿa al-awwal 1250). Ahmad's additional fortune did not benefit his heirs, however, since Ahmad owed large sums of money when he died. Most of his estate was consumed by these debts, but his heirs still had their interest in their grandfather's vast real estate holdings to fall back on.

21. See Chapter 2 for a discussion of family size.

22. MSA 133: 159–160 (3 Muharram 1201).

23. MSA 144/1: 109 (1 Dhu al-Hijja 1210).

24. MSA 134: 193–194 (24 Safar 1203); 152: 113–117 (20 Shawwal 1216).

25. MSA 191: 140 (9 Rabiʿa al-awwal 1236); 197: 79–80 (6 Shaʿban 1237).

26. Mundy, "Women's Inheritance," p. 164.

27. Annelies Moors has an interesting discussion of an apparent urban-rural dichotomy in the literature on women and inheritance and the way in which it is correlated to a disciplinary divide between historians and anthropologists, with the historians, who generally focus on cities, emphasizing that women did inherit and the anthropologists, who generally focus on villages or pastoral communities, arguing that women rarely inherited. As she points out, it is, of course, not that simple. See Moors, *Women, Property, and Islam,* pp. 48–50.

28. Peters, "Status of Women," p. 324.

29. Aswad, *Property Control,* p.55.

30. Peters, "Status of Women," p. 337.

31. For a full discussion of women and property, see Meriwether, "Women and Economic Change in Nineteenth-Century Syria: The Case of Aleppo," in *Arab Women: Old Boundaries, New Frontiers,* ed. Judith Tucker, pp. 69–72.

32. Faroqhi, *Men of Modest Substance,* p. 180. What Faroqhi found was that women sold property much more frequently than they bought it, to an extent that suggests that though women inherited property, they generally did not hold on to it.

33. MSA 107: 411–415 (15 Muharram 1188).

34. For an example of the former, see MSA 144/1: 109 (1 Dhu al-Hijja 1210).

35. MSA 228: 332 (25 Jumada al-akhira 1251).

36. Peters, "Status of Women," p. 325; Moors, *Women, Property, and Islam,* p. 54. See similar comments by Aswad, *Property Control,* p. 53, and Jack Goody, *The Oriental, the Ancient, and the Primitive,* pp. 373–377.

37. MSA 152: 113–117 (20 Shawwal 1217); 134: 193–194 (24 Safar 1203); 158: 239–240 (17 Shawwal 1220).

38. MSA 201: 177–178 (18 Safar 1239).

39. MSA 201: 142 (19 Safar 1239).

40. MSA 108: 429 (17 Rajab 1188).

41. MSA 219: 190–191 (28 Dhu al-Qada 1245).

42. MSA 201: 118 (27 Safar 1139).

43. Coulson, *Succession,* p. 33.

44. Powers, "Islamic Inheritance System," p. 12, summarizing Coulson's conclusions.

45. MSA 197: 77–80 (6 Sha'ban 1237).

46. MSA 180: 170 (27 Jumada al-ula 1228).

47. See Jack Goody's comments on the preference for daughters as heirs over distant male agnates in Europe and parts of Asia ("Inheritance, Property, and Women," p. 10).

48. See Chapter 3 for a complete discussion of marriage patterns and marriage strategies.

49. Goody, *The Oriental, the Ancient, and the Primitive,* p. 2.

CHAPTER 5

1. Beshara Doumani has written an excellent article in which he compares endowments in two cities, Nablus and Tripoli, and shows how they reflected different visions of the family and of gender. See "Endowing Family."

2. The way these endowment deeds were drawn up enhances their value as a source of information about the family. They specify who the beneficiaries and ad-

ministrators of the endowment will be over time, and they often include specific conditions relating to the endowment (e.g., whether women remain beneficiaries if they
marry, whether the property includes the family residence, etc.). From this we are
able to determine something about family structure and relationships, the role of
women, attitudes toward more distant relatives, and the disposition of authority and
control of resources within the family. The fullness of the documentation in these
sources and the large number of them also contribute to their usefulness as a source.
It is important to emphasize that the waqfiyyat themselves are valuable as an indication of preferences, and therefore of attitudes and values, not necessarily of actual
arrangements within the family. Other information in the mahkama shar'iyya archives,
however, does allow us to see to what extent these preferences were put into practice.

3. For a discussion of Ottoman attempts to control waqfs, see John Robert
Barnes, *Introduction to Religious Foundations in the Ottoman Empire*, chs. 2–3.

4. James Reilly, "Rural Waqfs of Ottoman Damascus: Rights of Ownership,
Possession, and Tenancy," *Acta Orientalia* 51 (1990), pp. 28–29.

5. Summaries of these waqfiyyat are provided by al-Ghazzi in *Nahr al-dhahab*, 2:
47–52, 113–124, 535–537, 605–630.

6. Raymond, "Great Arab Towns," pp. 87–89, 94–95.

7. Ibid., p. 95. The village of Haylan, northeast of the city, also formed part of
this endowment, as did 30,000 gold dinars. See al-Ghazzi, *Nahr al-dhahab*, 2: 113–
115. For an interesting discussion of the issue of cash endowments, see Jon Mandaville, "Usurious Piety: The Cash-Waqf Controversy in the Ottoman Empire," *International Journal of Middle East Studies* 10 (1979): 289–308.

8. See Jean-Claude David, *Le waqf d'Ibshir Pasa à Alep*, for a discussion of this
endowment and the development of the Judayda neighborhood.

9. Compare Reilly's comments on Damascus, "Rural Waqfs," p. 29.

10. These figures are based on the lists of endowments given by al-Ghazzi in *Nahr
al-dhahab*, 2: 535–586, 605–609, and 610–630.

11. This number was reached by combining the figures given in al-Ghazzi with
the additional waqfiyyat found in the mahkama shar'iyya archives that did not appear
in al-Ghazzi's list.

12. Al-Muradi, *Silk al-durar*, 3: 151–159.

13. An example of this would be the waqf of Hajj Musa Amiri, one of the three
largest created in the eighteenth century. Al-Ghazzi provides a summary of this waqf
in *Nahr al-dhahab*, vol. 2. For a similar trend in Damascus, see Reilly, "Rural Waqfs,"
pp. 36–37.

14. The subject of women and waqf is an interesting and important one by itself.
For a discussion of women and waqfs in Aleppo that goes into more detail and deals
with more questions than can be covered here, see Margaret L. Meriwether, "Women
and *Waqf* Revisited: The Case of Aleppo, 1770–1840," in *Women in the Ottoman
Empire*, ed. Madeline C. Zilfi.

15. In the seventeenth and eighteenth centuries, 52 percent were waqf khayri. The percentage was lower in the sixteenth century (41 percent) and higher in the nineteenth century (59 percent). These percentages are derived from the information in al-Ghazzi, *Nahr al-dhahab,* 2: 561–586, 605–630.

16. Ruth Roded has written an interesting article on the kinds of charitable endowments being set up in Aleppo during this period. She found that most were founded to benefit either the Great Mosque, neighborhood mosques, or *zawiya*s (Sufi lodges). See Roded, "Great Mosques, Zawiyas, and Neighborhood Mosques: Popular Beneficiaries of Waqf Endowments in Eighteenth- and Nineteenth-Century Aleppo," *Journal of the American Oriental Society* 110 (1990): 33–38.

17. MSA 211: 268 (27 Sha'ban 1242).

18. MSA 149: 5–6 and 7–8 (25 Sha'ban 1216).

19. MSA 225: 21–23 (no date).

20. Tucker, *Women in Egypt,* pp. 95–96.

21. MSA 162: 223–224 (29 Muharram 1222).

22. MSA 149: 116–117 (7 Rabi' al-awwal 1217).

23. Tucker, "Ties That Bound," p. 248.

24. MSA 182: 101 (8 Shawwal 1229).

25. MSA 141: 143 (10 Ramadan 1206).

26. MSA 132: 17–18 (25 Rabi' al-thani 1201).

27. Because of the importance of the large endowments to the city and therefore their highly visible nature, there is material in the sources not only on the large endowments created between 1770 and 1840, but also on many of the larger endowments established before 1770. Although we do not have the actual deeds of endowment for the time prior to 1770, as we do for the period under study, summaries of some of the large endowments are found in al-Ghazzi; moreover, quite a few court cases deal with questions about them. Consequently, we can look at some of these endowments at the time of their establishment and answer certain questions about the relationship between endowment and family structure, but there is the additional advantage of seeing the impact of these large endowments on the family over time and of thus being able to evaluate their significance from a different perspective.

28. The information on the size of endowments is taken from al-Ghazzi's list in *Nahr al-dhahab,* 2: 535–537, 561–586, 605–630. He gives a number for most of these endowments that indicates size, although he does not give a precise scale to correspond to these numbers. The largest endowments were those designated as a one or two, of which there were thirteen.

29. MSA 108: 22 (no date).

30. Al-Tabbakh, *I'lam al-nubala,* 7: 109–111; MSA 182: 16, 20–21 (16 Rajab 1229).

31. See al-Ghazzi, *Nahr al-dhahab,* 2: 53–63, 157–173, for a summary of the waqfiyyat of these endowments.

32. In counting up the number of large endowments during this period, I have treated multiple endowments created by one person as a single endowment, and I have also treated the waqfs set up by Mustafa Jabiri and his sons as a single endowment. Conceptually this makes sense because the beneficiaries and the conditions of these endowments were virtually the same.

33. MSA 111: 60 (15 Shawwal 1189).

34. See earlier discussion in this chapter as well as Barnes, *Introduction,* chs. 2–3.

35. MSA 117: 90 (21 Sha'ban 1192); also see Meriwether, "Urban Notables and Rural Resources," pp. 55–73, for a fuller discussion of the relationship between urban notables and rural resources and the issue of indebtedness.

36. MSA 121: 111 (23 Shawwal 1195).

37. MSA 116: 86 (1 Safar 1191).

38. For the endowments established in the early part of the eighteenth century, like those of Ahmad Taha and 'Uthman Pasha, these earlier generations went back to the last part of the seventeenth century.

39. See Ruth Roded's discussion of this issue in her article "The Waqf and the Social Elite of Aleppo in the Eighteenth and Nineteenth Centuries," *Turcica* 20 (1988): 71–91.

40. Al-Ghazzi, *Nahr al-dhahab,* 3: 334; Bodman, *Political Factions,* pp. 136–137.

41. MSA 227: 240–243 (17 Muharram 1250); 228: 26–28 (21 Rajab 1250).

42. MSA 130: 190–191 (23 Rabi' al-awwal 1201).

43. MSA 149: 149–150 (20 Sha'ban 1216).

44. Ibid.

45. MSA 127: 196–207 (23 Rabi' al-awwal 1199); 227: 240–243 (17 Muharram 1250).

46. MSA 129: 134–137 (18 Rabi' al-awwal 1200).

47. MSA 140: 204–205 (7 Dhi al-Qa'da 1209).

48. MSA 184: 217–220 (26 Jumada al-ula 1231).

49. MSA 224: 112–113 (25 Rajab 1248).

50. MSA 224: 382 (1 Rajab 1249); 182: 16 and 20 (29 Rajab 1229); 220: 88 (1 Rabi' al-thani 1246).

51. MSA 204: 7–11 (6 Sha'ban 1240).

52. Roded, "The Waqf and the Social Elite of Aleppo," 71–91 passim.

CONCLUSION

1. Peirce, *Imperial Harem,* especially Chapter 9.

Bibliography

ARCHIVAL SOURCES

Damascus. Mudiriyyat al-wathaʿiq al-taʾrikhiyya (National Historical Archives). Archives of the mahkama sharʿiyya of Aleppo, vols. 103–226 (1182–1257/1769–1841). (Cited as MSA.)

London. Public Record Office: State Papers 105, vols. 120–142, 212–218, 334, 340; State Papers 110, vols. 40–53, 58–59, 72–74, 87; Foreign Office Documents, vols. 78, 195, 198, 406, 876.

PUBLISHED SOURCES

Abdal-Rehim, Abdal-Rehim Abdal-Rahman. "The Family and Gender Laws in Egypt during the Ottoman Period." In *Women, the Family, and Divorce Laws in Islamic History,* ed. Amira E. Sonbol. Syracuse: Syracuse University Press, 1996.

Abdel-Nour, Antoine. *Introduction a l'histoire urbaine de la Syrie ottomane.* Beirut: Librarie Orientale, 1982.

Abou-el-Haj, Rifaat Ali. "The Ottoman Vezir and Pasa Households, 1683–1703: A Preliminary Report." *Journal of the American Oriental Society* (1973): 438–447.

Ahmed, Leila. "Women and the Advent of Islam." *Signs* 11 (1986): 665-691.

———. *Women and Gender in Islam: Historical Roots of a Modern Debate.* New Haven: Yale University Press, 1992.

Alberti, Leon. *The Family in Renaissance Florence.* Columbia, S.C.: University of South Carolina Press, 1969.

Anderson, James. "The Eclipse of the Patriarchal Family in Contemporary Islamic Law." In *Family Law in Asia and Africa,* ed. James N. D. Anderson. New York: Frederick A. Praeger, 1968. pp. 221–234.

Anderson, Michael. *Approaches to the History of the Western Family, 1500–1914.* London: Macmillan Press, 1980.

Antoun, Richard. "Anthropology." In *The Study of the Middle East,* ed. Leonard Binder. New York: Wiley, 1976.

———. "Social Organization and the Life Cycle of an Arab Village." *Ethnology* 6 (1967): 294–308.

Aries, Philippe. *Centuries of Childhood.* New York: Vintage, 1962.

d'Arvieux, Laurent. *Memoires de Chevalier d'Arvieux.* 6 vols. Paris: C. J. B. Delespine, 1735.

Aswad, Barbara C. "Key and Peripheral Roles of Noble Women in a Middle Eastern Plains Village." *Anthropological Quarterly* 40 (1967): 139–153.

———. *Property Control and Social Strategies in Settlers on a Middle Eastern Plain.* Anthropological Paper 44. Ann Arbor: University of Michigan Museum of Anthropology, 1971.

Baraket, Halim. "The Arab Family and the Challenge of Social Transformation." In *Women and the Family in the Middle East,* ed. Elizabeth Fernea. Austin: University of Texas Press, 1985.

Barbir, Karl K. *Ottoman Rule in Damascus, 1708–1758.* Princeton: Princeton University Press, 1980.

———. "From Pasha to Effendi: The Assimilation of Ottomans in Damascene Society." *International Journal of Turkish Studies* 1 (1980): 68–83.

Barkan, Omer Lutfi. "Essai sur les données statistiques de registres de recensement dans l'Empire ottomane au XVe et XVIe siècles." *Journal of the Economic and Social History of the Orient* 1 (1958): 9–36.

———. "Research in the Ottoman Fiscal Surveys." In *Studies in the Economic History of the Middle East,* ed. M. A. Cook. London: Oxford University Press, 1970.

Barker, Edward B. B. *Syria and Egypt under the Last Five Sultans of Turkey: Being the Experiences during Fifty Years of Mr. Consul-General Barker.* 2 vols. London: Tinsley, 1876.

Barnes, John Robert. *An Introduction to Religious Foundations in the Ottoman Empire.* Leiden: E. J. Brill, 1986.

Baron, Beth. "The Making and Breaking of Marital Bonds in Modern Egypt." In *Women in Middle Eastern History: Shifting Boundaries in Sex and Gender,* ed. Nikki Keddie and Beth Baron. New Haven: Yale University Press, 1991.

Barth, Frederick. "Father's Brother's Daughter's Marriage in Kurdistan." *Southwestern Journal of Anthropology* 10 (1954): 164–171.

Batatu, Hanna. *Old Social Classes and the Revolutionary Movements of Iraq.* Princeton: Princeton University Press, 1979.

Berkner, Lutz K. "Inheritance, Land Tenure, and Peasant Family Structure: A German Regional Comparison." In *Family and Inheritance: Rural Society in Western Europe, 1200–1800,* ed. Jack Goody, Joan Thirsk, and E. P. Thompson. Cambridge: Cambridge University Press, 1976.

Berkner, Lutz K., and Franklin F. Mendels. "Inheritance Systems, Family Structure, and Demographic Patterns in Western Europe, 1700–1900." In *Historical Studies in Changing Fertility,* ed. Charles Tilly. Princeton: Princeton University Press, 1978.

Bodman, Herbert L. *Political Factions in Aleppo, 1760–1826.* Chapel Hill: University of North Carolina Press, 1963.

Bowring, John. *Report on the Commercial Statistics of Syria.* 1840. Reprint, New York: Arno Press, 1973.

Browne, William G. *Travels in Africa, Egypt, and Syria.* London: T. Cadell and W. Davis, 1799.

Brunschvig, Robert. "'Abd." In *Encyclopedia of Islam.* 2d ed., vol. 1. Leiden: E. J. Brill, 1960.

Bulliet, Richard. *Conversion to Islam in the Medieval Period.* Cambridge, Mass.: Harvard University Press, 1979.

———. *The Patricians of Nishapur.* Cambridge, Mass.: Harvard University Press, 1972.

Burckhardt, John Lewis. *Travels in Syria and the Holy Land.* London: J. Murray, 1822.

Charles-Roux, François. *Les Échelles de Syrie et de Palestine au XVIIIe siècle.* Paris: Librairie Orientaliste Paul Geuthner, 1928.

Chevallier, Dominique. "Aspects sociaux de la question d'Orient." *Annales* 14 (1959): 35–64.

———. "A Damas, production et société a la fin du XIXe siècle." *Annales* 19 (1964): 966–975.

———. "Un exemple de résistance technique de l'artisan syrien aux XIXe et XXe siècles" *Syria* (1962): 300–324.

———. "Techniques et société en Syrie." *Bulletin des études orientales* 18 (1963–1964): 85–93.

———. "Western Development and Eastern Crisis in the Mid-Nineteenth Century: Syria Confronted with the European Economy." In *Beginnings of Modernization in the Middle East,* ed. William Polk and Richard Chambers. Chicago: University of Chicago Press, 1966.

Coulson, Noel J. *Succession in Islamic Family Law.* Cambridge: Cambridge University Press, 1972.

Cuno, Kenneth. "Egyptian Rural Notable Families: The Village of Sandub, 1847–68." Paper presented to the Third Carleton Conference on the History of the Family, Ottawa, May 1997.

———. "Joint Family Households and Rural Notables in Nineteenth-Century Egypt." *International Journal of Middle East Studies* 27 (1995): 485–502.

———. *The Pasha's Peasants: Land, Society, and Economy in Lower Egypt, 1740–1858.* Cambridge: Cambridge University Press, 1992.

———. "A Tale of Two Villages: Family, Property, and Economic Activity in Rural Egypt in the 1840's." In *Agriculture in Egypt from Pharaonic to Modern Times,* ed. Eugene Rogan and Alan Bowman. Oxford: Oxford University Press, 1998.

Cusinier, Jean. "The Domestic Cycle in the Traditional Family Organization in

Tunisia." In *Mediterranean Family Structure*, ed. J. G. Peristany. Cambridge: Cambridge University Press, 1976.

Daghestani, Kazem. *Étude sociologique sur la famille musulmane contemporaine en Syrie.* Paris: E. Leroux, 1932.

David, Jean-Claude. "Alep, dégradation et tentative actuelle de réadaptation des structures urbaines traditionnelles." *Bulletin des études orientales* 28 (1975): 19–56.

———. "Évolution et déplacement des fonctions centrales à Alep aux XIXe et XXe siècles." In *La Ville Arabe dans l'Islam*, ed. Abdelwahab Bouhdiba and Dominique Chevallier. Tunis: Imprimerie al-Asria, 1982.

———. "Les quartiers anciens dans la croissance de la ville moderne d'Alep." In *L'Espace social de la ville arabe*, ed. Dominique Chevallier et al. Paris: Maisonerie et Larose, 1979.

———. *Le waqf d'Ibshir Pasa à Alep (1063/1653): Étude d'urbanisme historique.* Damascus: Editions d'Amerique et d'Orient, 1982.

Davis, Ralph. *Aleppo and Devonshire Square.* London: Macmillan, 1967.

Doumani, Beshara. *Rediscovering Palestine: Merchants and Peasants in Jabal Nablus, 1700–1900.* Berkeley: University of California Press, 1995.

———. "Endowing Family: *Waqf*, Property Devolution, and Gender in Greater Syria, 1800–1860." *Comparative Studies in Society and History* 40 (1998): 3–41.

Duben, Alan. "Turkish Families and Households in Historical Perspective." *Journal of Family History* 10 (1985): 75–97.

———. "Understanding Muslim Households in the late Ottoman Period." *Journal of Family History* 15 (1990): 71–86.

Duben, Alan, and Cem Behar. *Istanbul Households: Marriage, Family, and Fertility, 1880–1940.* Cambridge: Cambridge University Press, 1991.

Eberhard, Wolfram. "Change in Leading Families in Southern Turkey." In *Peoples and Cultures of the Middle East;* Vol. 2, *Life in the Cities, Towns, and Countryside,* ed. Louise E. Sweet. Garden City, N.Y.: Natural History Press, 1970.

Eickelman, Dale F. *The Middle East and Central Asia: An Anthropological Approach.* 3d ed.. Upper Saddle, N. J.: Prentice Hall, 1997.

Elder, Glen H. "Approaches to Social Change and the Family." In *Turning Points: Historical and Sociological Essays on the Family,* ed. John Demos and Sarane Spence Babcock. Chicago: University of Chicago Press, 1978.

Erder, Laila. "The Measurement of Preindustrial Population Changes: Ottoman Empire from the Fifteenth to the Seventeenth Centuries." *Middle Eastern Studies* (1975): 284–301.

Esposito, John. *Women in Muslim Family Law.* Syracuse: Syracuse University Press, 1982.

Farley, J. Lewis. *Two Years in Syria.* London: Saunders and Otley, 1858.

Faroqhi, Suraiya. *Men of Modest Substance: House Owners and House Property in Seventeenth-Century Ankara and Kayseri.* Cambridge: Cambridge University Press, 1986.

Faroqhi, Suraiya, Bruce McGowen, and Donald Quataert. *An Economic and Social History of the Ottoman Empire*. Vol. 2. Cambridge: Cambridge University Press, 1995.

Farques, Philippe. "Le monde arabe: La citadelle domestique." In *Histoire de la famille*, ed. A. Burguiere et al. 2 vols. Paris: A. Colin, 1986.

Fay, Mary Ann. "The Ties That Bound: Women and Household in Eighteenth-Century Egypt." In *Women, the Family, and Divorce Laws in Islamic History*, ed. Amira E. Sonbol. Syracuse: Syracuse University Press, 1996.

Findley, Carter V. *Bureaucratic Reform in the Ottoman Empire*. Princeton: Princeton University Press, 1980.

———. *Ottoman Civil Officialdom: A Social History*. Princeton: Princeton University Press, 1988.

Flandrin, Jean-Louis. *Families in Former Times: Kinship, Household, and Sexuality in Early Modern France*. Translated by Richard Southern. Cambridge: Cambridge University Press, 1979.

Geertz, Hilda. "The Meaning of Family Ties." In *Meaning and Order in Moroccan Society*, ed. Clifford Geertz, Hilda Geertz, and Lawrence Rosen. Cambridge: Cambridge University Press, 1979.

Gerber, Haim. "Anthropology and Family History: The Ottoman and Turkish Families." *Journal of Family History* 14 (1989): 409–421.

———. "Sharia, Kanun, and Custom in Ottoman Law: Court Records of Seventeenth-Century Bursa." *International Journal of Turkish Studies* 2 (1982): 131–147.

———. "Social and Economic Position of Women in an Ottoman City, Bursa, 1600–1700." *International Journal of Middle East Studies* 12 (1980): 231–244.

———. *State, Society, and Law in Islam: Ottoman Law in Comparative Perspective*. Syracuse: Syracuse University Press, 1995.

al-Ghazzi, Kamil. *Nahr al-dhahab fi ta'rikh halab*. 3 vols. Aleppo: Maronite Press, 1923.

Goitein, Shlomo D. *A Mediterranean Society*. Vol. 3, *The Family*. Berkeley and Los Angeles: University of California Press, 1978.

Goode, William. *World Revolutions and Family Patterns*. New York: Glencoe Free Press, 1963.

Goody, Jack. "Inheritance, Property, and Women." In *Family and Society*, ed. Robert Forster and Orest Ranum. Baltimore: Johns Hopkins University Press, 1976.

———. *The Oriental, the Ancient, and the Primitive: Systems of Marriage and the Family in Preindustrial Societies in Eurasia*. Cambridge: Cambridge University Press, 1990.

Goody, Jack, Joan Thirsk, and E. P. Thompson. *Family and Inheritance: Rural Sociology in Western Europe, 1200–1800*. Cambridge: Cambridge University Press, 1976.

Gottlieb, Beatrice. *The Family in the Western World from the Black Death to the Industrial Age*. Oxford: Oxford University Press, 1993.

Gran, Peter. "Organization of Culture and the Construction of the Family in the Modern Middle East." In *Women, the Family, and Divorce Laws in Islamic History*, ed. Amira E. Sonbol. Syracuse: Syracuse University Press, 1996.

Granquist, Hilda. *Marriage Conditions in a Palestinian Village.* Helsinki: Societas Scientiarium Fennica, 1931, 1935.

Guys, Henri. *Essai sur la statistique politique et religieuse du Pachalik d'Alep, en 1845.* Marseilles, 1857.

Hajnal, John. "European Marriage Patterns in Perspective." In *Population and History,* ed. D. V. Glass and D. E. C. Eversley. London: Edward Arnold, 1965.

Hamide, Abdul Rahman. *La Ville d'Alep: Étude de geographie urbaine.* Paris: Imprimerie Université de Damas, 1959.

Hanna, Nelly. "Marriage among Merchant Families in Seventeenth-Century Cairo." In *Women, the Family, and Divorce Laws in Islamic History,* ed. Amira E. Sonbol. Syracuse: Syracuse University Press, 1996.

Harris, Christina Phelps. *The Syrian Desert: Caravan, Travel, and Exploration.* New York: Macmillan, 1938.

Hatem, Mervat. "Class and Patriarchy as Competing Paradigms for the Study of Middle Eastern Women." *Comparative Studies in Society and History* 29 (1987): 811–818.

———. "Politics of Sexuality and Gender in Segregated Patriarchal Systems: The Case of Egypt in the Eighteenth and Nineteenth Centuries." *Feminist Studies* 12 (1986): 251–274.

Hathaway, Jane. *The Politics of Households in Ottoman Egypt.* Cambridge: Cambridge University Press, 1997.

Hodgson, Marshall G. S. *Venture of Islam: Conscience and History in a World Civilization.* 3 vols. Chicago: University of Chicago Press, 1974.

Hourani, Albert. "Ottoman Reform and the Politics of Notables." In *Beginnings of Modernization in the Middle East,* ed. William Polk and Richard Chambers. Chicago: University of Chicago, 1966.

Hughes, Diane Owen. "From Brideprice to Dowry in Mediterranean Europe." *Journal of Family History* 3 (1978): 262–296.

———. "Toward a Historical Ethnography: Notarial Records and Family History in the Middle Ages." *Historical Methods Newsletter* 7 (1974): 61–71.

Inalcik, Halil. "Capital Formation in the Ottoman Empire." *Journal of Economic History* 19 (1964): 97–140.

———. "Centralization and Decentralization in Ottoman Administration." In *Studies in Eighteenth-Century Islamic History,* ed. Thomas Naff and Roger Owen. Carbondale, Ill.: Southern Illinois University Press, 1977.

Issawi, Charles. "British Consular Views on Syria's Economy in the 1850's–1860's." In *American University in Beirut Festival Book.* Beirut: American University of Beirut Press, 1967.

———. "Economic Change and Urbanization in the Middle East." In *Middle Eastern Cities,* ed. Ira M. Lapidus. Berkeley: University of California Press, 1969.

———. "Population and Resources in the Ottoman Empire and Iran." In *Studies in*

Eighteenth-Century Islamic History, ed. Thomas Naff and Roger Owen. Carbondale, Ill.: Southern Illinois University Press, 1977.

Ivanona, Svetlana. "The Divorce between Zubaida Hatun and Esseid Osman Aga: Women in the Eighteenth-Century Shariʿa Court of Rumelia." In *Women, the Family, and Divorce Laws in Islamic History,* ed. Amira E. Sonbol. Syracuse: Syracuse University Press, 1996.

Jennings, Ronald. "Women in Early Seventeenth-Century Ottoman Judicial Records—the Sharia Court of Anatolian Kayseri." *Journal of the Economic and Social History of the Orient* 18 (1975): 53–114.

Kandiyoti, Deniz. "Islam and Patriarchy: A Comparative Perspective." In *Women in Middle Eastern History: Shifting Boundaries in Sex and Gender,* ed. Nikki Keddie and Beth Baron. New Haven: Yale University Press, 1991.

Karpat, Kemal. "Ottoman Population Records and the Census of 1881/82–83." *International Journal of Middle East Studies* 9 (1978): 237–274.

———. "Some Historical and Methodological Considerations Concerning Social Stratification in the Middle East." In *Commoners, Climbers, and Notables: A Sample of Studies on Social Ranking in the Middle East,* ed. C. A. O. Nieuwenhuijze. Leiden: E. J. Brill, 1977.

———. "The Transformation of the Ottoman State, 1789–1908." *International Journal of Middle East Studies* 3 (1972): 243–281.

Keddie, Nikki, and Beth Baron, eds. *Women in Middle Eastern History: Shifting Boundaries in Sex and Gender.* New Haven: Yale University Press, 1991.

Keyser, James M. B. "The Middle Eastern Case: Is There a Marriage Rule?" *Ethnology* 13 (1974): 293–309.

Khadduri, Majid, and Herbert J. Liebisney, ed. *Law in the Middle East.* Washington: Middle East Institute, 1955.

Khoury, Philip. *Urban Notables and Arab Nationalism: The Politics of Damascus, 1860–1920.* Cambridge: Cambridge University Press, 1983.

Khuri, Fuad I. "Parallel Cousin Marriage Reconsidered: A Middle East Practice That Nullifies the Effects of Marriage on the Intensity of Family Relations." *Man* 5 (1970): 597–618.

Kirshner, Julius. "Some Problems in the Interpretation of Legal Texts *re* the Italian City-States." *Archiv für Begriffgeschichte* 19 (1975): 16–27.

Lapidus, Ira. "The Evolution of Muslim Urban Society." *Comparative Studies in Society and History* 15 (1973): 21–50.

———. *Muslim Cities in the Later Middle Ages.* Cambridge: Cambridge University Press, 1984.

Laslett, Peter. *Household and Family in Past Time.* Cambridge: Cambridge University Press, 1972.

Latron, A. *La vie rurale en Syrie et au Liban.* Beirut: N.p., 1936.

Lee, James, and Jon Gjerde. "Comparative Household Morphology of Stem, Joint, and Nuclear Household Systems: Norway, China, and the United States" *Continuity and Change* 1 (1986): 90–105.

Mandaville, Jon. "Usurious Piety: The Cash-Waqf Controversy in the Ottoman Empire." *International Journal of Middle East Studies* 10 (1979): 289–308.

Marcus, Abraham. "Men, Women, and Property: Dealers in Real Estate in Eighteenth-Century Aleppo." *Journal of the Economic and Social History of the Orient* 26 (1984): 138–163.

———. *The Middle East on the Eve of Modernity: Aleppo in the Eighteenth Century.* New York: Columbia University Press, 1989.

———. "Privacy in Eighteenth-Century Aleppo: The Limits of a Cultural Ideal." *International Journal of Middle East Studies* 18 (1986): 165–183.

———. "Real Property and Social Structure in the Premodern Middle East: A Case Study." In *Property, Social Structure, and Law in the Modern Middle East,* ed. Ann Elizabeth Mayer. Albany: State University of New York Press, 1985.

Marmon, S. E. "Concubinage, Islamic." In *Dictionary of the Middle Ages,* vol. 3, ed. Joseph R. Strayer et al., 527–529. New York: Charles Scribner's Sons, 1983.

Marsot, Afaf. "The Revolutionary Gentlewoman." In *Women in the Muslim Middle East,* ed. Lois Beck and Nikki Keddie. Cambridge, Mass.: Harvard University Press, 1978.

———. *Women and Men in Eighteenth-Century Egypt.* Austin: University of Texas Press, 1995.

Masson, Paul. *Histoire du commerce français dans le Levant au XVIIe siècle.* Paris: Hachette, 1896.

———. *Histoire du commerce français dans le Levant au XVIIIe siècle.* Paris: Hachette, 1911.

Masters, Bruce. "The 1850 Events in Aleppo: An Aftershock of Syria's Incorporation into the World Capitalist System." *International Journal of Middle East Studies* 22 (1990): 3–20.

———. *The Origins of Western Economic Dominance in the Middle East: Mercantilism and the Islamic Economy in Aleppo, 1600–1750.* New York: New York University Press, 1988.

———. "Patterns of Migration to Ottoman Aleppo in the Seventeenth and Eighteenth Centuries." *International Journal of Turkish Studies* 4 (1987): 75–89.

McCarthy, Justin. "Age, Family, and Migration in Nineteenth-Century Black Sea Provinces of the Ottoman Empire." *International Journal of Middle East Studies* 10 (1979): 309–323.

Meeker, Michael E. "The Great Family Aghas of Turkey." In *Rural Politics and Social Change in the Middle East,* ed. Richard T. Antoun and Iliya Harik. Bloomington: Indiana University Press, 1972.

———. "Meaning and Society in the Near East: Examples from the Black Sea Turks and Levantine Arabs." *International Journal of Middle East Studies* 7 (1976): 243–270, 383–422.

Meriwether, Margaret L. The Notable Families of Aleppo, 1770–1830: Networks and Social Structure. Ph.D. diss. University of Pennsylvania, 1981.

———. "The Rights of Children and the Responsibilities of Women: Women as Wasis in Ottoman Aleppo, 1770–1840." In *Women, the Family, and Divorce Laws in Islamic History,* ed. Amira E. Sonbol. Syracuse: Syracuse University Press, 1996.

———. "Urban Notables and Rural Resources in Ottoman Aleppo, 1770–1830." *International Journal of Turkish Studies* 4 (1987): 55–73.

———. "Women and Economic Change in Nineteenth-Century Syria: The Case of Aleppo." In *Arab Women: Old Boundaries, New Frontiers,* ed. Judith Tucker. Bloomington: Indiana University Press, 1993.

———. "Women and Waqf Revisited: The Case of Aleppo, 1770–1840." In *Women in the Ottoman Empire: Middle Eastern Women in the Early Modern Era,* ed. Madeline Zilfi. Leiden: E. J. Brill, 1997.

Moors, Annelies. "Debating Islamic Family Law: Legal Texts and Social Practices." In *Social History of Women and Gender in the Middle East,* ed. Margaret L. Meriwether and Judith Tucker. Boulder: Westview Press, forthcoming in 1999.

———. *Women, Property, and Islam: Palestinian Experiences, 1920–1990.* Cambridge: Cambridge University Press, 1995.

al-Muhibbi, Muhammad Amin. *Khulasat al-athar fi tarajim ahal al-qarn al-hadi ʿashar.* 4 vols. Cairo: Matbaʿa Wahbiyya, 1869.

Mundy, Martha. "The Family, Inheritance, and Islam: A Re-examination of the Sociology of Faraʾid Law." In *Islamic Law: Social and Historical Context,* ed. Aziz al-Azmeh. London and New York: Routledge, 1988.

———. "Women's Inheritance of Land in Highland Yemen." *Arabian Studies* 5 (1979): 161–187.

al-Muradi, Muhammad Khalil. *Silk al-durar fi aʿyan al-qarn al-thani ʿashar.* 4 vols. Baghdad: Matbaʿa Muthni, 1874–1883.

Murphy, R. F., and Leonard Kasdan. "Agnation and Endogamy: Some Further Considerations." *Southwestern Journal of Anthropology* 23 (1959): 1–14.

Musallam, Basim. *Sex and Society in Medieval Islam.* Cambridge: Cambridge University Press, 1983.

al-Nahal, Gamal. *Judicial Administration in Ottoman Egypt in the Seventeenth Century.* Minneapolis: Bibliotheca Islamica, 1985.

Oehler, Julie. "Bibi Maryam: A Bakhtiyari Tribal Woman." In *Struggle and Survival in the Modern Middle East,* ed. Edmund Burke. University of California, 1993.

Panzac, Daniel. *La Peste dans l'Empire Ottomane.* Louvain: Peeters, 1985.

Patai, Raphael. *Society, Culture, and Change in the Middle East.* Philadelphia: University of Pennsylvania Press, 1974.

———. "Structure of Endogamous Unilineal Descent Groups." *Southwestern Journal of Anthropology* 21 (1965): 325–350.

Peirce, Leslie P. *The Imperial Harem: Women and Sovereignty in the Ottoman Empire.* Oxford: Oxford University Press, 1993.

————. "Seniority, Sexuality, and Social Order: The Vocabulary of Gender in Early Modern Ottoman Society." In *Women in the Ottoman Empire: Middle Eastern Women in the Early Modern Era,* ed. Madeline C. Zilfi. Leiden: E. J. Brill, 1997.

Peters, Emrys L. "Status of Women in Four Middle Eastern Communities." In *Women in the Muslim World,* ed. Lois Beck and Nikki Keddie. Cambridge, Mass.: Harvard University Press, 1978.

Petry, Carl. "Class Solidarity versus Gender Gain: Women as Custodians of Property in Later Medieval Egypt." In *Women in Middle Eastern History: Shifting Boundaries in Sex and Gender,* ed. Nikki Keddie and Beth Baron. New Haven: Yale University Press, 1991.

Plakans, Andrejs. *Kinship in the Past: An Anthropology of European Family Life: 1500–1900.* Oxford: Basil Blackwell, 1984.

Powers, David S. "The Islamic Inheritance System: A Sociohistorical Approach." In *Islamic Family Law,* ed. Chibli Mallat and Jane Connors. London: Graham and Trotman, 1993.

————. *Studies in Qurʾan and Hadith: The Formation of the Islamic Law of Inheritance.* Berkeley: University of California Press, 1986.

Protho, Edwin, and Lutfy Najib Diab. *Changing Family Patterns in the Arab East.* Beirut: American University in Beirut Press, 1974.

Raymond, André. *Artisans et commerçants au Caire au XVIIIe siècle.* 2 vols. Damascus: Institut Français de Damas, 1973–1974.

————. *The Great Arab Cities from the Sixteenth to the Eighteenth Centuries: An Introduction.* New York: New York University Press, 1984.

————. "The Ottoman Conquest and the Development of the Great Arab Towns." *International Journal of Turkish Studies* 1 (1980): 94–95.

————. "Signes urbains et étude de la population des grandes villes arabes à l'epoque ottomane." *Bulletin des études orientales* 27 (1974): 182–193.

Reilly, James. "Rural Waqfs of Ottoman Damascus: Rights of Ownership, Possession, and Tenancy." *Acta Orientalia* 51 (1990): 27–46.

Roded, Ruth. "Great Mosques, Zawiyas, and Neighborhood Mosques: Popular Beneficiaries of *Waqf* Endowments in Eighteenth- and Nineteenth-Century Aleppo." *Journal of the American Oriental Society* 110 (1990): 33–38.

————. "Social Patterns among the Urban Elite of Syria during the Late Ottoman Period (1876–1918)." In *Palestine in the Late Ottoman Period: Political, Social, and Economic Transformation,* ed. David Kushner. Leiden: E. J. Brill, 1986.

————. "The Waqf and the Social Elite of Aleppo in the Eighteenth and Nineteenth Centuries." *Turcica* 20 (1988): 71–91.

Russell, Alexander. *The Natural History of Aleppo.* 2d ed. 2 vols. London: G. G. and J. Robinson, 1794.

Sauvaget, Jean. *Alep: Essai sur le développement d'une grande ville syrienne, des origines au milieu du XIXe siècle.* Paris: Librarie Orientaliste Paul Geuthner, 1941.

Schact, Joseph. *An Introduction to Islamic Law.* Oxford: Clarendon University Press, 1964.

———. "Umm al-walad." In *Encyclopedia of Islam.* 1st ed., vol. 8. London: Luzac & Co., 1928.

Schilcher, Linda S. *Families in Politics: Damascene Factions and Estates in the Eighteenth and Nineteenth Centuries.* Wiesbaden: Franz Steiner Verlag GMBH, 1985.

———. "The Lore and Reality of Middle Eastern Patriarchy." *Die Welt des Islams* 28 (1988): 496–512.

Shaw, Stanford. "The Ottoman Census System and Population, 1831–1914." *International Journal of Middle East Studies* 9 (1978): 325–338.

Sluglett, Peter, and Marion Farouk-Sluglett. "The Application of the 1858 Land Code in Greater Syria: Some Preliminary Observations." In *Land Tenure and Social Transformation in the Middle East,* ed. Tarif Khalidi. Beirut: American University of Beirut, 1984.

———. "Early, Recent, and Future Research on the Modern History of Aleppo: A Review and Some Proposals." In *Middle Eastern Cities in Comparative Perspective,* ed. Kenneth Brown. London: Ithaca University Press, 1986.

Smilianskaya, I. M. "Syria: From Subsistence to Market Economy." In *The Economic History of the Middle East,* ed. Charles Issawi. Chicago: University of Chicago Press, 1966.

Sonbol, Amira E., ed. *Women, the Family, and Divorce Laws in Islamic History.* Syracuse: Syracuse University Press, 1996.

Steensgaard, Niels. *The Asian Trade Revolution of the Seventeenth Century: The East India Company and the Decline of the Caravan Trade.* Chicago: University of Chicago Press, 1973.

Stone, Lawrence. "Family History in the 1980's." *Journal of Interdisciplinary History* 12 (1981): 51–87.

———. "Prosopography." *Daedalus: Historical Studies Today* 100 (1971): 46–79.

al-Tabbakh, Muhammad Raghib. *I'lam al-nubala bi ta'rikh halab al-shahba.* 7 vols. Aleppo: Maronite Press, 1923–1926.

Todorova, Maria N. *Balkan Family Structure and the European Pattern: Demographic Developments in Ottoman Bulgaria.* Washington: American University Press, 1993.

Tucker, Judith. "The Arab Family in History." In *Arab Women: Old Boundaries, New Frontiers,* ed. Judith Tucker. Bloomington: University of Indiana Press, 1993.

———. *In the House of the Law: Gender and Islamic Law in Ottoman Syria and Palestine.* Berkeley: University of California Press, 1998.

———. "Marriage and Family in Nablus, 1720–1856: Towards a History of Arab Marriage." *Journal of Family History* 13 (1988): 165–179.

———. "Ties That Bound: Women and Family in Eighteenth- and Nineteenth-Century Nablus." In *Women in Middle Eastern History: Shifting Boundaries in Sex and Gender,* ed. Nikki Keddie and Beth Baron. New Haven: Yale University Press, 1991.

———. *Women in Nineteenth-Century Egypt.* Cambridge: Cambridge University Press, 1985.

————, ed. *Arab Women: Old Boundaries, New Frontiers.* Bloomington: University of Indiana Press, 1993.

Tugay, Emine Foat. *Three Centuries: Family Chronicles of Egypt and Turkey.* Oxford: Oxford University Press, 1963.

Vann, Richard T. "The New Demographic History." In *International Handbook of Historical Studies: Contemporary Research and Theory,* ed. George E. Izzus and Harold T. Parker. Westport, Conn.: Greenwood Press, 1979.

Watt, W. Montgomery. *Muhammad: Prophet and Statesman.* Oxford: Oxford University Press, 1961.

Wrigley, E. Anthony. "Reflections on the History of the Family." *Daedalus: The Family* 106 (1977): 71–85.

Ze'ev, Dror. "Women in Seventeenth-Century Jerusalem." *International Journal of Middle East Studies* 27 (1995): 157–173.

Zilfi, Madeline C. "Elite Circulation in the Ottoman Empire: The Great Mollas of the Eighteenth Century." *Journal of the Economic and Social History of the Orient* 26 (1983):318–364.

————. "'We Don't Get Along': Women and *Hul* Divorce in the Eighteenth Century." In *Women in the Ottoman Empire: Middle Eastern Women in the Early Modern Period,* ed. Madeline C. Zilfi. Leiden: E. J. Brill, 1997.

————, ed. *Women in the Ottoman Empire: Middle Eastern Women in the Early Modern Period.* Leiden: E. J. Brill, 1997.

Index